How To Build a
Small-Block Chevy
for the Street

Jim Richardson

MOTORBOOKS

First published in 2002 by Motorbooks, an imprint of
MBI Publishing Company, Galtier Plaza, Suite 200, 380
Jackson Street, St. Paul, MN 55101-3885 USA

Motorbooks titles are also available at discounts in bulk
quantity for industrial or sales-promotional use. For
details write to Special Sales Manager at MBI Publishing
Company, Galtier Plaza, Suite 200, 380 Jackson Street,
St. Paul, MN 55101-3885 USA.

ISBN 13: 978-0-7603-1096-0
ISBN 10: 0-7603-1096-3

On the front cover, main: Author Jim Richardson
performs some fine-tuning on the small-block Chevy
installed in this street rod. *David Gooley.* **Small:** Clean the
saddles with lacquer thinner, then press in the main
bearing shells.

On the back cover: The big Roots-type blower on this
Corvette is enough to intimidate the competition, but is
gross overkill for street use.

About the author:
Jim Richardson is a life-long car buff and has been an
automotive writer for many years. His work appears
regularly in *Car Collector, Special Interest Autos, Auto Restorer,*
and *Custom & Classic Trucks*. His other books include *The
Classic Car Restoration Handbook* and the *Tri-Five Chevy
Handbook,* published by HP, and *The Do It Yourself Guide to
Engine and Chassis Detailing,* published by CarTech. He also
appears on *My Classic Car TV* and *Classic Car Garage.* Jim
and his wife divide their time between Long Beach,
California, and Tairua, New Zealand where Jim is a regular
contributor to *New Zealand Classic Car* and *Australian
Classic Car.*

Editor: Peter Bodensteiner
Designer: Stephanie Michaud
Layout by Katie Sonmor

Printed in Hong Kong

TABLE OF CONTENTS

ACKNOWLEDGMENTS

Many people helped with this book, and most are acknowledged in the appropriate chapters; but two good friends have been especially generous with their time. Both helped extensively with the wrenching, and both shared their vast knowledge of engines with me. These are John Jaroch, professional auto and truck mechanic, and John Miller, who was an aircraft engine mechanic for the Australian Navy for much of his life. I'd also like to thank my wife Bette for her much needed support and encouragement.

HISTORY
Who Started It All?

If one four-barrel is good on a street rod, two are better, or so the thinking went until recently.

Chevrolet was losing ground in the early 1950s. Any old-time hot rodder can tell you why. It wasn't because the Bow Tie offerings of the era were bad cars—indeed, they were good looking, dependable, and long lasting. However, largely because of Chevy's obsolescent inline six-cylinder motors, Chevys were regarded as "old people's cars."

The earlier stovebolt-six with its cast-iron pistons and poured babbitt rod bearings was slow off the line and couldn't take much revving, though it was a smooth, long-lived engine when operated within its design envelope. Of course, by the early 1950s Chevy's new Blue Flame 235 six-cylinder engine was thoroughly modern, with insert bearings, aluminum pistons, and pressure lubrication to its connecting rods. But it was too little too late. By that time the company's reputation was established and it needed something dramatic to make a change.

Ford began winning over the younger crowd way back in the 1930s with its inexpensive new flathead V-8s. Then Oldsmobile heated up the horsepower race by introducing its overhead valve, high-compression V-8 in 1948. Cadillac followed in 1949 with its own modern V-8. But Chevy and Plymouth still remained slow, solid, six-cylinder alternatives to the peppy new Fords.

By 1952 the brass at General Motors—the automobile colossus that produced nearly half of all the cars sold in the 1950s—knew they had to do something quickly about the division's image, because it accounted for 25 percent of profits and they were losing market share rapidly. General Motors appointed engineer Ed Cole—World War II production wonder boy and designer of the new Cadillac V-8—to the task of turning Chevy's image around.

General Motors gave him just two years, instead of the usual four, to do it.

Early 1955 motors didn't have a cast-in oil filter boss, so an external bypass-type filter was a must.

than continuing it on down below the main bearings. As a result, Chevrolet's small-block crankshaft hangs out into the pan, unlike Ford's heavier Y-block V-8 of the time period.

Stamped-steel rocker arms that pivoted on studs (rather than the standard heavier, cast rockers that rotated on shafts) and light, hollow pushrods were also added. Cole's division borrowed these innovations from the new 1955 Pontiac engine: they made the Bow Tie engine cheaper to produce, while the lower reciprocating mass allowed higher rpm.

The new V-8's crankshaft was short and sturdy and made of forged, pressed steel rather than nodular iron (although many later crankshafts were made of nodular iron). In addition, all of the rotating assembly components were balanced independently so that they could be used interchangeably. (The later 400-ci engines are externally balanced, so if you use a 400 crank in a 350, you will need a 400 flywheel and vibration damper to make it properly balanced. Otherwise, it will vibrate.)

Styling for the 1955 models was already in the works by the time Cole came aboard, but previous efforts to come up with a new engine had fallen flat. A V-6 the company developed in the late 1940s didn't produce enough power, so that project was scrapped. Then Chevrolet's chief engineer and designer of the inline six-cylinder engine (I-6), Edward H. "Crankshaft" Kelly, came up with a smaller (230 ci) knock-off of the Cadillac V-8. However, Kelly's model was too expensive to produce.

When Cole took over the division, he doubled the size of the engineering staff and began working on an entirely new engine. What they came up with in just 14 months was probably the best American production engine ever. Fifty years later it is still being built, though in a very updated form. Chevy's new V-8 for 1955 was smaller, lighter (50 pounds lighter than the Ford V-8), and more powerful than anything the other low-priced car makers had to offer.

Much of the weight savings was achieved by developing thin-wall casting techniques, and by ending the crankcase at the centerline of the crankshaft rather

Power steering, power brakes, air conditioning, Powerglide, Turboglide, and other accessories were popular on tri-five Chevys, and the small block had the muscle to handle them.

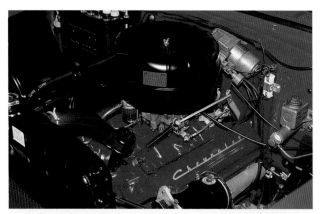

1956 V-8 engines were actually painted red as opposed to Chevy orange for that year only.

Even the magnificent Italian Bizzarrinis of the 1960s were Chevy small-block powered.

The intake manifold was designed to be efficient. Indeed, Chevy small blocks have never had problems breathing well on the intake side, though the exhaust valves and manifolds are somewhat limited for high-performance purposes. The intake manifold also acts as the lifter valley cover, saving weight and simplifying the engine further.

The exhaust port runners on the heads were short, and they went up and out through Chevy's trademark ram's horn cast-iron manifolds for better breathing efficiency and more effective cooling. Also, the new heads were cast to be interchangeable left-to-right, with the intake manifold providing a common water outlet for each of them, making production much simpler.

Chevrolet dubbed the new V-8 the Turbofire. Equipped with a two-barrel carburetor, it produced 162 horsepower on regular gasoline with a fairly low 8:1 compression ratio. This was a big leap over the traditional six's 136 horsepower, and the V-8 was 40 pounds lighter to boot.

At midyear in 1955, a Super Turbofire option was offered that included a Rochester four-barrel carburetor and dual exhausts to boost the engine to 180 horsepower. Hot on its heels came the Special Power Pack kit, intended primarily for racing, which pumped the ponies up to 195.

Stock car racers soon took advantage of the newfound horsepower and torque. Chevy racers won at Darlington and 13 other races that year as well. The little V-8 became known among racers as the "Mighty Mouse," named for a popular cartoon character of the time. The small block's racing career was truly launched and it is still going strong today. Chevy mouse motors have been put in almost everything that moves, from handmade Italian Bizzarrini sports cars to Indy cars to 1941 Willys coupes.

In 1957, the renowned engineer Arkus Duntov—designer of the Ardun overhead-valve conversion for the Ford flathead V-8—was hired by Chevrolet to make its engines even hotter because Ford and Chrysler were mounting stout competition of their own. His innovations made it possible for a

The 283 for 1957 was a hot performer, but it didn't prevent Ford from outselling Chevrolet that year.

Small-block Chevys are still hair-raising performers, especially when built to the hilt, blown, and injected.

small-block Chevy engine to run up Pike's Peak in a record-breaking 17 minutes—2 minutes faster than the Ford of that year.

The new V-8 wasn't an unalloyed success at first. Early 1955 engines burned a quart of oil every 200 miles, apparently because the rings would not seat against the cylinder bores. Legend has it that some mechanics of the era even resorted to putting a little Bon Ami cleanser down the carb to help scuff the cylinder walls and make the rings seat. Also, the early 265-ci engines had no cast-in oil filter boss.

Because the engine came with hydraulic lifters, fitting an accessory bypass oil filter became a must to prevent lifter wear and eventual collapse from oil contamination. This problem

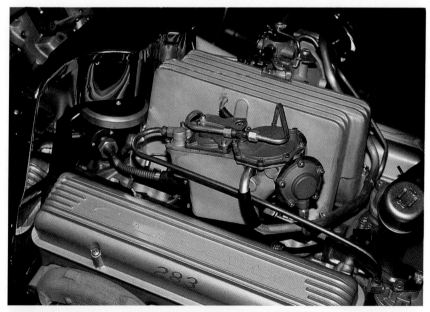

Rochester fuel injection, first available in 1957, made an impressive 283 horsepower from 283 ci.

The Chevy V-8 was pure magic in the Corvette, making it America's first real sports car.

was soon rectified with a cast-in oil filter boss at the rear of the engine for a full-flow filter. As a result of these initial shortcomings, in models as late as 1956, almost half of the Chevys sold had the old six-cylinder engine in them.

The car that gained the most from the new engine was the Corvette. Equipped with an inline six and a two-speed Power-glide transmission upon its introduction in 1953, the car enjoyed only limited success. When the 265-ci V-8 and manual transmission were added in 1955, Chevrolet's sports car became a real contender to the European Ferraris, Jaguars, and Alfa Romeos on the road racing tracks of the United States.

Birth of the 283

Ford and Chrysler were mounting their own performance efforts by the mid-1950s, so Chevrolet could not rest on its laurels for long. The 283 made its debut in 1957—the most sought-after year of the classic tri-five Chevys—even though Ford outsold Chevrolet that year. What cost Chevy its sales was not horsepower, but warmed-over styling compared with Ford and Plymouth's fresh new appearances. In fact, in 1957 Chevy was the first of the low-priced three to be able to boast one horsepower per cubic inch out of its new fuel injection–equipped engine.

The 283 engine with two four-barrels pumped out 270 horsepower at 6,000 rpm.

The 283 was a 265 bored out to 3.88 inches. Its stroke remained at 3.00. The Turbofire single four-barrel version made 185 horsepower and had a compression ratio of 8.5:1. The Super Turbofire came with a 9.5:1 compression ratio and, equipped with a single four-barrel, it made 220 horsepower at 4,800 rpm. With two four-barrels, the 283 pumped out 245 horsepower at 5,000 rpm.

A high-lift cam version of the twin four-barrel 283, which was available only with a three-speed, close-ratio manual transmission, yielded 270 horsepower at 6,000 rpm. The injection-equipped engines with a 10.5:1 compression ratio made an honest 283 horsepower at 6,200 rpm. The 283 was such a success that it was built essentially unaltered for the next 10 years. It, along with the later 327, 302, 350, and 400 engines, made the Chevrolet small-block V-8 the most popular performance engine of all time.

FINDING AN ENGINE
The Search Is On

Chevy small blocks have been put into everything from Italian sports cars to modified Model Ts because they are the best American production engines ever.

There are many reasons why you may have to hunt down a new engine. It could be that the one in your classic is too far gone to rebuild, or possibly you just want to swap out a smaller engine for a 350 or 400. Whatever the case may be, you will need to make sure you are getting what you bargained for.

The biggest problem with finding exactly what you want is that Chevy small-block engines almost all look alike. The newest Generation III computerized, injected engines certainly have a distinctive look, but the earlier blocks from the 1980s back to the 1950s are so similar in appearance that it is hard to tell whether you are looking at a 400, 350, 327, 307, 305, or 283 block, unless you know them well or have access to the casting numbers.

With the possible exception of the 262, which was an ill-fated attempt to meet the smog laws and fuel restrictions of the 1970s, they are all great engines. (Even the 262 was dependable enough, but it lacked power and provided

A later, super-tuned small block will drop right in a mid-1950s Chevy pickup.

only marginal fuel economy.) Almost any small-block Chevy engine can be made to perform well, but if you are looking for a 350-ci engine, you won't want to buy a 283 or 305 by mistake. Here's how you can tell them apart:

265
(Bore: 3.770"/Stroke: 3")
This was Chevrolet's first modern V-8. (Chevy's first V-8 came out much earlier, but it was not successful.) The new engine made its debut in the 1955 model year and was produced until 1957, when the 283 replaced it. This early engine is fairly uncommon these days, except in original cars from the era. However, the 265 was still available in 1957 and was common in trucks. You can spot a 1957 model year 265 by its distinctive yellow color.

These early engines are also easy to identify because the oil vent tube is cast-in, and the early 265s made in 1954 and 1955 have no cast-in boss for an oil filter. An accessory bypass filter can be added to such motors and it's a good idea to do so, because these engines came with hydraulic lifters that need a steady supply of clean oil to operate properly.

A 265 can withstand being bored a maximum of .125," which essentially makes them into a 302. The crankshaft journals in this engine are 2.30" and the crankshafts are forged.

They were good motors and can be made to perform. However, unless you are restoring an original Chevy and want to keep it stock, you'd be better off with one of the later engines with the bigger bores and crankshaft journals.

You don't want the engine out of this car. The driveline is bent and bashed, and who knows what happened to the rapidly spinning crankshaft.

283
(Bore: 3.875" Stroke: 3")
This was Chevy's mainstay for years and was a superb engine. Because they were produced for a long time, they are not nearly as rare as 265 motors. Those made in 1957 can be safely bored .125" over, but blocks from 1958 to 1962 can only be over bored .060" at a maximum. General Motors went back to thinner cylinder walls again from 1963 to 1967, so motors from these years can only safely stand a .060" overbore. Crank journals are small, at 2.30", and crankshafts are cast.

The 283 can be super-tuned to give good performance, though it is limited somewhat by its displacement. However, unless you are going to get into serious bracket racing, a 283 is a great street mill. It is rugged, dependable, and made of good stuff. Parts are also plentiful to rebuild and performance-tune this engine.

327
(Bore: 4" Stroke: 3.25")
This engine debuted in 1962 in the Corvette and served as Chevy's performance engine for years. Both the bore and stroke were increased for this engine, and that necessitated a redesigned bottom end to allow for larger counterweights on the crank. By the mid-1960s, these engines were producing 375 horsepower with fuel injection, and 365 horsepower normally carbureted. The 327 powered the mighty Corvettes of the 1960s and achieved glory for the Chaparral team in 1966.

The 327 is valued for its comparative rarity these days and because it can really pump out the power at higher rpms. These engines have no real shortcomings, and they can be made to perform with a little work. The 327 blocks were all equipped with two-bolt main bearing caps. Earlier engines had 2.30" small-crank journals, but in 1968, Chevy went to midsize 2.45" journals. These engines will easily handle a .040" rebore, but .060" is risky.

302
(Bore: 4" Stroke: 3")
These engines were designed for racing in the Trans-Am series, and they are real screamers, literally. When the prototypes were dynoed at 8,000 rpm by its designers, the exhaust—which was piped directly out of the lab—made people nearby think they were hearing an air raid siren. It was the short stroke and big bore that made these engines such capable revvers. What they lacked in torque at the bottom end, they more than made up for in horsepower at the top end.

The painted numbers at the upper left indicate the block has been bored .030" over. The 010 below tells you that the block is 10 percent nickel, making it stronger.

In 1967 these engines came with small (2.30") crank journals and two-bolt mains, but in 1968 and 1969 they sported 2.45" crank journals and four-bolt mains, making them extremely rugged. If you find a rebuildable 302 of either configuration, grab it. They are very sought-after today. They go like stink right out of the box, and with a little massaging they can be awesome performers.

307
(Bore: 3.875" Stroke: 3.25")

At the time, the 327 was blowing the doors off of everything and it was considered Chevy's high-performance engine. The company decided it also needed a V-8 for Joe Station Wagon, hence the 307. It only came with a two-barrel and no high-performance goodies, but it can be made to run like a scared cat with a few performance add-ons. The heads and other castings are thick and the metallurgy is good.

Most 307 blocks can be easily opened up .060" over. All of these engines had two-bolt mains and used the same stroke as the 327, which is 3.25". The 307 was used from 1968 through 1973 in a number of applications. It had a stroke of 3.25". If you find one of these at a cheap price and in good condition, you might want to give it some thought.

350
(Bore: 4" Stroke: 3.48")

It's been put into every kind of race car, hot rod, dragster, and speedboat imaginable. Everything is available for the 350 at competitive prices, making it the most popular engine of all time to build up for the street. Millions of 350s have been produced, and they're still making them in one form or another today.

The 350 was first offered in the 1967 Camaro. The earlier engines can easily be bored .040" over and will often go to .060", though I wouldn't recommend it. All Generation I and II motors came with medium-sized crank journals of 2.45" and 3.48" strokes. These engines were also available with two- or four-bolt main bearing caps. Since 1986, these engines were designed to take one-piece rear main bearing seals, and since 1987 they were also available with roller cams.

Generation III 350s came out in the 1997 Corvettes. They have aluminum blocks and six-bolt main bearing caps, making them very light and strong powerplants. These engines use iron cylinder sleeves bored to 3.90," and have 3.62" strokes, to provide an actual displacement of 346-ci. Over-boring is limited to cleaning up the cylinder walls because of their thin iron cylinder liners.

267
(Bore: 3.50" Stroke: 3.48")

Produced between 1979 and 1982, these engines were designed to meet the smog and fuel economy restrictions

Even essentially stock small blocks can kick up dust with a little tweaking.

Casting Number	Displacement	Years	Installed In:
3703524	265	1955	Cars (No oil filter)
3720991	265	1956–1957	Cars, trucks
3731548	283	1957	Cars (No side motor mounts)
3556519, 3737739 3837739, 3756519 3794226	283	1958–1963	Cars, trucks
3789935, 3849852, 3864812, 3790721 3792582,3834812	283	1962–1965	Cars, trucks
3782870, 3789817 3852174, 3858180 3959512	327	1962–1964	Cars, trucks
3834810	283	1964–1966	Cars, trucks
3849852, 3849935, 3896944, 393288 3862194, 3849935 3896944,	283	1965–1967	Cars, trucks
3782870, 3789817 3792563, 3794460 3814660, 3830944 3852174, 3858174 3858180, 3892657 3903352, 3914660 3970041	327	1964–1967	Cars, trucks
3892657, 3914678 3932386, 3956618 3970010	302	1967–1969	Z-28 Camaro
3814660, 3914678 3932386, 3955618	327	1968–1969	Corvette, Camaro, High-performance applications
376450, 3855961 3914678, 3932386 3932388, 3958618 6259425	350	1967–1976	Cars (Two-bolt 3858618, 3892657mains)
3956618, 3970010 3932386	350	1968–1973	High-performance, trucks (Four-bolt mains)
3970014	350	1972	Two- and four-bolt mains
362245, 366287 460703	350	1978–1979	

Casting Number	Displacement	Years	Installed In:
366299	350	1978–1979	Aluminum. Four-bolt mains
3914636, 3914653 3932371, 3932373 3956632, 3970020	307	1968–1973	Cars, trucks
3951511	400	1970–1973	Cars, trucks (Four-bolt mains)
330817	400	1972–1980	(Two-bolt mains)
3951509, 3030817	400	1974–1978	Cars, trucks (Two-bolt mains)
355909, 360851	262	1975–1976	Nova, Monza
361979, 460776 460777, 460778 4715111	305	1978–1980	Cars, trucks

Look for the engine-casting number on the back of the engine, behind the head on the driver's side. The arrow and dots on the right indicate on which shift the block was cast.

of the era. A 267 can only be safely bored .030" over, due to its thin-wall block casting. All of them had two-bolt mains. These are good motors, with no special problems, but they are not good candidates for street rod use because of their small displacement and low-compression heads.

400
(Bore: 4.125" Stroke: 3.76")

This was the biggest small-block of them all. To make this displacement happen within the confines of the original external configuration, the cylinders had to be siamesed together, allowing no water to circulate between them. These blocks can be bored .040" over and can occasionally go to .060." Yet, if their water jackets are badly corroded, heating problems may develop, even if the block cleans up at .060. The 400-ci blocks were available with either two- or four-bolt mains from 1970 through 1980. The 400 was also the only configuration available with 2.65" crank journals and 3.76" strokes.

The 400 small block was externally balanced, meaning that the rotating assembly was balanced as a whole, so you can't just switch flywheels without rebalancing the rest of the engine. The same applies if you make your 350 into a stroker 383. You will need to provide your engine balancer with a 400 flywheel or flexplate.

Check any prospective purchase for cracks using a Magnaflux Spotcheck Jr. kit.

305
(Bore: 3.75" Stroke 3.48")

The 305s—especially the later, Vortec 5000 models—are gaining in popularity among street rodders. With the stroke of a 350 and the bore of a 283, these engines are torquey, and you can use many of the same go-fast goodies on them as the other engines. Blocks manufactured since 1986 have a one-piece rear main seal. Also, many later blocks have been cast for use with roller cams.

WHEN ORIGINALITY COUNTS

If you are doing a meticulous restoration and need to have all the numbers match, or if you are driving a rare car such as a 1955 Chevy equipped with one of those early 265 engines that has no cast-in oil filter boss, you may want to have your old block fixed. In many cases fractures can be welded, but the process is expensive.

To weld up a cast-iron engine block requires a specialist, and the block must be heated in an oven to cherry-red first. This can cause warping, stresses, and other problems, so the block must then be remachined and align-bored. If you decide to go this route, Excelsweld U.S.A. in Oakland, California (1-800-743-HEADS), can help you.

If a broken rod damaged a cylinder bore, you could be in trouble. Deep damage to cylinder walls can only be fixed by boring them away completely and wet sleeving the block.

Just keep in mind that the most common reason an old engine self-destructs is overheating caused by a corroded cooling system. Cylinder walls on the water-jacket side rust away and become too thin to dissipate heat properly, which causes the engine to fail. Having a machinist install wet sleeves in all the cylinders is one answer to this problem if you must stick with an original block.

Cracked heads can be fixed, too, but if the cracks are between valve seats, the repairs may not last because of the fragile castings in those areas. It is better look for a replacement head in sound condition, rather than attempting to fix an old one. You'll most likely be money ahead, and you won't have to worry about problems later.

The alternative to fixing a bad engine is to look for another with the same numbers. If your car came from the local area, there is a good chance that a bunch of cars, equipped the same way and made around the same time, were sent to the same place. Check local salvage yards and swap meets; also join the Chevy club in your area to find another block with the same numbers and casting date.

THE SHORT AND LONG OF IT

You will hear the terms "short" and "long" block when checking around for engines. A short block only includes the bottom end of an engine, or the block, crank, and pistons, but it does not include the heads, manifolds, or accessories. If all you did was damage the block in an otherwise decent engine, the short block may be just what you need. A long block is a complete engine, including heads and valve train, but you still need to use your old manifolds and accessories with them.

SALVAGE YARD TREASURES

Whoever said one man's junk is another man's treasure knew what they were talking about. But just to make sure you don't buy a pig in a poke, take the time to carefully examine your prospective purchase. Here are a few tips on what to look for and what to avoid:

Don't accept a junk engine that has been hit in its vibration damper or timing gear housing. Such an engine could easily have a damaged

After some tests, it was discovered that this old Chevy still had a good block in it, although the engine was tired.

Judging from the odometer and the old Chevy's condition, we would assume that the reading is in fact more like 132,456.

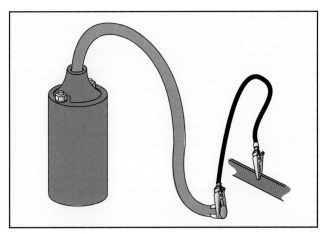

Ground the coil high-tension wire to the block using a couple of alligator clips and a piece of 10–inch-gauge wire.

crankshaft or camshaft. You don't want an engine and transmission combination that has been hit hard from the rear, either, because the entire driveline could have been knocked out of alignment. Also, inspect the donor car, if possible. If it appears to have been well maintained until an accident, its engine is probably sound. But if the car was sadly neglected or is worn out, the engine will be too. It's not out of the question to buy a non-running engine, but be sure to remove the heads and inspect it before making a purchase.

Most junkyards will start an engine for you if you ask, whether it is in a car or not. But hearing it run won't tell you much more than whether there are major problems. Look for

blue smoke, which is an indication of worn rings or leaking valve guides, causing oil consumption problems. Listen for rhythmic clunks, clanks, and bonks that would indicate rod or main bearing wear.

To really determine your prospective engine's condition, warm it up for 15 to 20 minutes, then shut it off, block its choke and throttle open, and run a compression check. To do that, you need to remove all of the spark plugs, and ground the coil high-tension lead to prevent a fire from starting. Of course, you will also need to know the correct compression spec for that particular engine, which can be found in a shop manual.

Your donor engine's cylinders should be within six pounds of the specification. If the compression is 10 pounds or lower all across, the engine is in need of an overhaul. If the compression is down in two adjacent cylinders, it probably has a leaking head gasket or a cracked head or block. If the compression is down in just one cylinder, it could be rings, valves, a holed piston, or a bad head gasket. If you shoot a little oil down the cylinder, re-test it, and the compression comes up, the problem is rings. If the compression stays down, it is probably valves. If it only comes up a little, both the rings and the valves need work.

Look the plugs over too. If they are wet with oil or rusty, avoid that engine. Oil on the plugs indicates ring or valve guide problems, and water in the combustion chambers means a leaky head gasket or a cracked block or head.

If you can't hear a prospective purchase run, take a head off and look inside it before making a purchase.

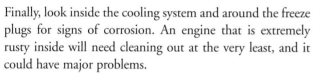

This isn't such a bad deal because you can check everything out before you make the purchase. And I'll bet that price becomes more flexible as the afternoon wears on.

If you've got the money, you can buy all the go-fast parts with one check and easily bolt together a pretty hot street machine.

Finally, look inside the cooling system and around the freeze plugs for signs of corrosion. An engine that is extremely rusty inside will need cleaning out at the very least, and it could have major problems.

Another thing to keep in mind while engine hunting is that you want the entire engine, including brackets, manifolds, valve covers, carb, and so on, if it is coming from a car that is not the exact year and model of yours. Some items can be very similar and yet not fit from engine to engine. It is a good idea to also get the throttle linkage because bending new linkage to fit is no easy task.

HOT SWAPS

There is nothing more appealing at a show than a correct, original, restored car, but some such cars just don't make very good drivers. There are cases where the engine for your particular year wasn't as good as the one in next year's model, or perhaps your car is equipped with a six and you'd like to put in a V-8. Well, you can do it, but it might be more complicated than you think.

Plan ahead, talk to people who have made the swap you intend to make, and be sure to get all of the accessories and the throttle linkage when you find your replacement engine. Just remember, the bigger and more powerful the new engine is, the more stress you will be placing on a classic's stock driveline. Another problem is that some smaller unit-bodied cars have actually been known to crack, due to metal fatigue at their door frames from being twisted by the torque of a big mill, which makes them very dangerous vehicles to drive.

REMOVAL A COMPLICATED DIVORCE

COST LESS THAN $200

SKILL LEVEL

TIME 4 HOURS

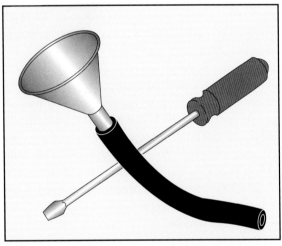

A long screwdriver and a funnel with a bit of rubber tubing can be used to pinpoint ominous engine noises.

Is it really necessary to extricate your engine?

Car magazines are full of ads selling "Bolt-on horsepower" components that work well. If your engine is fresh with little mileage on it, there is probably no need to jerk it out of the chassis and go through it. It's pretty easy just to bolt on manifolds, carbs, and heads. You can install headers and even racing cams in most cars without pulling the motor. Unless you are a contortionist with very small hands, however, it's quite difficult to do much to the rotating assembly (pistons, rods, crankshaft, and flywheel or flex-plate) without pulling the engine.

A compression test will tell you most of what you need to know about your engine's health. One end of the tester is pushed or screwed into the spark plug hole and then the engine is cranked to test the pressure.

CHECKING COMPRESSION

The most common procedure for determining an engine's condition is the compression test. It has been around since the horseless carriage, it is simple to do, and it is accurate enough to tell you almost everything you need to know about your engine's top end. But before attempting it, make sure your engine is in proper tune, with its valves correctly adjusted if they use solid lifters, and its battery fully charged. Otherwise, your readings will be faulty.

Compression should always be checked with the engine at full operating temperature. Take your car out for

Block the throttle and choke wide open before testing your engine's compression.

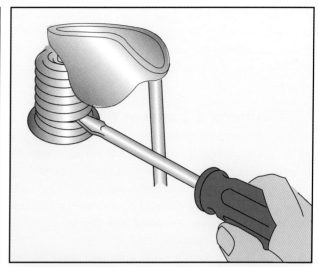
A long screwdriver can be used to check the strength of valve springs. Simply insert it and twist it. If the idle smooths out, the valve spring is weak.

at least a 20-minute drive on a nice warm day so all of its metal parts can warm up and expand to their correct clearances. Don't go by the temperature gauge. That only tells you localized temperature. Next, check a shop manual to verify what the compression should be for your engine.

Shut the engine off, block the choke and throttle wide open, and remove the spark plugs. Ground the coil wire to prevent sparks. Have a friend crank the engine while you check the compression. Push the nipple of the gauge into each spark plug hole while the engine turns over several times. Note each cylinder's reading, and return the gauge to zero before testing the next cylinder.

As a general rule, a difference of up to 6 psi is acceptable from one cylinder to another for normal use. If your engine is consistently a few pounds lower than the specified compression in your shop manual, it just means it has aged due to use. But, if any of the cylinders are more than 10 pounds

low, your engine needs work. If the cylinders are all 10 pounds low or lower, you're in for an overhaul if you intend to push the engine at all.

If your compression checks out low in any cylinder, the problem could be rings or valves, or a combination of the two. To determine if you have worn rings, squirt a little oil in the spark plug hole for that cylinder, and then test it again. If the compression test comes up to normal, rings are your trouble and an overhaul is in order.

If the compression does not come up on re-testing, a burned valve or a blown head gasket is the likely problem. If the compression comes up a little upon oiling and re-testing, but not enough, the problem may be rings and valves.

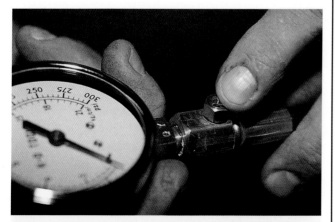
Be sure to take note of your results, then set the tester back to zero before testing the next cylinder.

Use a vacuum gauge to check your engine's health. Maybe you don't need to pull it from the car.

If the compression is down in two adjacent cylinders, the problem is likely to be a blown head gasket. Sometimes, re-torqueing the head will solve the problem, but most likely you will need to remove the head and replace the gasket.

USING A VACUUM GAUGE

Because an internal combustion engine is essentially a big air pump, much can be learned about its condition by monitoring the flow of air being sucked into it during operation. For that you need a vacuum gauge. A vacuum gauge will indicate the difference between the air pressure inside the intake manifold and the atmospheric pressure outside the manifold.

If you know how to use one, a vacuum gauge can tell you a number of things about your engine. Not only can it tell you about manifold leaks and burned valves, but it can also tell you about late ignition timing, poor carburetor adjustment, and exhaust back pressure problems. For our purposes, we'll be using a vacuum gauge to determine your small block's overall condition, but it would pay to learn how to use one for other things too.

Because a vacuum gauge measures the difference between atmospheric pressure and the pressure in your intake manifold (rather than measuring from some fixed benchmark), if you live above sea level you need to take into account the lower atmospheric pressure when using your gauge. The following table lists what can be expected at various altitudes. The readings are measured in inches of mercury, which refers to the number of inches the pressure would cause mercury to move up a glass tube in an old-fashioned barometric gauge.

The following figures are normal for a well-tuned engine at idle:

Sea level to 1,000 feet	18 to 22 inches
1,000 to 2,000 feet	17 to 21 inches
2,000 to 3,000 feet	16 to 20 inches
3,000 to 4,000 feet	15 to 19 inches
4,000 to 5,000 feet	14 to 18 inches
5,000 to 6,000 feet	13 to 17 inches

To use a vacuum gauge, you will need to remove a plug on the intake manifold or carb, and install a fitting that will let you hook up the rubber tubing from your vacuum gauge. Set the idle, then warm the engine thoroughly before beginning the test. Use a tachometer, if you have one, to make sure your engine is idling at the correct speed

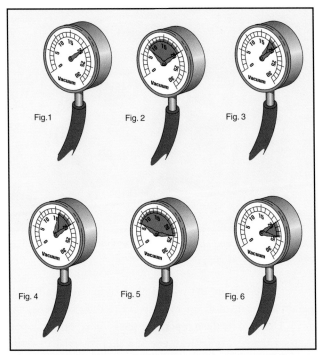

Another valuable diagnostic tool for old car engines is a vacuum gauge. It's good for diagnosing manifold leaks, valve problems, carb malfunctions, and a number of other things.

while testing. A shop manual will give you the exact figure to expect.

On cars not equipped with a tach, you can simply adjust the throttle so the car will roll along at about 7 to 10 miles an hour in low gear with your foot off of the gas. Assuming the test is being done at sea level, if your engine is in good condition your vacuum gauge should show a steady reading between 18 and 22 inches at idle (figure 1).

Open and close the throttle quickly and observe the results on your gauge. The reading should drop down to 2 inches when the throttle is all the way open, but should bounce up to 25 momentarily as soon as you let up.

If the needle fluctuates below normal with the engine idling (figure 2), it could indicate an air leak at the intake manifold, its gasket, or at the carburetor gasket. It could also indicate a leaking head gasket.

A regular, intermittent drop below normal (figure 3) indicates a leaking valve. Most likely it will be an exhaust valve that is adjusted too tight, in the case of solid lifters, or perhaps burned. Readjust the valves and check the vacuum again.

A rapid intermittent dropping from normal reading (figure 4) indicates sticking valves or dirty hydraulic lifters. Next, try vacuum readings with open and closed throttle. If

Each cylinder must be brought up to Top Dead Center (TDC) on the compression stroke, so that both valves are closed before the test can be performed. Of course, you can do a simple leak-down test just by pumping compressed air into the cylinder and then listening using a funnel and rubber tube. You can hear the air leaking out, just as it would from a bad tire if the rings or valves were not up to par.

In addition to the leak-down tester, you will need a source of compressed air capable of at least 80 pounds of pressure. The tester costs about $100 and can be a little hard to find. Try professional tool sources. If you are going to race seriously, you'll want to have one.

EXTRICATING YOUR ENGINE

Getting the engine out of the car is the dirtiest and toughest part of the whole job. It's not that it takes much skill, it's just that our classic Chevys were designed to be put together, not taken apart. At the other end of this project, you'll find that installing a clean new engine and buttoning things up isn't any big deal. You see, a great deal of engineering goes into making production cars easy to put together on a moving assembly line. But not much thought is given to the fact that 5, 10, or 20 years down the line, the engine might need to be taken apart and rebuilt.

To begin with, for safety reasons you'll need a place to work that is off-limits to little kids and inquisitive pets. Chevy small-block V-8s are heavy and full of old oil and toxic coolant. You'll need to keep your wits about you while you work to prevent making a poisonous mess. You

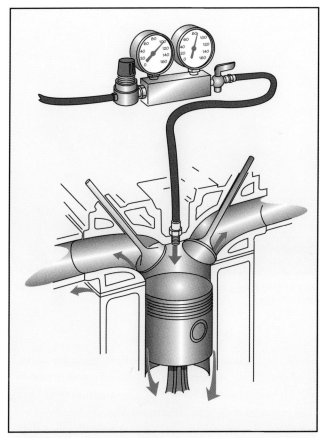

A more sophisticated way of checking for upper cylinder problems is the leak-down test. Air is pumped into the cylinder and then checked to see how fast it leaks down past rings and valves.

you see fluctuations increasing with engine speed (figure 5), the problem is weak valve springs.

If, with the engine idling, fast vibrations of normal vacuum are evident (figure 6) it is an indication of ignition trouble. On the other hand, slow movement at normal vacuum indicates incorrect carburetor adjustment.

LEAK-DOWN TEST

This is a technique used by aircraft engine mechanics that has become popular with street rodders recently. It is probably the most accurate type of test for determining the sealing abilities of an engine's valves and piston rings. Leak-down testing involves pumping compressed air into a cylinder through a spark plug hole and verifying how long it takes for the air to leak down past the rings and valves.

Attach your engine to an engine stand at the bell housing.

If you clean your engine before removing it, you'll stay cleaner and the work will be easier.

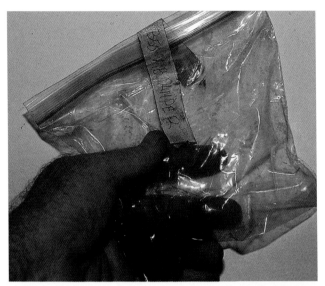

As you take things apart, take pictures and save parts in labeled plastic bags.

will want a friend who doesn't mind getting dirty to help you. You will also need a camera nearby.

THE MOST IMPORTANT TOOL

By far the most important tool you have is your brain. If you use it correctly, everything will fall into place. But if you allow your emotions to take over, you can easily ruin expensive parts. Be patient and analytical. If a part doesn't fit, find out why. Never try to force-fit anything on an engine. You'll just damage parts if you do. If a fastener won't come loose, don't get a three-feet-long extension and try to muscle it. That's a great way to run headlong into a wall and break off a fastener.

Instead, shoot on a little penetrating oil and let the item sit overnight. If that doesn't help, get a brass hammer and tap on the fastener rapidly and repeatedly. Hitting it hard will just swage the bolt into place and damage things, but a rapid tapping can break the molecular bond. If that doesn't work, try heating the head of the fastener with a propane torch and then letting it cool down. This helps break the corrosion loose. Never heat the surrounding metal, though, because you can do serious damage that way.

Cast iron crumbles when overheated, and aluminum will suddenly melt without even glowing red when the temperature gets too high. Steel will lose its strength, and many parts will warp and distort under high heat. Be patient, and if none of your approaches does the job, try combinations, such as heating, then tapping. If you do break off a bolt head, find a professional who can weld on a lever to turn the fastener, or have the item drilled out on a drill press.

When loosening a tight bolt, never push the wrench away from you. Always arrange yourself so you pull the wrench toward you. That way if you slip, you won't bang your knuckles on nearby structures. Also, if a stubborn bolt or nut won't turn, and you can't pull it toward you, slap the wrench with your hand or a rubber mallet, but don't just throw all your weight into it. If you do, you could easily wind up with a broken-off stub instead of a freed fastener.

TAKE PICTURES

Unless you've taken apart a lot of Chevys, you won't remember how that throttle linkage was set up, how that alternator was wired, or how that air conditioning bracket was attached several weeks from now when you are ready to put your engine back in. Take pictures of each assembly before you take it apart, and label each item with a felt pen or china marker before storing it. Use bits of masking tape to label small items.

If your engine is extremely filthy, you may want to take your car to one of those do-it-yourself car washes. Before you start blasting, though, make sure you cover all the electrics—such as the distributor, coil, alternator, voltage regulator, and starter—with plastic to keep them from getting wet and ruined. Wet down the engine, shake a little trisodium phosphate or Tide laundry detergent on it, let that sit for a few minutes, then go over it with a scrub brush before blasting off the dirt with the steam wand.

To take out the driveshaft, you must split the rear U joint. Do that by loosening and removing the yokes that hold the bearings in.

Pull the yokes out carefully and don't let the bearing caps fall off in the process.

Wrap tape around the bearing caps to hold them in place, and then pull the driveshaft out. The slip joint up front can be pulled off by pulling straight back on the shaft.

When you get your car home and in a spot where it can be left until you are ready to put the engine back in, take out the battery, clean it up, and store it on a wooden shelf. Do not leave it on a concrete floor. You'll also need to remove the hood on your car. Scribe around its hinges so you can reposition the hood correctly when you put it back on, and save any accompanying shims. Get a friend to help lift the hood off so you won't damage it or scratch your paint.

DRAIN THE FLUIDS

Jack the car up, put it on jack stands, and drain the engine oil into a waiting receptacle. Twist off the oil filter and drain it too. You will also need to drain the radiator. There is a small petcock at the bottom of the radiator that can be opened to drain it, but a little coolant will still remain in the engine block. Keep this in mind when lifting the engine out.

If the little petcock on the radiator is stuck, don't try to force it with pliers because it is made of thin brass, and you could end up just twisting it off. Instead, cut the lower radiator hose with a sharp knife, but be ready for a torrent. Drain the coolant into a drip pan and dispose of it according to local ordinances. Coolant is deceptively dangerous stuff. Although it looks innocuous, it is highly toxic and pets like the taste of it.

While you are under the car, disconnect the exhaust system and strap it up with coat hanger wire. Also disconnect the transmission cooler if you have an automatic. A golf tee and some duct tape can be used to minimize the loss of transmission fluid through the connecting hoses. Loosen its clamp and pull the lower radiator hose free of the radiator. Finally, take the battery cable and wires loose from the starter. Be sure to label all wires, describing where they are supposed to go.

Take off the air filter, throttle linkage, and alternator or generator, making sure to label all wires. Any other accessories such as power steering, air conditioning, and so on, should be taken off the engine now as well. If possible, leave the compressor for the air conditioning system hooked up to the system and just gently lift it out of the way. Otherwise you will need to bleed off the refrigerant and have the system replenished after you reinstall the engine. In any case, keep in mind that it is illegal to dump R-12 refrigerant into the atmosphere, and it is expensive to refill the system.

CHOICES

At this point, there are several ways you can extricate the engine. You can support the transmission on a transmission jack, then separate the engine from the transmission, and lift it up and out; or you can remove the radiator and pull the engine and transmission, as a unit, up and out through the front of the car. If you choose the latter, plastic plugs are available that can be used to plug the output shaft hole and prevent a mess of spilled transmission fluid from the rear of the transmission (this can happen even if the transmission has been drained). Another approach I happen to like is to remove the whole front clip, consisting of the bumper, grille, radiator cradle, and front fenders, then lift the transmission and engine out of the chassis as a unit.

Taking off the front clip isn't as tough as it might sound. Comparatively few bolts hold it in place. Without the front clip, getting the engine in and out and hooking it up is easy. Just make sure you have a couple of hefty friends to help you lift the clip off and place it on some heavy moving quilts to avoid damage.

If you decide to take apart as little as possible and leave the front clip in place, be sure to put layers of corrugated cardboard on the back of the radiator to protect its core. Personally, on any Chevy I would remove the radiator. Most likely, you'll want to have it serviced at a radiator shop or replaced with a new unit if you're planning to run a small block that is modified for performance. Next, remove the fan shroud, water pump, fan, and pulley before lifting the engine out. If you're removing only the engine, support the transmission using the car's chassis so that the car can be moved. If you're not going to move the car, a transmission jack provides good support, or you can build a cradle out of pieces 2x4s. Just make sure you don't put the weight of an automatic transmission on its pan because it could crush the pan.

If you decide to take the transmission out with the engine, split the rear universal joint and tape its bearing caps in place so the needle bearings inside will not get lost or contaminated. Pull the driveshaft straight back, so that the sleeve on the transmission output shaft slides off, allowing the driveshaft to be pulled out from under the car.

LIFTING THE ENGINE

Buy, borrow, or rent a sturdy cherry picker hoist. Don't try to pull your engine out using a chainfall attached to your garage rafters. Chevy small blocks weigh approximately 500 pounds and can easily come crashing down if not properly supported. On the hoist, use at least three feet of chain with welded links that are at least 1/4-inch in diameter. If you don't need all of the chain, you can pile it on top of the engine. Never try to use a short chain because it will create dangerous side loads on its attaching bolts. Your engine can also slip in the hook because of the shallow angles created by a short chain.

If your engine uses a cast-iron intake manifold, you can remove the carburetor and attach a welded plate and hook that will allow you to lift the engine easily. Otherwise, you can lift the engine out by installing a couple of longer bolts in place of intake manifold bolts. Use big fender washers under the bolts, backed up with other washers, and attach one end of the chain under a bolt near the front of the engine on one side, and another in the rear on the other.

Take up the slack in the chain on the hoist using the lever. Loosen the motor mounts and remove their bolts. If you are separating the engine from its bell housing and leaving the transmission in place, you may need to pry the engine loose with a big screwdriver. Inspect the engine one more time to make sure there are no fuel lines, electrical wires, ground straps, or linkages attached to it anywhere. Have a friend stand by to guide it, and then start lifting the engine slowly. Take it up a little and look things over again. The body of the car will come up with the engine because of the relieved tension on the front springs.

Take the engine up until it clears the front radiator cradle, then pull the engine clear or roll the car out from under the engine. Swing the engine around and unbolt the transmission. Pull it straight back to disengage it. Next, unbolt the bell housing and set it aside. With automatics, be careful not to let the torque converter drop out and spill fluid all over the place. For standard-shift cars, evenly loosen the bolts holding the pressure plate in place, half a turn at a time, until the tension is relieved. Otherwise, you risk warping the pressure plate. Now remove the flywheel or flexplate. Lower the engine slowly until you can slide it home in the engine stand. After a little cleanup, you will be ready for the fun of taking the engine apart and figuring out what it needs.

COST LESS THAN $200 INCLUDING HOIST AND SPECIAL TOOLS

SKILL LEVEL

TIME  4 - 6 HOURS

✔ YOU'LL NEED:

- ❑ 3/8-, 1/2-inch-drive socket sets
- ❑ Combination wrenches
- ❑ Putty knife
- ❑ Engine stand
- ❑ Plastic concrete mixing tray
- ❑ Puller for vibration damper
- ❑ Pressure blaster (optional)
- ❑ Gunk or other engine degreaser
- ❑ Laundry detergent
- ❑ Small ball peen hammer and prick punch
- ❑ Camera
- ❑ Ziploc plastic bags
- ❑ Clean rags

- ❑ Paper towels, several rolls
- ❑ 2x4 or 4x4 pieces of wood
- ❑ Large plastic bag (for storage of clutch assembly)
- ❑ Duct tape
- ❑ Four long, heat-treated bolts
- ❑ Scrub brush
- ❑ Felt pen or china marker
- ❑ Wire
- ❑ Corrugated cardboard
- ❑ Rubber/plastic tubing
- ❑ Masking tape
- ❑ Propane torch
- ❑ Plastic tarp
- ❑ Rifle bore cleaning kit
- ❑ WD-40

Place a concrete mixing tray (available from home improvement stores) under the engine stand during disassembly to catch drips.

The first time I tore an engine down, I was amazed at how it was designed and how it worked. The experience was a little like opening a birthday gift. I got so excited about what was being revealed at each stage that I just kept taking things apart at a furious pace and didn't organize or label anything.

I was 16 years old at the time and couldn't wait to get that engine done and back in the car. As it turned out, I never did. Instead, I ended up giving the disassembled engine to my cousin a few months after that. Later, my uncle sold it for next to nothing at a garage sale.

This pan has been removed before and whoever took it off didn't take much care when doing so. A new pan is in order. Remove the old bolts evenly, and then tap the pan with a rubber mallet to pop it free.

Back then, I didn't know that the disassembly of an engine needs to be approached with almost as much care as putting one together. In fact, there was a lot I didn't know back then. For instance, I didn't know that you don't want to mix up lifters, rods, pistons, pushrods, and other components unless you are going to replace them completely, because they have worn in together.

I also didn't realize how easy it is to forget how accessories and linkages were designed and installed. I didn't comprehend that, if you aren't careful, you could easily wind up with a big, bewildering, cast-iron jigsaw puzzle—especially if it's your first time tearing down an engine.

To ensure that won't happen to you if you're a first-timer, let's take disassembly one step at a time. It really isn't difficult or mysterious, and only a couple of special hand tools are required. We have allowed four to six hours to dismantle your engine, and that is what it will take if you are doing it for the first time and doing it right. A professional can do it in less than half that time. Here's how to do it:

This engine has seen a lot of miles and few oil changes. Oil has burnt under the heat riser in the intake manifold and formed a nasty sludge.

SEPARATE THE ENGINE AND TRANSMISSION

If you pulled your engine and transmission out of the car as a unit, find some short pieces of 2x4 or 4x4 to place under it at strategic points, and then let it down gently with the hoist. Never let the weight of an engine rest on its oil pan. You'll crush it if you do, or at least dent or buckle it.

Once you have the engine propped up and braced so it won't roll over onto your foot, separate the transmission from the bell housing, but don't take the engine loose from

Rust and corrosion in the water jacket may mean real problems if it is extensive.

the hoist. After that, if your car is an automatic, slide the torque converter off. Be careful not to dump its fluid all over your garage floor. Finally, remove the flexplate and bell housing.

If your car has a standard transmission, remove the throwout bearing and pivot arm, then loosen the bolts, holding the clutch plate in place, half a turn at a time until the spring tension is relieved. Wear a particle mask while working on the clutch and never use compressed air to blow out the dust. Chances are it is lined with asbestos, which is a known carcinogen. Store the clutch assembly in a plastic bag so it won't get oil or dirt on its lining and pressure plate.

CHECK THE FLYWHEEL

Inspect the flywheel. If it is scorched and discolored, cracked, or checked, it will need to be resurfaced or even replaced if it won't clean up completely. Let your local machine shop be the judge. A defective flywheel can be extremely dangerous because it can go off like a grenade at high rpms. If there is any doubt—especially if you are building a performance engine—get a new flywheel rather than risk injury.

PUT THE ENGINE ON THE STAND

Jack the engine back up with the hoist and attach it to the engine stand using four long, heat-treated bolts. Place a plastic concrete-mixing tray under the engine to catch

Attach the engine adapter (part of the engine stand) while the engine or block is still hanging from the hoist, then slip the adapter into the collar on the stand. Put the pin in the hole at the top to hold the engine in place.

A special puller is needed to remove the vibration damper. Don't try to pry it off with big screwdrivers. You may damage the timing gear cover and damper if you do.

drips. (Mixing trays are available at hardware and building supply stores.) Place a plastic bag over the mouth of the carburetor and tape it in place with duct tape. Cover the hole where the distributor was inserted with duct tape too.

WASH IT DOWN

Now is a good time to wash the engine down again. It'll be easier to work on and you'll stay cleaner if you do. Start by digging off any caked-on filth using a putty knife and an old screwdriver. When you've scraped off all you can, shoot on a good engine degreaser, let it soak in for a few minutes, then blast the rest off using a pressure blaster or garden hose and nozzle. If you can hook up to a source of hot water, such as at your washing machine or the bottom of the water heater, so much the better.

When you've blasted all the degreaser off, shake a little powdered laundry detergent on the wet engine and let that soak in for a few minutes. Finally, using a scrub brush, give the engine a good scrubbing. Rinse and dry the engine.

TAKE IT APART

Remove the intake manifold and carburetor as a unit. Remove the exhaust manifolds. Take off the fuel pump. Remove any other accessories you didn't take off before pulling the engine. Store everything in an orderly fashion out of the way of your work.

PULL THE VIBRATION DAMPER

Remove the accessory drive pulley by removing the three bolts holding it in place. (Early engines may only have two bolts holding the pulley on.) On some small-block Chevys there will be a large bolt and heavy washer holding the vibration damper in place. To remove it, you may need to remove the pan and wedge a piece of 2x4 between the crankshaft and the edge of the block to keep the crank from turning. If the rubber on the damper is swollen, or if its outer ring is out of alignment with the center, replace it.

You will need a special puller, available from tool stores, to remove your vibration damper. Attach the damper puller using the bolts that came with the tool. Be careful to use only bolts with the correct threads. (They can be coarse on one Chevy small block and fine on the next, so be careful.) Make sure the bolts are threaded in at least 3/8-inch so you don't end up pulling the threads out and leaving the vibration damper in place.

The damper puller should have a flat end with a small cone to center it on the nose of the crankshaft. If it doesn't, make sure you place a flat plate or other protection on the nose of the crankshaft to protect the threads in its center. Turn the puller slowly, using a large wrench, until the damper pops loose.

REMOVE THE HEADS

Next, remove the valve covers. Put their screws in a Ziploc bag and label it with a felt pen or china marker.

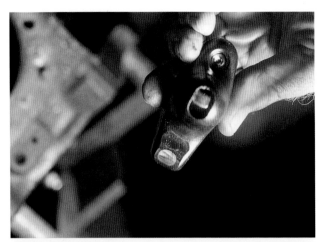

Rockers that are cracked or badly worn like these should also be replaced.

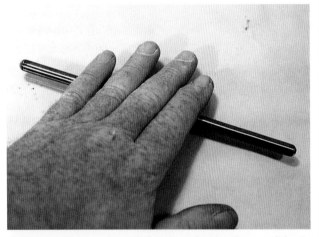

Roll pushrods on a piece of glass to make sure they aren't bent.

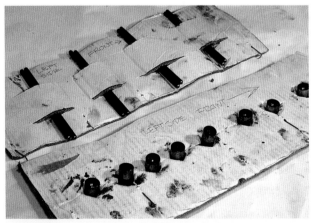

Store lifters and pushrods by slotting them into corrugated cardboard (in order) and don't mix them up.

Wipe any excess oil out of the valve covers and set them aside for now. Loosen and remove the rocker arms from their studs one by one, and string them on a piece of wire in order (from the front to the back of the heads). This is a critical step if you intend to reuse them.

Pull the pushrods out next, and then ease out the lifters. You may have to turn the cam to pop the lifers out if the interior of the engine is excessively dirty. Store the pushrods and lifters so they can be put back in the same location from which they were removed. I cut Xs and slots in corrugated cardboard and slip these items into them, but any way you have for keeping these items organized is fine.

The reason for keeping things separate and organized is that these components have worn themselves into a good working relationship. If you disturb that, the engine will never be the same unless you replace all the mixed-up components with new ones. An old egg carton is good for lifters, and pushrods can be cleaned and then labeled using tape too. Or, you can drill 16 holes in a board to hold the pushrods. Just make sure you know which cylinder on which side of the engine the component fits and whether it goes with the intake or exhaust valve.

Finally, with a 1/2–inch-drive socket wrench and breaker bar, loosen and remove the head bolts, bag and label them, and lift the heads off. An impact wrench can be used, but don't reuse those bolts. If the heads seem to be stuck, thread two bolts back on a couple of turns, insert a pry bar or breaker bar handle in the center exhaust port, and give a quick pull up to loosen the head. You can also try using a sharp putty knife to pop the heads loose from the block. Pull the head gaskets off, label them "right" and "left" according to their orientation, then save them so you can verify that your replacements have all the right holes in the appropriate places.

CHECK THE BORES

An engine that has seen a lot of service will have a fair amount of wear just down from the tops of the cylinder bores, where the rings ride up and down. This wear leaves a ridge at the top of the cylinder, making it impossible to get the pistons out through the top, due to ring expansion. If you find such ridges at the tops of your engine's cylinders, you will need to use a ridge reamer to remove them.

Ridge reamers are available from larger tool stores. Turn the crankshaft until each piston in turn is at or near the bottom of its stroke. Stuff oily rags in the barrels to pick up the swarf

Healthy lifters should be reground like this so they are slightly domed.

This lifter is dished and worn out. It must be replaced.

(metal shavings) from the ridge reamer so you won't damage the pistons when you remove them.

Oil the reamer's cutting blades with motor oil, then insert the reamer. Tighten it out against the ridge so it will make a slight cut, and then turn the reamer slowly with a large wrench. Keep the cylinder walls well lubricated as you rotate the cutter. Don't get too aggressive with the reamer. Just remove a little at a time, and then adjust the blades to cut a little more. Otherwise, you will damage the cutting blades and make chatter grooves and ridges in the cylinder walls.

BOTTOMS UP

Turn the engine over on the stand so you can get at the bottom end of the engine. Remove the screws holding the pan in place, then bag and tag them. Gently pop the pan off by tapping it at the corners with a rubber mallet or by using a putty knife. Wipe any excess oil or sludge out of the pan with paper towels and set it aside. Remove the oil pump filter basket and then remove the oil pump and its drive.

REMOVE THE RODS AND PISTONS

Next, look the connecting rods over carefully to make sure they are numbered, and that the numbers are in order. Most of the time they are labeled on the sides of the rods and caps so you can't mix them up. The engine originally came from the factory with the rods in the correct sequence from front to back, but they could easily have been mixed up during a later overhaul, so be careful. If the numbering is out of sequence, nonexistent, or for some reason unclear, use a prick punch and small ball peen hammer to number them in the correct order, away from the parting line making small marks.

Also make sure that each rod and end cap is labeled so you know which cap goes with which rod, and which way the cap faces. If bearing caps get mixed up or turned around, bearing failure could be the result. This is a critical step, so don't neglect to do it unless you will be replacing all of the rods and pistons anyway.

One at a time, remove the rod bearing caps. Slip rubber or plastic tubing on the threaded parts of the rod bolts to protect the cylinder bores and crank journals before pushing each piston out through the top of the block. Alternatively, you can wrap them with a couple of layers of masking tape, or buy special plastic protectors for this purpose.

With a prick punch, number each piston on the front quadrant of its top so you'll know which hole it goes in and which way it faces. It is possible to install pistons and rods backwards, and the result of this mistake can be disastrous. Even if you decide to install new pistons, it is nice to be able to use your old ones for reference if you are a novice.

You may have to gently tap on the pistons with the wooden handle of a hammer to get them past any slight remaining ridge, but don't use a lot of force. If you encounter resistance, make sure that the rod bolt or shoulder is not hanging up on the cylinder lip at the

A thick ridge at the tops of the cylinders prevents pushing pistons out from below. It also indicates wear.

Use a ridge reamer to cut out overhanging ridges so piston rings can slide up past them.

If they aren't clearly marked already, mark the rod caps and rods in order so you won't mix them up.

bottom. Novices have been known to damage pistons and rods and fracture lower cylinder walls by pounding too hard. Store the pistons and rods in order in a box so they won't get mixed up.

If your engine has been sitting out and is rusty internally, spray a little penetrating oil down each cylinder barrel from both top and bottom and let the block sit overnight. You can also try heating the pistons with a propane torch, but never heat the block itself. They will expand, crushing the corosion, then cool to pull away from it. You won't be reusing the pistons from a rusty block in any case, so if you damage them it doesn't matter; but if you heat the cylinder block too much in one place you could crack it, and besides, excessive heat can destroy cast iron.

REMOVE THE TIMING GEAR

Take off the timing gear cover and set it aside. Remove the bolts holding the cam timing gear in place, and slip the gear off with the timing chain. Never reuse a timing chain, and if the timing gears are notched or worn, you will need to replace them too. In some cases, the cam timing gear is made of nylon and it will be less noisy. I always replace nylon gears with metal ones because they hold up much better. This is a must for performance engines.

Break loose and remove rod bolts, then push pistons out through the top of the engine.

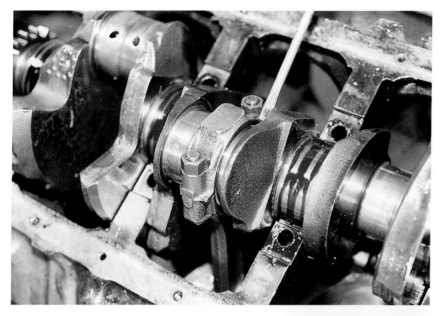

The fact that the rods can be moved around so easily in this engine means that bearings are worn and the engine probably wasn't holding proper oil pressure.

Pop off the timing cover, then remove the bolts holding the cam timing gear in place.

Timing gears that are notched and worn like this must be replaced, along with the timing chain.

Freeze plugs like these will have to come out so the water jacket can be cleaned properly.

A punch and hammer are good for popping the plugs loose.

Use a screwdriver to position the plug to pull it out.

LIFT OUT THE CRANK

Number the main bearing caps down one side so you know which way they are supposed to face, then break loose their bolts and remove them. Finally, lift the crankshaft out of the block. Unless you are a rather strong sort, I recommend having a friend help with this. Crankshafts are slippery and heavier than you might think. Put the main bearing caps back in place, facing the right way, and tighten their bolts finger-tight.

Store the crankshaft standing upright. If you lay it flat, it can actually warp under its own weight. I like to put it next to a vertical timber in my garage, then loop wire around the top of the crankshaft and wrap it around a couple of nails driven into the timber to prevent the crankshaft from falling over and getting damaged, or damaging me.

Cams come out the front of the engine only. The bearings are larger in front and smaller in back, so never try to drive the cam out the back of an engine. (Some later, roller-cam engines have a thrust plate to keep the cam from walking in the block. If your engine does, you will need to remove the two locating screws and the thrust plate before extricating the cam.) Put one of the timing gear screws back in a little bit and use it as a handle to pull the cam out. Ease the cam out carefully, using two hands, to avoid bumping its lobes or damaging its bearings.

If you wish to use your cam again, wrap it in plastic and hang it on a piece of coat hanger wire. In my experience, it is not usually worth trying to reuse a cam from a small block unless it is almost new. You run the risk of having marginal performance caused by flat or worn lobes. New cams are not expensive, especially in stock form. Also, never combine used lifters with a new cam.

PULL THE PLUGS

You will need to remove the freeze plugs, the plug at the rear of the cam, and the little oil gallery plugs nearby so your engine block can be hot-tanked and baked clean. Drive an old screwdriver into each one near the edge, and then use the screwdriver as a lever to pop it out. You may find a pair of vise grips necessary to help pull the plugs out.

Use a screwdriver to dig as much rust and scale out of the water jackets in the block and heads as possible. This

Needle-nose pliers or vise grips make popping the freeze plugs easy.

Use a rifle bore cleaning kit to remove sludge from oil galleries in the block and crankshaft.

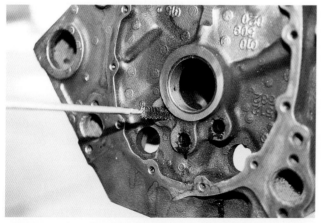
Make sure you clean out the galleries adjacent to the rear cam bearing too.

will aid in getting the block clean and will help prevent your rebuilt engine from overheating. Finally, use a rifle bore cleaning kit and soft wire bottle brushes to clean out the oil galleries in the crankshaft and main bearing saddles. Also, clean out the galleries at the rear of the engine next to the cam retainer. Scrub until your brush comes out clean.

If you have a parts cleaning tub, clean all of your engine components of grease, dirt, and sludge. It is preferable to use a water-soluable, biodegradable degreaser, but you can also use a little kerosene and rags to do your cleanup. Just be careful because kerosene is flammable and its fumes can be dangerous. After washing everything with solvent, kerosene, or a good degreaser, shoot on a little WD-40 to keep things from rusting. Store all of your engine components in an orderly fashion so they won't get mixed up, lost, or damaged. Wrap big components in supermarket plastic bags to prevent rust and dirt from attacking them.

MEASURING TOOLS
Taking the Measure of Your Engine

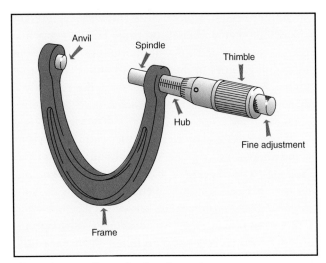

Shown here are the parts of a micrometer.

MEASURING TOOLS

Once, when I went to my favorite machine shop to drop off a 350 block and heads for some machine work, another guy was dropping his mouse motor off as well. The difference between his engine and mine was, his was still all together, right down to the carburetor and oil filter. It also appeared to be dripping a brown, thick, mixture of coolant and oil from somewhere. The fellow mumbled something about overheating as the engine was lifted off his truck.

It occurred to me that his bill might very well include an extra zero or two over what my trip to the machinist was going to cost because I had taken the time to tear my engine down, clean it up, and check it out. You see, it strikes me as folly to pay a high-end machine shop to degrease and disassemble an engine. Why would you pay skilled craftsmen the going rate to do work you can do yourself?

Judging from the chocolate pudding oozing from his engine's cooling system, the machinist's efforts may well have been for nothing. Besides, the block may have already been bored out as far as it can go. Oh, well. It's his money. Personally I would rather tear down an engine myself, figure out what it needs, and know what I am getting into before taking it to a machine shop.

I disassembled my engine completely, found out that it still had an overhaul left in it, and figured out what needed to be done before I ever dropped it off. I knew the block had been bored .040" over in a previous overhaul, and that the taper in the cylinders was beyond cleaning up with a hone and a drill. I also determined that the main bearings were still in alignment and that the decks (mating surfaces for the heads) and the heads themselves were not cracked, but were nice and flat.

I verified that the crankshaft was in good shape, but not so with the cam—pretty much what I expected. You might think figuring out what an engine needs would require years of experience and that a novice would not be able to do it. Actually, the process is pretty simple. It just takes a few very precise hand tools and the know-how to use them. Here are the tools you'll use:

Calipers are great for taking quick measurements to .001" and are easy to use. Vernier calipers are the standard at machine shops, but a dial caliper like this one is easier to read.

Calipers

These devices can measure any length up to 7.5 inches accurately to within .001" (1/1,000 of an inch). They are very handy and easy to use for a quick check of engine components, if you do not require more accurate measurements. There are three styles of calipers. Which style you choose depends on how much you are willing to learn, and how much you want to spend. If you need to measure beyond 7.5 inches, extended calipers are available, but you won't need such large ones for engine work.

There are smooth calipers that have no measuring scale on them at all, and those are just for transferring a particular dimension to another measuring device, such as an inside micrometer. They can be handy for getting into tight places, and when combined with micrometers, can provide accurate information. Using them does require some skill and experience, because two measurements have to be taken instead of one. However, uncalibrated

HOW TO READ A VERNIER SCALE

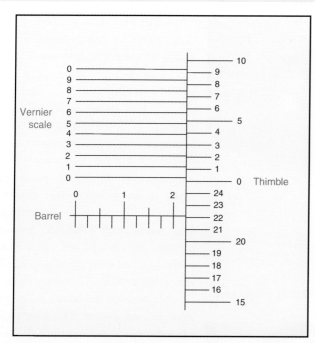

Shown here is a vernier scale laid out flat.

The scale shown in our illustration looks as if it were unwrapped from around the hub and thimble, and then placed flat on a table. In reality, you will have to rotate the instrument slightly to read the entire scale.

Adjust the thimble to a bit larger than the item to be measured, and then turn the fine adjustment slowly until it clicks. Make sure the item to be adjusted is not slightly cockeyed between the thimble and anvil, and then begin reading the scale.

Observe the number of lines revealed on the hub, or barrel. In the case of our diagram the thimble has moved out beyond the 2 mark, but not quite to the next mark beyond it. Note the number, which is 0.2000.

Next, note the number on the thimble, which most closely aligns with the line on the barrel. In this case, it is 22 or .0220.

Find the line on the vernier scale that exactly lines up with one of the marks on the thimble. In this case, it is the 3 line. This translates to .0003, or three ten-thousandths of an inch.

Barrel =	.2000
Thimble =	.0220
Vernier scale =	.0003
	————
Total reading is	.2223

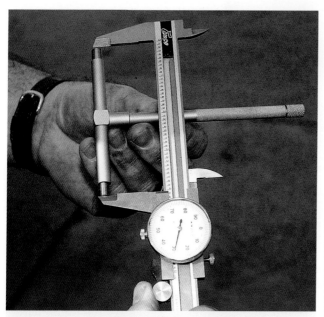

Snap gauges are only used to transfer an inside dimension to an outside micrometer or calipers.

calipers are inexpensive, and can be a handy addition to your tool chest.

The most accurate and durable caliper is the vernier caliper. The device is called that because it has a vernier scale etched into it that tells you the dimension you are measuring to the thousandth of an inch. Vernier scales can be a little confusing until you get the hang of reading them. On the other hand, most professional machinists will use nothing else. We'll show you how to read a vernier scale a little later.

If you don't want to bother with the vernier scale, for a few bucks more you can get a dial caliper. As the name indicates, these have an analog dial built into them that will tell you dimensions in thousandths of an inch. You just zero out the dial with the calipers closed or zeroed on a measuring standard, then take your measurement. If you buy a quality dial caliper, accuracy will not be a problem and they are easy to use.

Then there is the new kid on the block—the digital caliper. This is the most expensive of the choices. It comes

Micrometers can measure to .0001" accurately and are essential for close engine work.

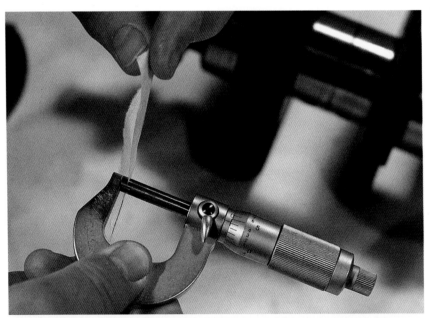

Clean the anvil and spindle tips of your micrometer after each measurement using a piece of paper or a lint-free rag. Clean the part to be measured too.

Micrometers

There are times when measuring engine components to one-thousandth of an inch isn't close enough. For instance, the stock, cast-aluminum piston clearance in a Chevy 350 is .0015" to .0025". This means a piston with a clearance of .0012" could seize in the bore when the engine warms up, and a piston that has a clearance of .0027" is in danger of developing piston slap when it wears in. If you can only measure to the nearest thousandth, you can't verify such clearances precisely enough. As a result, you could have a problem if you went ahead and installed new pistons without checking them.

Micrometers are what you need to measure your pistons. The most precise micrometers can measure to .0001" using a combination vernier scale. Such tools can be pricey if you want the finest, and even the less expensive alternatives aren't cheap. Sears sells a Craftsman 0- to 4-inch set of four micrometers for $279.99 at this writing, but Starrett, Mitutoyo, Fowler, and Mahr Federal—the brands favored by the pros—cost more.

Craftsman micrometers are excellent, as are many other less expensive brands, but beware of extremely low-priced, imported micrometers. Rather than buying those to save money, do as I did and pick up a set of micrometers at a pawn shop. You can sometimes find name brands for a fraction of what they cost new. Just make sure you get the proper measuring standards with them, and make sure the scale on each mic zeros out at the correct dimension.

Micrometers that are out of adjustment can be recalibrated professionally by the manufacturer, but that will cost money. To check the calibration, clean the measuring points (the anvil and spindle tips) and the measuring standard with a piece of paper or a lint-free cloth, then turn the fine adjustment on the end of the thimble in until it clicks. The scale should zero out at the dimension of the measuring standard.

with a battery-powered digital readout that is simple to comprehend, but it becomes a paperweight if the battery dies. Digital calipers can also be confining in the same way that learning to drive a car with an automatic—but never mastering a standard shift—can cut down on your options. Someday you might be in a situation where all that is available to you is a vernier caliper, and you won't be able to use it if you have never learned how.

Snap gauges are a less expensive alternative to inside micrometers, but they take a little finesse to use correctly.

A dial gauge mounted in a special jig is the most reliable way to measure for taper and out-of-roundness in cylinder bores.

Never oil a micrometer, because doing so will cause it to read incorrectly. Also, treat your micrometers with the respect delicate measuring tools deserve. Avoid dropping them or treating them roughly, and never use a micrometer as a C clamp. This last bit of advice should be obvious, but every auto shop teacher can tell you stories about people who have done such things.

Ideally, your selection of engine-measuring micrometers would include inside and outside mics, but you can get by using a telescope gauge set and your outside micrometers. Telescoping gauges are also called snap gauges, because you insert them in the opening to be measured and snap them out against the surfaces. You then lock the snap gauge

using the twist barrel on top and slip it out of the hole. Use an outside micrometer to measure the snap gauge and you have the dimension you are looking for.

Whether you use inside micrometers or snap gauges, the key to measuring correctly is having the gauge or inside mic exactly 90 degrees to the surfaces being measured. You can make a light pencil line on the extension of the snap gauge, and then watch the line move in and out when you rock the mic back and forth slightly. When the line is in as far as it will go before it starts to come back out, you are at exactly 90 degrees.

In the case of a cylinder bore, you can also push a piston up from underneath to help line up your mic or snap gauge. But the most accurate way to measure a cylinder bore is using a dial indicator mounted in a special jig that holds it straight while you move it up and down inside the bore.

Dial indicators

These are invaluable devices that can perform all sorts of automotive tasks. For example, they can measure gear lash on a differential and run-out in a transmission or flywheel. And they are indispensable for checking crankshaft straightness, finding precisely TDC for pistons when you are degreeing in a cam, and determining cylinder bore taper. Dial indicators aren't terribly expensive, and they are vital for careful engine rebuilding. New indicators can run around $80, but, you may be able to beat this price at the pawn shop.

When you purchase your dial indicator, be sure to pick up a good magnetic base as well. You'll want one with a minimum 90-pound pull so it will hold firm to the part on which it is placed. A complete magnetic base with attachments from Craftsman retails for around $50.

Machinist's straightedges

These are great for measuring valve spring height and checking flatness of heads and decks. They are also great for determining whether an engine needs its main bearing journals align-bored or not. Don't be tempted to use an ordinary straightedge, because it may not be straight enough to give you an accurate reading. A machinist's straightedge can be found for under $10.

You don't need all or any of these tools to build an engine. But the fewer measuring tools you have, the more you will be required to depend on your machinist to tell you what needs to be done, you will have to trust that the job was done correctly, and your machining bill will be much bigger.

Also, to really blueprint an engine and make it better than the factory original—something you will want to do if you are planning to pump more performance out of your small block—you will need to understand how to take precise measurements. We'll tell you what blueprinting means and how it is done in the next chapter.

MEASURING
Lessons in Tolerance

COST $100 – $500 (FOR TOOLS)

SKILL LEVEL

TIME 3 HOURS

I hear some of the guys at meets tossing around the term "blueprinting" when talking about engines, but I don't think many of them know what the term really means. They usually use it to imply that an engine was carefully machined and assembled, and that's close enough to loosely fit the modern definition of the word blueprinting. But my sarcastic side sometimes tempts me to ask them to which blueprint they referred when they built their engines.

Back in the late 1950s, in the days of such drivers as Fireball Roberts and Marvin Panch, stock cars were really stock. The race car builders would go to the factories and rummage through the parts bins until they found pistons, rods, crankshafts, and blocks that were manufactured and machined as close to the specifications on the original blueprints as possible. Such components produced the best engines for the track, hence the term blueprinting.

Race car builders did this because the engines that came off Detroit assembly lines back then were only approximately within tolerance. When you realize that these cars were cranked out at about the rate of one per minute, you can understand why. That's not a lot of time to spend making sure everything is perfect. On motors, valves were manipulated to get them to seat, pistons were put in blocks by trial and error, and the assemblers worked at a brisk pace.

As a result, very few of our cars' engines performed quite to their potential, even from the factory. And that is why you can often make them better than new when you overhaul them. In addition, machining has come a long way in the past 50 years, and careful work can make a big difference in your engine's performance and longevity.

Also, most racers prefer blocks that have been around awhile because it means the stresses cast into them at the factory have had time to work themselves out, so they will be more stable and will hold their dimensions better. Some of the manufacturers of the great hand-made classics even let their block castings age for as long as six months before doing any machine work on them. We're talking clearances of only thousandths of an inch, after all, so any warping will throw them off.

The keys to having powerful, smooth, long-lived engines are good measuring, careful machining, and meticulous assembly. Most of us can't do our own machine work, but we can take careful measurements to determine what our engine needs, then verify that the machine shop did the job correctly. And we can do a top-quality job of assembly if we try.

Measuring in thousandths of an inch takes care and a little experience, but it is not as difficult as you might think. Read chapter 5 and spend a little time practicing before you try measuring your motor. If you're just refurbishing, and especially if you are building a performance engine, you will want to take such measurements. They can tell you what an engine needs, and even tell you if a trip to the machine shop is necessary. Sometimes all an engine needs is honing, new rings, and a valve job.

If your engine has a lot of miles on it and is well-worn, or if it has been sitting for years, you will want to have a machine shop go through it to make it as close to optimum as possible. Whatever your particular situation is, if at all possible, you will want to check your engine yourself before and after having any machine work done to it.

Check each cylinder bore for taper and wear using a micrometer or bore gauge.

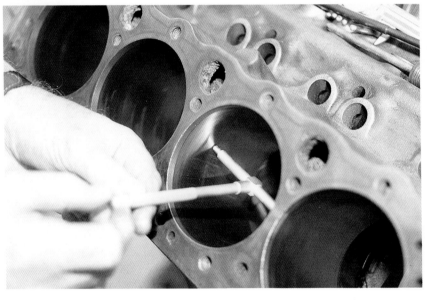

An inside micrometer can also be used to check taper. Tip it back and forth until you have the minimum dimension and the gauge is at a right angle to the bore.

Cylinders

At the top of each cylinder bore on a worn engine, you will find a ridge just above where the rings moved up and down in service. The ridge extends from the top of the bore down about 1/4 inch. If it is thick (.003 or .004), or hangs up when you pass your fingernail over it, the engine will need to be rebored. In any case, you will most likely have used a ridge reamer to cut down this lip at the top of the cylinder to remove the pistons and rods.

If the ridge is thin or nonexistent, use a bore gauge or inside micrometer to see how much taper there is in the cylinders. Check at right angles and near the top and bottom of where the rings travel. Use an old piston to help get an inside mic perpendicular to the bore, as described in chapter 5. Cylinder wall

taper develops when the compression and oil rings on the piston scrape along the upper parts of the cylinder bore, eventually causing it to wear and get larger in diameter than the lower area and top 1/4- inch that the rings never touch.

Taper isn't the only problem. Be sure to use your bore gauge to check along the axis of the crankshaft, and then again at right angles from top to bottom, because cylinders wear out of round. If the taper is within .003 from top to bottom, and the cylinders are no more than .0025 out of round, you can overhaul your engine. Use its original pistons and new rings by cleaning the bores and knocking off the glaze with a cylinder hone chucked into a 3/8-inch multi-speed drill.

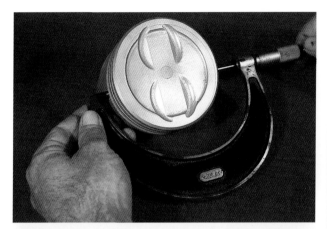

Measure the piston at the wrist pin and perpendicular to it, top and bottom.

Use a machinist's straightedge to determine if heads and decks are flat. If a .004" feeler gauge will slide under it at any point, the surface will need to be ground flat.

Check heads and decks for flatness along the length and diagonally, both ways.

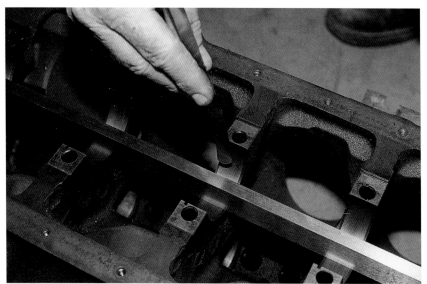

Use a machinist's straightedge (not an ordinary metal ruler) and feeler gauge to check the alignment of your engine's main bearings. If they are out by more than .004" from one to another, have the block align bored.

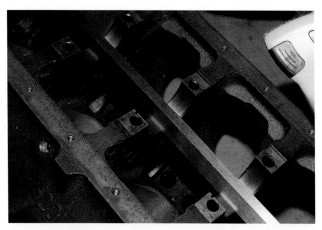

Be sure to check both the sides and bottoms of the mains to make sure they are in alignment.

You can even clean cylinder bores without removing the crankshaft by carefully wrapping the crank with rags to catch any grit from the hone. Liberally coat the cylinder walls with kerosene or an oil-and-solvent mix, then run the hone slowly up and down in the bores. Make sure all of the glaze is gone and there is a faint cross-hatch pattern on all the surfaces. Be careful not to push the hone down so far that its stones come out down below the bores. You will ruin the tool and risk damaging the crankshaft. A ball hone is the best glaze breaker. A sunken stone hone is best left to a professional. Ball hones can be rented. After honing, clean the bores with soapy water and oil them. Solvent alone will not lift out the honing grit.

Pistons

Measure your old pistons top, bottom, and parallel to the wrist pin, as well as 90 degrees to it, using an outside micrometer. Next, check the figures against the pistons specifications. Pistons wear out eventually, and sometimes their skirts shrink or collapse if the engine seriously overheats. Worn and collapsed pistons wobble in their bores and cause an annoying clatter called piston slap. They will eventually fail, and their rings will wear unnecessarily too.

Rings

Even if you are simply putting new rings on your original pistons, you will need to use flat-stock feeler gauges to verify that the rings have the correct tolerances in their grooves and that the ring gaps are the correct width. Specs are supplied with the ring set. Make sure the rings are not too thick for their grooves and that the ring gaps are not too small. Otherwise, when the engine warms up and the pistons expand under running conditions, the rings will not be able to move in their lands and the engine will seize.

Connecting rods

Your engine's rods must withstand a great deal of punishment because of the push and pull they have to deal with over the years. They can stretch, bend, and even crack, especially in performance engines. You can check length, and look for cracks at home, but it is pretty hard to accurately check for bending and twisting.

To check for cracks, use a Magnaflux Spotcheck Jr. kit. If you find cracks in any of your rods, it's best to replace them all. You can get away with changing out just one rod, but if an engine has been pushed to the point of cracking one connecting rod, chances are the others have been overstressed too. You can check rods for length using vernier calipers, and if any are stretched, replace them all. Stretched rods can result in spun bearings and will be prone to cracking and failure, often with catastrophic results for your engine.

On the other hand, also make sure the rods are not bent or twisted. If rods are bent or twisted, they can create friction due to misaligned bearings and pistons. Slightly bent or twisted rods can be straightened, and for general street use

Using a micrometer, check each of the rod journals for out-of-roundness.

Check each of the crankshaft journals for out-of-roundness as well as taper using a micrometer.

engine's heads or block decks are warped, the head gaskets will leak. Then you will lose compression and you can easily damage your engine. The simplest way to tell if you have a warped head or deck is with a steel machinist's straightedge and flashlight.

Place the straightedge on its edge across each head lengthwise, then sight under it with a flashlight. Make several checks with the straightedge parallel to the head, diagonally across it, and across its narrow dimension in several places to make sure it is completely flat. Do the same with the mating surfaces of the block (decks).

If you see light under the straightedge, check the gap with a feeler gauge. If a .004"-thick gauge will fit under the straightedge, the block or head will need to be resurfaced. You can also check the main-bearing saddles for the crankshaft with your steel straightedge to see if they are aligned properly. If they are out of alignment more than .0015", the block should be align-bored.

Check the crank

Put the crankshaft in the block with only the front and rear main-bearing shells in place, then turn it and watch for wobble at the center mains, or use a dial indicator to measure the wobble. Hold a feeler gauge (the thickness of a bearing shell) next to a center-bearing journal and see if you can spot any side-to-side movement. If you do, the crankshaft will need to be straightened.

Check the main- and rod-bearing journals for roundness and taper using an outside micrometer. You will need to take the following four measurements: two at the front of each journal at right angles to each other, and two at the back in the same manner. These measurements will tell you if the crankshaft needs to be machined and undersize bearings fitted. Bearings and journals wear out of round from the pounding they get in operation. They often wear more at one end than the other as they work back and

they will in all likelihood perform well for years. Of course, if you are building a nitrous-burning racing engine, even new stock rods may not suffice. Have your machine shop make all the same checks you did, just to verify your findings, and then decide whether you want to stay with your stockers or buy replacements.

Checking for flatness

Engine blocks and heads warp due to repeated heating up and cooling down during operation. If your

Cams on old engines can be reground, but if they are chipped and worn through the hard chrome surface like this, they should be replaced.

It is important to measure the heel, or base circle, of the cam to make sure it is within tolerances.

Cam lobes wear flatter as engines age. Check the height of each lobe to make sure it meets the specifications in your manual.

forth in the block. If your crankshaft journals are more than .0005" out of round, or taper more than .0005", the crankshaft will have to be reground.

Cams

If you are doing more than a simple ring-and-valve job, remove your cam and check for wear and flattened lobes too. (I generally replace the cam as a matter of course during a complete overhaul because it takes a lot of punishment in service, and an uneven or worn cam can spoil an otherwise nice engine.) Verify the dimension across the heel, and from heel to toe of each lobe, using a micrometer. Replace the camshaft if it is not within specifications.

All of the valve springs should be inspected and measured using a steel straightedge. The springs should all be the height specified in your shop manual. If they aren't, replace them. Also, have a machinist measure the valve guides to see that they are in specs. If they aren't, they will need to be machined out and bushings will need to be

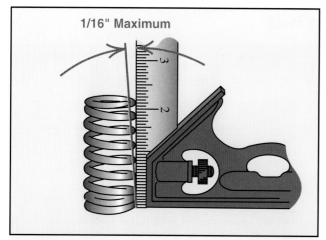

1/16" Maximum

If you want to reuse valve springs, you'll need to test them for correct height and make sure they aren't warped out of square.

installed. Otherwise, oil will run down through the valve guides and your engine will burn oil.

These basic checks will indicate your engine's condition and can help you make choices that will be the difference between a motor that will run well only for another year or two, and one that will last a lifetime. Take your time, take notes, and work carefully. Then, when you make that trip to the machine shop, you will know what your engine's needs are. And when you get it back, you will be able to verify that the job was done properly.

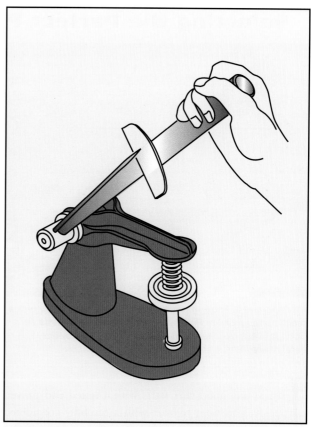

You must also test valve springs for correct tension. This is a device most machine shops have to do the job.

CHOOSING A MACHINE SHOP
Selecting the Perfect Partner

It's important to know who you are dealing with when you pick a machine shop. Larkin Ranney at L&R Automotive in Santa Fe Springs, California, has years of experience and provides careful, accurate, custom work at reasonable prices.

Magnaflux crack testing is the first thing that needs to be done on any block before any machine work is performed.

Just as any good chef starts with a tested and proven recipe, you need to start with a carefully considered plan, or mental blueprint, before having anything done to your engine. Do you want to build a radical, screaming fuelie that will leave everybody in your class in the weeds? Or do you just want to build a hot street machine that will stay together for a long time, but scare the stuffing out of you and your friends when you stand on it and make that awesome V-8 rumble as you roll into the local car show? You have to make such decisions before you go to the machine shop.

Machining an engine for a short-track sprint car is entirely different from building one for a Top Fuel dragster, or building one for the street. In some ways, the street engine is the biggest challenge. A short-track sprinter or an all-out dragster run at essentially fixed throttle. They don't have to idle, they don't have to pull away from a standing stop smoothly, and they don't have to start easily in rainy weather or avoid overheating in hot weather.

What you have the machinist do depends partly on what your engine needs in order to be brought back to health, and partly on what you want to do to it to make it more durable, more powerful, and more appropriate for your intended use. Because full racing engines have to be competitive, a lot of trick things need to be done to transform them into winners. On the other hand, a street

engine will be operating closer to its original design envelope, so less custom machine work will be needed.

Once you have your blueprint clearly in mind, start checking around for a good shop to do the machine work. Finding a custom shop isn't as easy as it once was. With the advent of more complex engines in modern cars, fewer professional mechanics are rebuilding engines one-by-one. Chances are, if you took a car with a tired engine to your local garage, they would simply replace the old motor with a rebuilt long-block obtained from a big production rebuilder. With the high costs of labor, small garages can't rebuild engines the old-fashioned way and remain competitive.

The economies of scale for large production shops make it possible for them to keep their equipment running constantly and allow them to employ people who only need

Honing is the final step to get cylinders ready for new pistons. It must be done with the block precisely aligned and exactly perpendicular with the crankshaft.

whose work they prefer. As an example, one of the reasons I use L&R in Santa Fe Springs, California, to do my engine work is because I know that the famous drag racer Junior Thompson also has his machine work done there. I spent a large part of my youth watching Thompson blow the doors off of everything that moved at the old Lions Drag Strip in Southern California. I figure if L&R is good enough for Junior, it's good enough for me.

Speed shops are another place to check who is hot and who is not. They can often recommend a good machine shop, and they generally have a better understanding of the specialty work you are looking for. Some may even do the work for you, but they can be a bit pricey. That's because most of them don't have their own facilities. They just "middle" the job as a service to their customers, send it out to people they know, and then mark things up a bit for their trouble.

I also know that my favorite local speed shop, California Discount Warehouse in Long Beach, California, has all of their machine work done at L&R too. Rocky at California Discount Warehouse has been around a long time and knows everyone in the business, so her choice of machinists is an informed one. How did I find out who she uses? I asked.

Block decks have to be perfectly flat, and properly aligned with cylinders.

to know how to run one machine all day long. That is not to say that such assembly-line production facilities don't do a good job. However, they may not be equipped, nor will they usually want to take the time, to do all the extra little things to make your hot street engine run its best.

On the other hand, if you are just overhauling your stock engine, a reputable production machine shop can save you money and will do a good job. They may not radius the crankshaft journals, do a three-way cut on the valve seats, or cross-drill the crank, but none of that is necessary for the longevity of a stock engine that will be driven moderately. If you are going to be putting the pedal to the metal, however, you'll want the machinist to pay a little more attention to details. That kind of work will require a custom shop.

So, how do you find a good custom machine shop? You can start by asking local rodders and mechanics

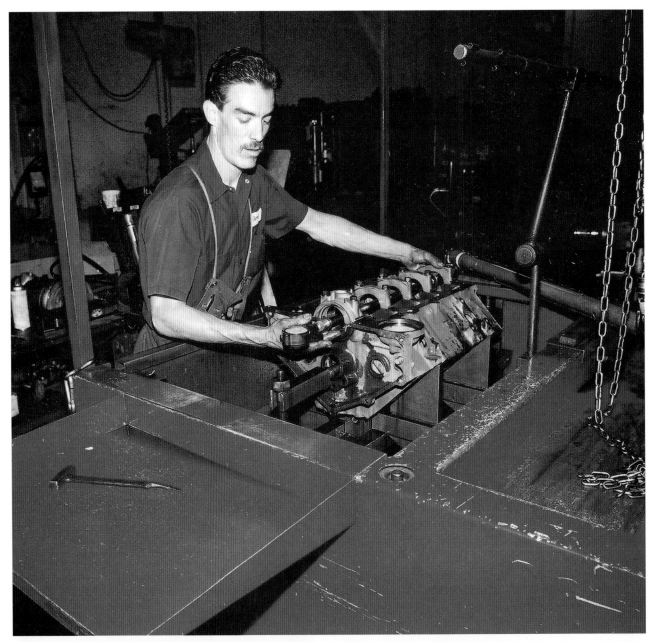

Align boring puts crankshaft-bearing journals in exact alignment so crankshaft bearings will be long-lived.

A few years ago, I had another local speed shop send out an engine I was working on and I got back a damaged crankshaft. It seems the people to whom they farmed out the crank grinding job drove a pin out of it from the wrong direction. They attempted to punch it from the big end and out through the little end, fracturing the crankshaft and rendering it useless in the process.

After discovering the problem, it took me a month to get the matter straightened out. The speed shop had to send my crank back to the machine shop, the shop had to replace it and do all of the work again, and then send the replacement crank back to the speed shop.

That's why these days I stick with Larkin and Darrick Ranney at L&R. They do custom work at fair prices, and nothing gets lost in the translation. I can verify for myself that the facility is clean and neat, and whether the work is done with precision and care. Quality machining takes meticulous attention and

good habits. It's one business where "good enough" isn't good enough.

Whatever you do, don't hand your parts over to a machine shop that has big heaps of greasy parts and oily messes everywhere. You want a group that is proud of their facility and proud of the work they do. If you find a dirty, disorganized, cluttered facility piled high with junk, and if the machines are old and neglected, keep on looking. The shop you trust with your precious parts must be clean and organized, and its machines should be well-maintained and properly calibrated.

For our purposes, it is important that the shop has experience with Chevy small-block engines. That's because each powerplant has a few of its own unique requirements. Though the same general procedures are done to all automotive engines in the process of machining them, what is critical on one engine may not be so important on another. In addition, the super-tuning tricks you use on a Chevy engine may not work as well on a Ford or Mopar motor.

Another possible problem with some machine shops is that you may not get the same components back that you brought in. To avoid this problem, mark your heads, block, connecting rods, and crankshaft with a prick punch to ensure that you can identify them. If you checked them out beforehand to make sure your parts were in good shape for a rebuild, you won't want someone else's tired, marginal components in exchange.

If you have followed along so far, you will have made the important measurements to determine the condition of your engine and you can inform the machine shop of your determinations, but let your machinist make his own measurements and tell you what he recommends. That way you can cross-check his findings with yours and decide what you want to do. If your information differs in any major way from the machinist's, ask questions and find out where the discrepancy lies. You may save yourself some headaches later and you will learn from the experience.

Keep in mind that if you just drop your engine off with a list of things you want done based on your own measurements, the machinist will do what you ask whether it is the best course of action or not. For example, if you tell him to bore the block .060" over, that is what he will do. Yet, he may be able to clean up the bores sufficiently at .040". That's why it's important to let the machinist measure everything carefully himself and tell you what needs to be done to your engine. Good, experienced machinists will know your engine and what can and cannot be done with it.

If you have a good idea of what your engine needs and you find out what each procedure will cost, you will be able to walk out of the machine shop with a pretty accurate idea of what the whole job will entail financially. Of course, as I mentioned before, you need to know what kind of engine you are building in the first place. Building an all-out racing engine and trying to squeeze out every last pound of torque entails much more than just building a nice street engine.

For instance, in situations where you won't be going over 7,000 rpm, you don't need to cross-drill the crankshaft. You also don't need to change to a custom-forged crankshaft or install special connecting rods. In that situation, as long as your originals are good, you can stick with them. If you do need to change crankshafts, a cast, aftermarket crankshaft will do very well.

If you are building a bracket racer or full-drag racing machine (where you will be revving in the 7,000–10,000+ rpm range) you will need a forged crankshaft, forged pistons, and better rods. And you will also want to drill any block equipped with two-bolt main bearing caps to allow for four-bolt caps. Use caps that allow you to splay the outer bolts on the mains for extra strength, rather than having them go in 90 degrees to the block.

Take your time to determine what your engine needs and what you want to do. Then find a good machine shop to do the work. These are critical steps that can make all the difference as to your satisfaction with your engine when you are finished.

WHAT MACHINE SHOPS DO
A Look behind Closed Doors

Now you know how engine measuring and blueprinting are done and how to find a good machine shop, but we must cover the specifics of what a machinist might need to do and why. Getting your engine to match your blueprint is a complex and exacting task that takes time, and as a consequence, a fair amount of money. The amount of money depends on what needs to be done and how far you want to take it.

Cylinder bores must be aligned perpendicular to the crankshaft, and the block deck height in relation to the crankshaft journal must be made the same for each cylinder. Cylinder bores must be made perfectly straight and round, with no taper top to bottom. Connecting rods and crankshafts must be perfectly straight too. Bearing clearances must be exact because if they are too loose, the engine won't hold oil pressure. If they are too tight, the bearings will overheat and destroy the crankshaft.

Cylinder heads must be milled flat and true, and valves and valve seats must be ground so they will seal properly. All of these items are basic and necessary when doing a complete, high-quality overhaul, but there is much more to do if you want to build a trick engine.

After the machinist has done all of the cleaning, measuring, and checking for cracks, you will want to sit down with him and discuss what you want him to do. There are the basic necessities that must be done to overhaul any engine, and then there are the little extras that make a difference to performance and durability. And there are a few tasks you can do at home to save money, if you choose.

Tell your machinist what you want to do with the engine, let him explain what each procedure costs, what your particular engine requires, and what he recommends. Then compare your findings with your budget to determine how much work you would like your machinist to do. If you have more money than time, have the machine shop do the whole job. Otherwise you may want to do some things yourself, and you may not want to go for some of the extra little tricks.

Let's look at the machine shop tasks and the components one at a time:

THE BLOCK

It is rare that a Chevy small block is in such bad shape that it cannot be restored to health. However, if the engine has been severely neglected or abused, the engine may easily be

Cylinders must be perpendicular to the decks for the heads, and crankshaft bearings must be an equal distance from the mating surfaces so each piston's stroke is the same.

damaged to the point that it must be scrapped. A few small blocks out of high-mileage trucks, taxis, or sorely neglected cars may not be salvageable for another rebuild.

Before any work is done on the block, have it hot-tanked and baked to flush out any sludge or filth. Next, make sure the block is Magnaflux tested for cracks, even if you checked it with a Spotcheck Jr. kit. As previously mentioned, unless you are doing a numbers-matching restoration, it makes no sense to try to fix a crack in a Bow Tie V-8 block. There are still plenty of cores out there and good cores only cost about $125 (at this writing). Blocks with four-bolt mains are a bit pricier, as are 400-cubic-inch blocks, but the cost still isn't outrageous.

It is also a good idea to sonic-test any prospective block as well. This is a process that uses sound waves to verify cylinder bore thickness and roundness. This test will also tell you if there was any core shift when the block was cast. If a casting core shifted during manufacture, some cylinders may be thick in certain areas and thin in others. Boring out a block with significant core shift can cause cylinder walls to be paper-thin in places, which will result in overheating and engine failure. Corrosion in the water jacket can also cause thin cylinder bores.

Next, have the decks (head mating surfaces) of the block checked for flatness, and have the distances from the center of the crankshaft to the decks checked. You could end up

If the main-bearing journals are out of alignment due to block warpage, they will have to be align-bored as shown here.

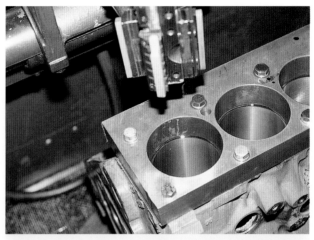

After cylinders are bored, they need to be honed. A torque plate (the 2-inch slab of metal on top) should be used before honing to eliminate any clamping distortion from head installation.

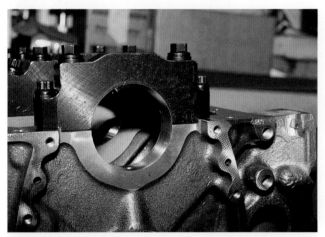

Bearing caps must never be mixed up or put on backward because they are matched to their journals during align boring.

Finished cylinders should have fine grooving like this to help rings seat when the engine is first run in.

with higher compression on one bank or in one cylinder if this dimension is neglected. Finally, have the main-bearing journals checked to see if they are in proper alignment. There is no point in having the block align-bored and honed if it isn't necessary.

Any block that is to the point where it needs to go to the machine shop should have its cylinders bored oversize and fitted with new pistons. Radically overboring a Chevy block just to gain displacement in a street motor is not a good idea. If you go too far, you could have trouble with overheating. You will also be shortening the useful life of the engine because you may not have another overbore left in it unless you use wet sleeves. Except for some early Chevy small blocks, .060" is about the maximum you can overbore your engine anyway.

If one cylinder is too badly worn, or if it is pitted, cracked, or otherwise ruined, the cylinder wall can be bored away completely and a wet sleeve can be installed. This will hold up well, but it is an expensive process. Besides, if one cylinder is that bad, often the others aren't much better. The most practical and least expensive thing to do would be to find another block, unless you must use the one you have for the sake of correct serial numbers in a restoration.

Don't buy new pistons until your machinist tells you what size you need. Small-block oversize pistons are commonly available in 20, 30, 40, and 60 thousandths over, but smaller and larger ones can be purchased on special order. Most Chevy blocks require a 30 thousandths over bore to clean up properly. And if the machinist tells you that your block will clean up at 30 thousandths, don't bore it to .060" over unless you are building a racing engine and are willing to risk thin cylinder walls and cylinder wall pits that won't clean up.

MAKING IT BETTER THAN NEW

Aside from more accurate machining than the factory provided, there are a couple of things you can do to a Chevy block that will make it better than new. You can clean away any flashing from around oil return holes, and round the sharp edges on bearing saddles to help prevent cracks by not giving them a place to start. The point isn't to make things look pretty, so don't remove all those little casting bumps in the block, because they increase its surface area and help with cooling.

Another thing the machine shop can do—or you may want to do at home—is to shot peen the bearing caps and even the webs around the main bearings to further strengthen them. Finally, you will want the machine shop to tap the cam-oil gallery plug holes at the back of the block and install pipe plugs. The standard little soft plugs that go in these holes are not likely to blow or leak, but it is better to play it safe.

Crankshaft journals often wear out of round, and can develop taper from front to rear. Regrinding the crankshaft and installing undersize bearings is the answer to this problem.

THE CRANKSHAFT

Just as with the block, the crankshaft should be steam-cleaned, baked, and Magnaflux tested before any work is done on it. Cracked crankshafts must be discarded. If you need another crankshaft, a cast crankshaft (or a forged crankshaft if you are building a high-rpm racing engine) from Scat Enterprises in Redondo Beach, California, is an excellent option. A Scat crank costs significantly less than a new crank from Chevrolet, and Scat's crankshafts are beautifully machined and made to last. You can also get a stroker crank from Scat that is better and easier to fit than an original 400 crank. If your stock crankshaft is sound, however, there is no need to replace it unless you are building a stroker motor.

Crankshaft bearing journals wear out of round, and they often wear to a taper too. If your crankshaft is too far out of specs to accept new bearings, have it reground and install undersize bearings. Again, let your machinist tell you which size bearings you need after he has done his own measurements.

If you do need to have the crankshaft turned to a smaller size, tell the machine shop to provide generous fillet radii where the main bearing journals meet the counterweights and throws. Turning a used crankshaft down 30 thousandths and building in large fillet radii can actually result in a crank that is less prone to cracking than the original, with its sharp corners at the bearing journal edges.

Crankshafts also sometimes warp as a result of all the inertial forces and shocks of acceleration. This is not generally a major problem with Chevy small-block V-8s because of their short, stout crankshafts. It does sometimes happen, and if you stick a bent crank back in an engine it will cause rapid bearing wear and oil pressure loss. Most bent cast-iron cranks are not out of spec by more than a few thousandths and they can be straightened, but the job requires the skills of a pro.

MAKING IT BETTER THAN NEW

Beyond the usual machining tasks required for renewing a crankshaft, there are some performance tricks worth thinking about. You can improve your stock crankshaft a little by grinding off all of the casting slag and roughness at home. Use #40 and #80 grit disks and abrasive rolls to do the job. Be sure to chamfer the oil holes in the bearing journals too. Sharp edges at these points can damage bearings and limit oiling.

Your machine shop can make your crankshaft last longer by cross-drilling or Tuftriding it. Do not try to cross-drill your crank at home. Cross-drilling provides your engine's bearings with more consistent oiling and prevents spun bearings at high revs. Tuftriding involves submerging the crankshaft in molten salt, which heat treats and hardens it.

A high-performance crankshaft should have a smooth surface, chamfered or radiused counterweights to help prevent cracks, and beveled leading edges to help it knife through air and oil while running.

Radius all sharp edges on the counterbalance weights too. This will help the crankshaft slip through the oil, and will help prevent cracks. Finally, before you have the crankshaft machined and balanced, you might want to have it shot peened, or even do it yourself at home.

If you really want to set up your engine's old crank for racing, but don't want to buy a new one from a source such as Scat, there are several other things you can do to make it slip through the oil in the pan. This may sound like gilding the lily, but it all makes a difference at higher rpms. At 6,000 rpm a crankshaft is spinning very quickly, so every little bit helps. Of course, you will want an oil pan with a windage tray if you are going to get serious about racing. This suggestion, and the following tips and tricks, will make your engine rev faster and produce more power.

The next level of making your crankshaft better than new is to remove all of the roughness from its counterweights to make it more slippery. After that, you can have your machinist bevel the forward edges of the counterweights to a 45 degree angle. Beveling will make them slip through the oil and air with less turbulence and friction. You can also have the counterweights lightened by removing metal to reduce radii, and this will make the engine respond faster. This task must be done as part of the balancing process.

HEADS

Cylinder heads have a tough job to do. They take much of the heat of combustion when the engine is running. Their seats and valves have to work in diabolical circumstances. Whether you disassemble and inspect your heads yourself or have the machine shop do it, the job should be done every time you have the heads off the engine.

Cylinder heads frequently warp and crack due to heat. Have them hot tanked and Magnaflux tested before you do anything else to them, because a cracked cast-iron head is best scrapped. It is possible, at some expense, to weld them, but the fix is often temporary. Besides, a new set of high-performance heads can be acquired for as little as $650, and a new set will be far more efficient than your originals.

Cracked aluminum heads can be welded easily by a skilled welder, and they are worth fixing unless they are badly damaged in some other way. The aluminum heads can be expensive to replace. It may be cheaper to purchase a set of rebuildable cast-iron heads. They can be found for as little as $225 (at this writing), and welding up cracked heads can cost at least that much because a head must be heated in an oven to cherry-red before welding it. Heating cracked heads almost inevitably causes warpage that must also be corrected, which is another disadvantage of welding damaged heads.

The first thing that must be done to most heads is to mill or grind them flat so they will seal against the block properly. This is critical. If the head is warped, the engine will not maintain compression, head gaskets can blow, and water can get into the cylinders with disastrous results. You will also want to have the mating surfaces for the manifolds checked and ground flat too. Don't forget to have the manifolds or headers ground to match.

Stamped rockers and their studs need to be checked for wear, and valve springs must be checked for proper height and resilience. Valves and valve seats need to be inspected to see if they are burned or cracked. If an engine has valves and seats that were not designed for unleaded fuel, either new, hardened valve seats should be installed, or valves designed for unleaded fuel will need to be put in. You don't generally need both, unless you are going racing.

Finally, the valve guides will need to be checked for wear. Chevy valve guides are integral to the head castings and are cast iron. If the guides are worn, oil will leak past the valve stems into the combustion chambers and the engine will burn oil. If your valve guides are worn, they can be cleaned up and valves with oversize stems can be installed. A better fix is to machine out the valve guides and install bronze inserts. Bronze inserts can either be screwed into place or press-fitted, but the job must be done at a machine shop.

Have the valves and valve seats ground, and if you are looking for performance, have the machinist do a three-way cut with the seat angle at 30 degrees instead of the usual 45 degrees. This makes for less turbulence and more

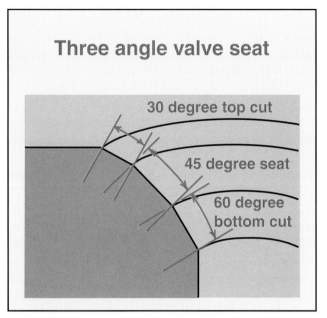

Three angle valve seat

30 degree top cut

45 degree seat

60 degree bottom cut

This is the best way to grind valve seats for maximum horsepower.

horsepower. Of course, if you want to go from 1.94"/1.50" valves to 2.02"/1.60" diameter valves, that will also have to be done by a good machine shop.

The life of your original valve guides can be extended somewhat by knurling them, which is the process of grooving the valve guides and forcing the surrounding metal out to where it was before the guides were worn. However, this is a temporary fix at best. Don't do it unless you just want an engine to last for few months until you can get another one. If you do not replace the engine after a short amount of time, you'll be dealing with the problem of oil consumption all over again.

MAKING IT BETTER THAN NEW

On stock Chevy cylinder heads, the rocker arm studs are merely pressed in. If yours are worn, of if you are building a high-performance engine, you will want to replace them with screw-in studs. Removing rocker arm studs is not a big deal, but don't try to cut threads for screw-in studs at home. If they are even the slightest bit misaligned, you can cause major problems with the valve train.

Instead, have the machine shop cut new threads. Then you can have them install the studs, or you can do it at home when you assemble the heads. Just use a little Lok-Tite and take them down until snug, but don't overtighten them. Studs and guide plates are a must on high-rpm engines, but they aren't really necessary for low-revving torquer motors.

Also, check out the porting chapter if you want to make big horsepower gains for very little money. If you invest a little time and effort into your stock heads, the performance potential can increase dramatically. Judicious pocket porting and cleaning up port runners can easily yield 17–25 more horsepower out of a 350, and that's a big gain over stock performance that will cost you next to nothing. And the porting process will actually make your stock heads better than new.

Of course, if you can spring for it financially, a set of World Products Sportsman II heads can make your engine a whole lot better than new. With their superior 72-cc combustion chambers, they can be run with flat-top pistons for maximum power without risking detonation. World's castings are much cleaner and higher quality than stock, and they will produce more horsepower right out of the box.

When you consider what it costs to have all the testing, machine work, and valve grinding done on a set of stock heads, you realize that aftermarket heads don't cost that much more money. The older, closed chamber heads (68 cc) are hard to find and are expensive. They also must be used with dished pistons to avoid detonation, unless they are made of aluminum. The heads most of us will have or will be able to find easily are the 74–76-cc smog heads, which have good performance potential. If you can afford them, World's 72-cc heads and a set of KB flat-top pistons will give you about the ultimate for a street engine on pump gas.

RODS

Connecting rods take a great deal of punishment during service and must be in tip-top shape if they are to hold up in a performance engine. Even though you checked them with a Spotcheck Jr. kit, have them Magnaflux tested at the machine shop for cracks as well. If a rod lets go, that could easily be the end of all your dreams of glory at the strip. Rods don't usually let go at their narrowest point. More often they break at fracture points, such as the sharp angular breaks where the rod bolts rest.

Your machine shop will also need to check your rods for straightness. Rods can easily get bent and twisted in service, especially if an engine is pushed to its limits. Big-end journals can become elongated too. Make sure the machine shop checks all of your rods for center-to-center length, from the wrist pin to the bearing journal. Also, make sure the machine shop checks the rod bolt surfaces to ensure that they are perfectly flat so the rod bolts won't be pulling at an angle.

Connecting rods must be weighed and balanced, along with the rest of the rotating assembly.

If any of your rods require more than minor correction, replace them. As we said before, you won't want to be running over your own parts in front of your friends. If the rod big ends get stretched, you can easily spin a bearing with catastrophic results. A new set of forged rods from Scat Enterprises can be had for a nominal cost and could be good insurance. Get the type with full-floating wrist pins because they will last longer and make the engine easier to work on.

MAKING THEM BETTER THAN NEW

Read the shot peening chapter for tips on making connecting rods the best they can be. Of course, if you are building a revver or racer you may want to use heavy-duty aluminum rods. They aren't necessary for most applications, but if you want to run nitrous, or a blower and high rpms, you might want to consider them.

Unless you are rebuilding a stock engine with relatively few miles on it, replace the pistons. Which pistons you choose will depend on what you want to do with the engine and how much metal the machinist must remove to clean up the bores. If you run closed-combustion chamber (68-cc) iron heads with flat-top pistons (flat except for valve relief slots), your engine will develop compression in the neighborhood of 10.5:1, which will cause detonation on pump gas.

You can usually get away with aluminum closed-chamber heads with flat-top pistons because of their superior heat-exchanging capacity, or you can use dished pistons and stay with cast-iron heads. Closed-combustion chamber heads are superior for all-out performance to open (74–76-cc) combustion chamber heads, but either can be made to perform well for the street, and open-chamber heads are what most of us will be able to find and afford.

Any small-block Chevy engine, whether it be a stocker, street rod, or racer, will benefit from proper balancing. Tiny amounts of weight (as little as one gram) can make your engine run at less than optimum performance and bigger imbalances can make it tear itself apart. All of the rotating assembly, including crankshaft, rods, and pistons, must be carefully balanced, as well as the flywheel and clutch, if the engine is going to be mated to a standard transmission.

Many stroker cranks, and any crank from a 400-ci engine, must be balanced with the vibration damper and the flywheel or flexplate attached because these engines were externally balanced originally. An externally balanced engine has some of its balancing and adjustments done on the vibration damper and flywheel or flexplate. The machine shop may do the balancing themselves or farm it out to a specialist. Either way, the crank will have to be spun and balanced dynamically, and the rods and pistons

A dynamically balanced crankshaft will make your engine smoother and it will last longer. This is the machine used to do the job.

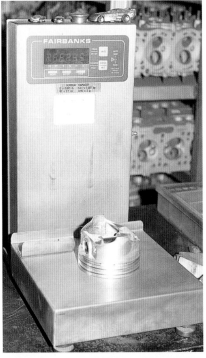

Have your engine carefully balanced whether you are building a stocker or a street rod. This scale is so sensitive that it can accurately measure below a gram in weight.

Stroker cranks must be balanced with the vibration damper and flywheel or flexplate attached.

will need to be carefully weighed, with adjustments made to correct any discrepancies.

Heavier pistons will be balanced to the lightest one, and the same is true of connecting rods. The flywheel may be drilled on one side or the other to correct any problems. Weights can be riveted to the clutch assembly to zero it out, and the crankshaft may be drilled, or drilled and filled with mallory plugs made of tungsten (heavier than steel) to deal with any imbalance.

MAKING IT BETTER THAN NEW

A good, accurate balancing job will be superior to what was done at the factory and will make your engine last longer as a result. Small soft plugs can be added in the drilled balance holes of the crankshaft to cut down turbulence, but that is only recommended for extreme-use engines.

Holes are often drilled in crankshaft counterweights to balance the engine.

Occasionally, weight must be added to balance a rotating assembly. Also, plugs are installed in holes to make the crank smooth again and to limit drag in racing engines.

HEADS

Have Your Heads Examined

✔ YOU'LL NEED:

- ❏ Valve spring compressor
- ❏ Sharp putty knife
- ❏ Soft wire brush
- ❏ Magnaflux Spotcheck Jr. kit.
- ❏ 1/2-inch socket set
- ❏ Old slothead screwdriver

Whether you use the original heads for your engine or decide to go with a set that better suits your goals, you will need to know how to disassemble and inspect a set of heads to make sure they are useable. This is an easy task that can save you money. You get to keep what the machine shop would charge to tear down your heads, and you avoid having costly machine work done on defective ones.

To begin with, look over the faces of the valves and inspect them for cracks or missing bits. Check the valve springs for looseness or breaks. Also check inside the water passages for extensive corrosion. You will find crust and rust in heads that have been in service for any length of time, but if passages are extensively clogged, the interiors of the water jackets may be in bad shape.

If the heads are off of an engine you are overhauling, you can tell a lot about the general health of the engine by looking at the combustion chambers and valves. If a combustion chamber is rusty, you may have had a leaking head gasket. This can usually be verified by inspecting the head gasket itself. A head or cylinder block may be cracked, which would indicate a more serious problem.

If a combustion chamber is particularly wet with oil and full of carbon, oil was probably leaking down the valve guides or blowing up past worn piston rings. Either condition means the engine should be inspected. Valve guides in Chevy heads are cast in, and knurling them to curb oil consumption is only a temporary solution. Machining out old guides and installing bushings is a better solution to the problem. And rings should always be replaced when an engine is down for servicing.

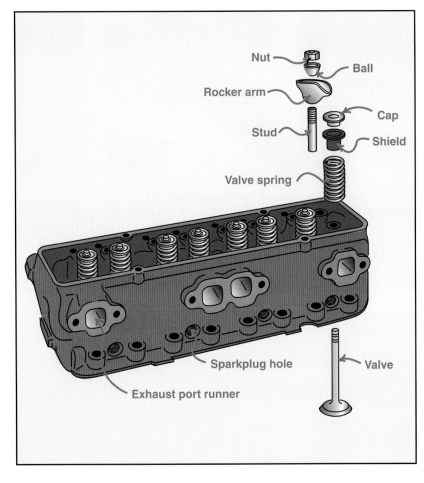

Next, clean the heads of carbon, gasket residue, and caked-on grease and filth. Another blast of degreaser followed by a little scrubbing and scraping with a soft wire brush and a putty knife will get most of the filth off. Later, after the heads are stripped for overhaul, you will want to have them hot-tanked and Magnaflux tested, but for right now a general cleanup will do.

TAKE OUT THE VALVES

You'll need a good-quality, sturdy valve compressor to remove the valves. Cheap valve compressors won't have the capability to compress the valve springs adequately. Slide the cupped part of the tool onto the valve spring keeper, and then slip the flat part of the tool onto the center of the valve face. Adjust the tool so that when you push down on the lever, the valve spring will be compressed enough to allow you to lift out the split keeper. A small pocket magnet helps to do this job. Be careful not to let your fingers get pinched during this process.

Lift off the retainer, the outer spring, and the inner, flat harmonic spring if there is one, and then slide the valve out the bottom of the head. Keep the valves in order on a piece of cardboard, and put the springs, retainers, and keepers in a plastic bag and label it as to which cylinder it came from and whether it went to the intake or exhaust valve.

Clean up the valve seats with a soft wire brush and solvent and examine them for cracks. It is generally not worth

continued on page 64

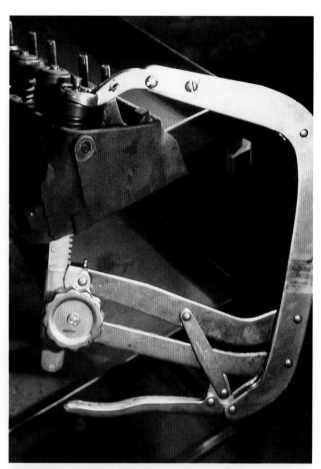

A sturdy valve-spring compressor is required to decrease the tension of valve springs so that valves can be removed.

Once a valve spring is compressed, keepers can be removed. Keep any parts that are to be reused separate from each other and labeled.

Once a keeper is out of the way, let the tension off the valve spring and remove the rest of the assembly.

Pull the rubber oil seal off and slip the valve out of its guide.

If you plan to reuse them, leave the rocker studs in place. Otherwise, remove them by using spacers and a nut to press against the head.

One way to check for cracks is to use a Spotcheck Jr. kit from Magnaflux.

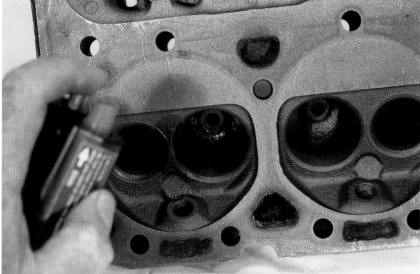

Clean the area to be checked using the included cleaner. Be sure to check around the valve seats and bolt-holes.

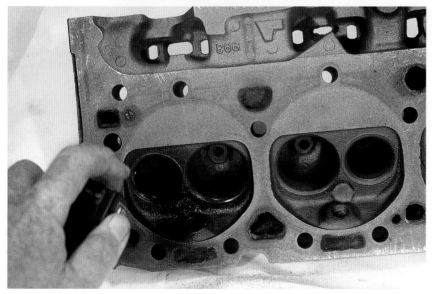

Shoot on a light coat of the red dye and let it soak in.

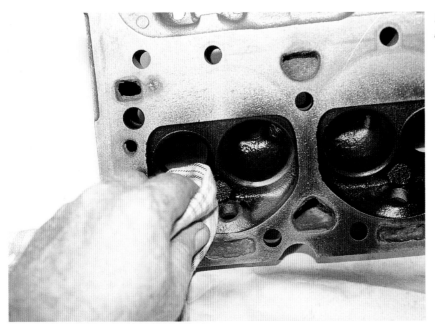

Next, shoot a little cleaner on a rag—not the part—and wipe off the red dye.

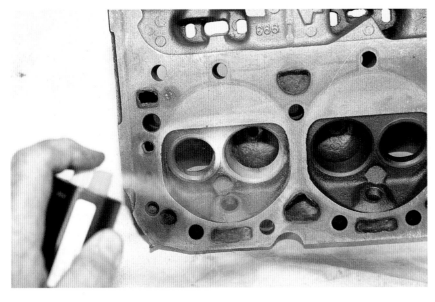

Spray on a light coat of the developing powder.

Continued from page 61

attempting to weld up cracks in cast-iron heads because the process is very costly and the results are most often marginal. Aluminum heads aqre able to be welded quite easily by a professional.

REMOVE THE ROCKER STUDS

If they are not damaged, rocker studs can be left in place, but if you are building a performance engine, remove them and have new, threaded studs installed. The originals can work loose under stress and pull out of their mounts.

Never try to cut new threads and replace the rocker studs yourself because it is easy to get them off-center or misaligned. Let a competent machinist do this job when the heads are being reconditioned.

The simplest way to remove rocker studs is to put spacers or a stack of washers on the stud and then tighten a nut down onto the washers to pull the stud out. As the stud is pulled up, you will need to add more washers so that you don't end up tightening the nut down to the limit of the threads.

CHECK FOR CRACKS

I like to do a preliminary check for cracks before I take a set of heads to the machine shop. If I find cracks, I can save myself a trip to the machinist, as well as the money it costs to have the heads hot-tanked and Magnaflux tested. You'll want to check around valve seats, combustion chambers, bolt-holes, and valve guides.

I use a little kit made by Magnaflux called the Spotcheck Jr. to do this inspection. It consists of a cleaner, a dye penetrant, and a developing powder. It will work on cast iron or aluminum and is very accurate, although I would still want to have cast-iron components Magnafluxed by a machinist before I did a lot of expensive work. Here's how to use the kit:

First, shoot on the cleaner and wipe down the part with a rag to rid it of dirt, oil, and grease. The surface to be tested needs to be clean for the process to work. Next, shoot on a little of the red dye. (The little aerosol canisters are color coded so you can't get confused.) Let the dye soak in for a couple of minutes.

When the dye gets tacky, shoot a little of the cleaner onto your rag and wipe off the red penetrating dye. Do not put the cleaner directly on the part because it will cause the red penetrant dye to diffuse too much and wash deep into small cracks. Finally, shoot on the white powder developer.

Even tiny hairline cracks will become visible almost immediately as bright red lines. You can also use a Spotcheck Jr. kit to check engine blocks and connecting rods, which will be covered later. At this point, we want to make sure we have a good set of rebuildable heads for our engine.

SWITCHING HEADS

There are certain small-block heads that are better for performance applications than others. You'll hear lots about 68-cc versus 74-cc heads, bigger valves versus smaller, aluminum heads versus cast iron, and "camel hump" versus other castings. All of these factors have advantages under certain circumstances.

Chevrolet has developed hundreds of different small-block head configurations over the years for all kinds of applications, so the possibilities are mind boggling. An entire book could be written about Chevy small-block head castings alone, but many of them wouldn't interest anyone except the historians. So which heads are best for you? That depends.

Some heads lend themselves to modifications better than others, and some of them cannot be used at all on cars that must meet today's air pollution standards. Of

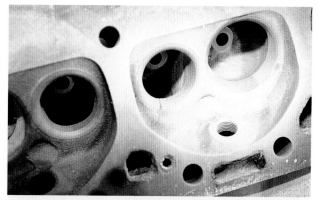

Cracks show up as red lines. Cracked Chevy heads aren't usually worth fixing.

This is a closed-combustion chamber head with big valves installed. They'll make mighty horsepower but will probably make your compression too high for the street.

course, aftermarket performance heads are available from a number of sources that will meet current pollution laws and give hotter performance. If you can afford them, they will save you the time and effort you would expend to modify a set of stock heads.

With a little work, the heads that came on your engine, or a set of used heads you find at a swap meet or wrecking yard, can be made to perform very well too. Just be careful when buying used heads. Make sure the vendor will allow you to exchange them for another set if the ones you he sells you turn out to be defective. And use casting numbers to verify whether you are getting the heads you want.

Closed- versus open-combustion chamber heads

Earlier, cast-iron small combustion chamber heads (64 cc) from the 1960s can be made to breathe very well and they can deliver more torque all across the rpm range. When they are surfaced and paired with flat-top pistons,

Later on, open-combustion chamber heads can be made to perform by pocket porting and will still keep your compression in the pump gas range.

These heat riser ports can be blocked to produce a cooler fuel-air mixture, provided you don't live in a cool climate.

they can easily bump your compression up over 10:1. At this point, your engine would suffer from detonation on pump gas, and that will ruin it in a hurry.

Aluminum closed-combustion chamber heads are better when combined with flat-top pistons because of their superior heat-conducting capacity, but they are more expensive and harder to find. Even cast-iron small combustion chamber heads are becoming pricey and rare these days. Dished pistons, when combined with closed-combustion chamber heads, will lower your compression ratio to around 9:1, so if you do find a good set of closed-combustion chamber heads for a reasonable price, grab them while you can.

Open-combustion chamber heads (72–74 cc) are not as good for all-out racing, but can be made to breathe very well for street use, and they are much more common and less expensive to acquire. Unless you live in a cold climate, you will want to block the heat riser ports that heat up the fuel mixture during cold starts because it also makes it less dense once the engine is warmed up, which cuts power. There is one caveat: These heat-riser ports were added partly to meet smog restrictions, so if you are going to put your engine in a later car that has to pass smog tests, you may not want to block them.

Bigger versus smaller valves

Most small-block 350 heads came with either 1.94"/1.5" intake and exhaust valves or slightly larger 2.02"/1.6" valves for performance situations. If you are going with a more radical cam in a 350 or are building a

stroker, you will definitely want to go with the larger 2.02"/1.6" valves. If you are leaving your engine basically stock you'd be better off leaving the valves at 1.94"/1.5" if that is how the engine was set up originally.

The bigger valves help you only at higher rpms, and then they only offer a significant increase in airflow if the intake valve is deshrouded and the head is pocket ported. The factory did this as a separate machining operation on heads in which bigger valves were installed. Otherwise, by just installing bigger valves, you will only incur added expense and you might actually hurt your engine's performance.

Aluminum versus iron

Aluminum heads have the advantage of conducting heat better than iron heads, so an engine equipped with them can run a slightly higher compression ratio without detonation, but aluminum heads do not add horsepower per se. Aluminum Corvette heads from engines of the late 1980s to early 1990s breathe well, but because of their small combustion chamber (58 cc) they won't accept larger valves. However, if you find a set in good shape for a decent price, purchase them. With a little judicious porting, they will perform very well indeed.

Many people tout the weight advantage of aluminum heads. And at only 20 pounds each, they weigh less than half as much as cast-iron heads, but we're only talking about a savings of about 44 pounds altogether. Unless you are putting your engine in a very light, purpose-built race car, that doesn't mean much. I don't know about you, but I could go on a diet and lose that much weight for free.

You can tell what kind of head you have by looking at the cast-in symbol on the end. Double-hump heads are good street rod candidates.

EARLY, SMALL-COMBUSTION CHAMBER HEADS

Casting No. 3782461

The 461 castings, produced from 1961–1966, were the first to have the double-hump symbol cast into their ends. Because, with few excep- tions, they were made for and installed on fuel-injected Corvettes, these heads are sought after but not common, especially in rebuildable condition.

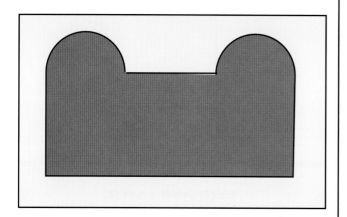

Casting No. 3782461X (1961–1963)

This is a very rare head because only a small batch was produced especially for drag racing. Strangely enough, a number of them wound up on truck engines. These heads are especially nice because they have larger intake port run-ners (175 cc as opposed to 158 cc) so they make more top-

end power. The combustion chamber also has a quench pad next to the spark plug hole, which is unique to this head. These heads were made in either large or small valve configurations.

Casting No. 3795896 (1963–1965)

These were used on the 283 Power Pack and 327-ci 250-horsepower Corvette; 58-cc combustion chambers might make compression quite high.

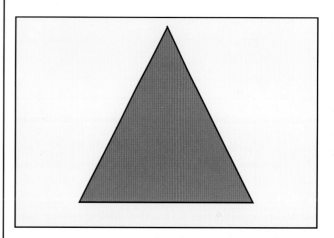

Casting No. 3890462 (1962–1967)

The double hump was also used to identify the more common 462 castings. Spark plugs are a little higher in the combustion chambers on these than they are in the 461 heads and that provides somewhat better performance. The quench pad behind the plug is relieved slightly. These some-what more com- mon double-hump heads came with large or small valves, depending on the application. One problem with these early heads is that they do not have accessory mounting holes in them.

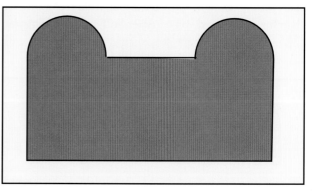

Casting No. 3917291 (1967–1968)

Almost identical to the 462 casting, these heads breathe well due to their larger port volumes. You'll find them on 302, 327, and 350 engines.

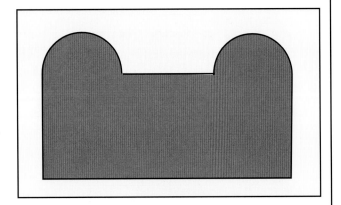

Casting No. 3927186 (1969–1970)

These were used on 302 and 350 high-performance engines and have small, 63-cc combustion chambers. These castings are very similar to the earlier 291s and 462s, but their big advantage is that they have accessory bolt-holes in them, making them very desirable (as well as rare and expensive) for street rod use.

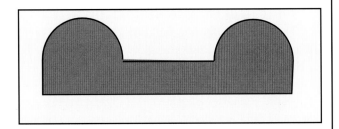

Casting No. 3991492 (1970 and up)

These heads came on LT1 350 engines and are available with a straight or angled plug. The combustion chamber is a closed, 64-cc type. Still available from your Chevrolet dealer, these heads can be purchased with screwed-in studs as part number PN3987376.

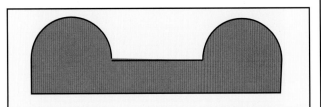

Casting No. 3947041 (1969–1970)

These are identical to the 186–187 heads and come in both closed (64 cc) and open (76 cc) when installed on the 400-ci engine. Both versions came with either 1.94"/1.5" diameter valves and 2.02" / 1.6" valves.

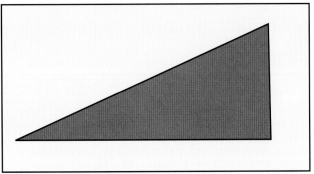

Casting No. 3917292 (1968)

These are closed-combustion chamber, high-compression Corvette heads and came on both the 327 and 350 engines. They do have the accessory bolt-holes, so they are very desirable.

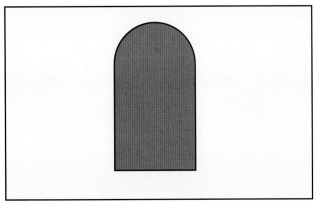

1970 AND LATER
OPEN-COMBUSTION CHAMBER HEADS

Casting No. 3932441 (1969–1970)

These first smog heads are sturdy and can be made to perform well for street use with pocket porting. Compression ratios will be kept in a usable range with pump gas if you use this type of head with flat-top pistons.

Head casting numbers are in the rocker arm area. The casting number tells us that these heads may be from a 350-ci motor.

This casting number indicates a later (after 1987) head. It won't take as much porting as an earlier head.

Casting No. 333882 (1974–1980)

Used on both the 350- and 400-ci engines, these heads are 76 cc.

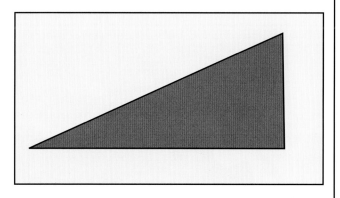

Casting No. 3986339 (1971)

307, 350; has 74.5-cc combustion chambers.

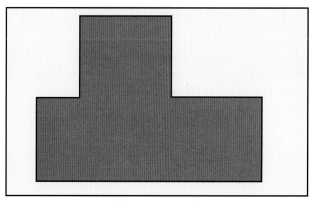

Casting No: 3998993 (In production)

Goodwrench 350 crate motor, made in Mexico.

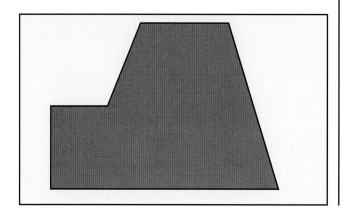

Later production heads

Generally, castings made after 1987 are thinner, more prone to cracking, and will stand less porting than earlier heads, so keep that in mind when you are looking around. There are some notable exceptions to this rule of thumb. The tuned-port fuel injected heads from 1986 and later, used on the 350 high-output engines such as those in the Trans-Ams and Camaros, are excellent because they have smaller, well-designed combustion chambers that are suitable for performance applications.

PORTING
Open Up and Say "Aaah"

COST $70

SKILL LEVEL

TIME 30 HOURS

I f there is a real art involved in performance engine building, it is head porting and polishing. Ported heads will add more horsepower than just about any other single thing you can do to your engine. The problem is, you can't easily accomplish it just by following a set of instructions.

If you really want to rework your engine's heads effectively without damaging them, practice on a set of scrap heads until you get the feel for what you are doing. Keep in mind that the point isn't to make the ports look pretty, or even to make them bigger. Rather, it is to allow more air to flow through them as quickly as possible.

Stock Chevy small blocks are great engines because they were beautifully designed to do the job they were intended to do. Yet, they were not made with the almost infinite care used to build a money-is-no-object racing engine. If they were, very few of us could afford Chevrolets. You see, machining and labor are the most costly

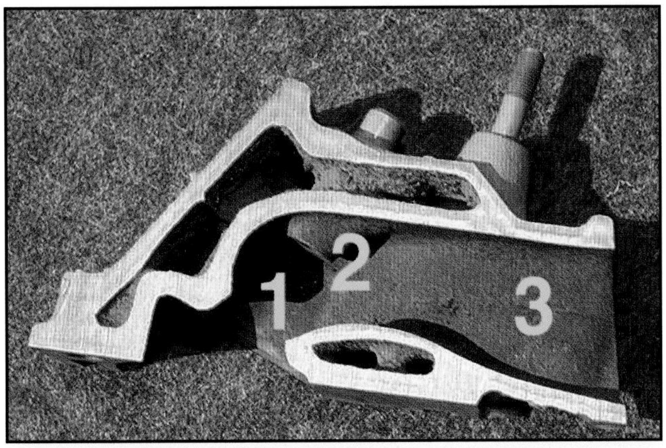

Area one benefits most from porting. Area two is next. Opening area three does little for all but radical drag-racing engines.

aspects of building engines, and porting heads is a labor-intensive process, so the factory didn't bother. But with a little work you can. Here's how:

A scrap Chevy head suitable to learn on can be obtained from any large machine shop, or you can pick one up at a nearby salvage yard. Most of us will be working with cast-iron heads, but if you are lucky enough to be installing a set of aluminum heads, you may want to rework them too. In this case, you will want to practice on scrap aluminum heads first.

When doing cast-iron heads, try the different types of cutters such as stones, carbide burrs, and sandpaper rolls to gauge their effects. Practice working deep into the ports without damaging valve seat faces. You might also want to actually grind through into the water jacket in one port of your scrap head, just to see how much metal is there to play with. If you can see into the water jacket, you've ruined a

PORTING

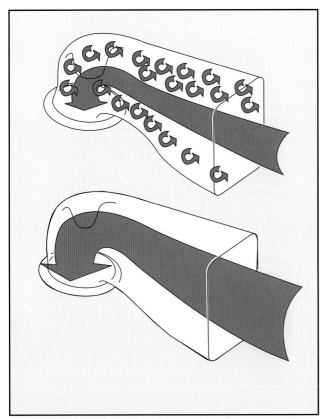

Cleaning up ports cuts down on turbulence, allowing more air in and out of your engine.

This set of late heads has had its exhaust ports done professionally.

head, and even if you only take off a bit too much, you will certainly shorten the life of a head.

The main reason for cleaning up ports and pockets in heads is that ridges and surface roughness cause turbulence that cuts down on airflow. Airplanes have flush riveting and retractable landing gear so air can travel over their external surfaces with minimal drag. Intake—and especially exhaust ports—in cylinder heads need to be as smooth and unrestricted as possible for the same reason. Making ports clean and smooth allows more air in and more air out of your engine, and a piston engine is really just an air pump.

IS BIGGER BETTER?

Just cleaning up the ports in your heads can be worth 15 to 20 horsepower. The point of what we're trying to do isn't primarily to make the ports and pockets bigger, but to make them smoother and less restrictive. If the intake ports are too large on an engine intended for the street, it won't run well at low rpm. This problem is caused by the atomized fuel in the intake charge, which can actually slow down on its way to the combustion chamber, condense out, and run down the cylinder walls.

Ports that have been opened too much will also cut down on the velocity of the air going into the cylinder as the piston is on the down stroke, thus creating a weaker mixture. But if the velocity is right and the throat is opened to about 85 percent of the valve opening, the cylinder can actually fill to 110 percent of capacity because of the force of the air rushing in. And that means a denser mixture and more horsepower. But if you open the ports out to 100 percent of the valve opening, you will only get about 90 percent of the potential air fuel mixture due to lack of velocity, and you'll actually lose power.

Also, lots of rodders think that going to bigger valves in Chevy heads will produce more horsepower. Not so. A set of heads equipped with 1.94/1.50-inch valves won't necessarily produce more power if the smaller valves are replaced with larger, 2.02/1.60-inch valves. In fact, doing so can actually hurt power output because of the restricted area immediately below the valve called the throat. Tests have shown that this configuration is actually detrimental to air flow unless you go to a lift of .600" or greater.

On the other hand, if you do a good job of opening the bowl area behind the valve (this is called pocket porting), switching to the larger valves can mean as much as 25 horsepower, and that's well worth the effort. Just remember, success when building engines depends on which combinations of things you do. Keep in mind that the tricks needed for a few seconds of awesome power in a funny car generally have no place in a street engine.

Radically ported heads can really pump out the ponies at high rpms (50–60 extra horsepower), but then there will not be enough air velocity at low rpms for the engine to perform properly for street use. If you want your cylinder heads reworked for maximum racing performance, take them to a professional porting facility that has a flow bench and experienced technicians.

SETTING UP SHOP

You will need to work in an area where you can make a mess, because iron filings will drift everywhere. Many people port their heads outdoors because the work area can then be hosed down afterward, and there is also usually plenty of light so you can see what you are doing. I chose to work inside because I have a workbench that fits my 6-foot, 2-inch height so I don't have to stoop or bend over. Comfort is an important factor to consider when choosing your work area, because porting heads takes a fair amount of time. It is safe to say that no one likes to be uncomfortable for hours on end.

STAYING CLEAN

One little trick I learned from a professional colleague named John Jaroch is to hook up about 2 feet of 1-1/4–inch-diameter clear vinyl tubing to a shop vacuum with a filter bag so you can suck the swarf out the back of the chamber while you're grinding. Without this setup, it doesn't take long for powdered black iron to blow everywhere. The stuff gets into and under your skin, and if you don't wear a particle mask, you will taste iron for days afterward.

Another clever innovation Jaroch taught me is to hook up a small desk lamp or other type of light and shine it into the vinyl tubing from behind. When you do that, the clear plastic tubing acts sort of like fiber optics because it directs light into the port from behind, allowing you to check your progress easily.

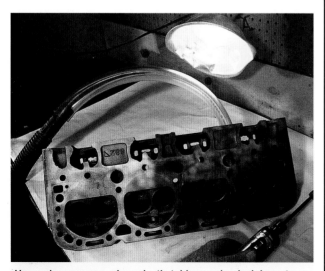

Use a shop vacuum, clear plastic tubing, and a desk lamp to remove swarf and allow you to see what you are doing.

TOOLS AND RULES

You will need a high-speed die grinder, and by that I mean one that can put out 20,000 rpm. A Dremel tool won't suffice. If you have a source of compressed air that can put out 4 cfm at 90 psi or more, go with an air-powered grinder because air grinders are smaller and lighter than electric grinders, and you will be able to control the speed with an air tool. Also, you will not risk the electrifying experience of having fine metal shavings get into the motor of an air tool and short it out, as is possible with an electric grinder. Don't forget to protect your lamp from metal particles as well.

You will also need an assortment of carbide burrs, stones, and abrasive rolls and tapers. Carbide burrs and cutting stones remove a lot of material in a hurry, so be careful when using them. And don't use stones or burrs on aluminum at all. Everything you need to do with aluminum heads can be done entirely with abrasive rolls.

If you can afford a nice assortment of carbide burrs, you can forget the abrasive stones, because they change shape as they are being used up, so they can be a bit erratic if you aren't careful. Long cylindrical burrs are dangerous, too, because the ends can make deep grooves that are hard to grind out. Personally, I prefer oval-shaped burrs for corners, and tapered burrs for flat areas. Keep beeswax nearby to clean carbide burrs, and use a little WD-40 to clean stones and abrasive rolls and tapers.

When you are working, wear a long-sleeve shirt and close-fitting gloves to protect your hands. This is especially important when using carbide burrs and until you get the feel for what you are doing. A carbide burr can easily hang up in the port and whip the die grinder loose from your hands, causing injury.

Also, wear a particle mask to prevent the inhalation of iron filings, and put on a safety shield or goggles to keep the stuff out of your eyes. Finally, the porting process can get pretty noisy with port grinding and a shop vacuum going all at once, so it would be a good idea to wear hearing protection or muffs too.

GETTING STARTED

Before you begin, make sure you have plenty of light and that you can move around the head you are porting to get at everything. Long bolts can be loosely installed to hold the head up off the bench and at different angles too. A few short pieces of 2x4 are also good to support the head.

The best way to determine how much you can enlarge the ports is to spray on a little machinist's bluing, let it dry,

If you can't find machinist's dye, you can use a fine felt-tip marker to outline the gasket openings.

On the left is a finished port runner. Radical porting in the runners is a waste of time. Never go beyond the gasket line.

Paint on the machinist's dye liberally to create an easily read scribe line.

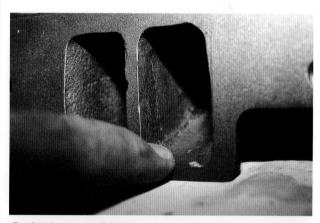

Don't take much off of the port runner floor. There is nothing to gain and you could weaken the head.

Open ports to the gasket edge and clean them up, but don't get carried away. Opening these areas does little to improve power in street engines.

then install a couple of manifold bolts. Place the gasket that will be used to seal the manifold on them. Hold the gasket carefully in place and, using an awl, scribe around the inner edge of the gasket opening for the port.

The gasket will be as little as 1/16-inch and as much as 1/8-inch bigger in places than the port opening. This will give you a good index as to how much to cut away, because you will want to remove material until the port is flush with the gasket. Don't remove any more than you have to from the floor of the port to clean it up. You can remove more from the top and sides. If you have followed the recommendation about practicing on a scrap head, you'll have a good idea about how much you can grind away without causing damage.

Getting aggressive in the port area leading up to the valve pocket is not very productive because the air has a pretty straight shot in this area, and you could actually make the head too thin in the pushrod area. Start by doing the corners first, then smoothing the flat surfaces level with them. All you are trying to do is clean up the long, straight area and open it out a little to match the gasket.

REMOVING ROUGHNESS

Intake ports should not be polished, but all the roughness should be gone. Exhaust ports and combustion chambers can benefit from polishing to a satin finish because doing so will help prevent carbon buildup. In any case, the most difficult area to get at is where the port makes a right-angle turn into the valve pocket. This is an area that will benefit greatly from smoothing and cleaning.

The area that will benefit the most from porting is the pocket, an inch or so behind the valve. The more easily that air can swoop around the valve in a perfect cone, the more power your engine will have. All roughness, ridges, and abrupt changes of angle should be smoothed to allow maximum flow and minimum turbulence.

An air-powered die grinder is easiest to control and you'll get your best results at around 10,000–12,000 rpm. Carbide burrs tend to chatter at high speeds, and stones can cut away too much before you realize it. Even after practicing on your scrap head you will want to work carefully and check your progress frequently.

As you are smoothing and cutting, shoot a little WD-40 on the stones or burrs periodically to keep them from gumming up. Also, check your progress frequently by wiping the port surface with a rag dampened with WD-40 to get the swarf out. Then run your finger inside on the surface to check for ridges, slag, or roughness. Your fingertip (unless it is very callused or damaged by chemicals)

Use sandpaper rolls and tapers to do your final finishing.

Check your progress frequently using your finger. You can feel roughness with your fingertip to within a few thousandths.

You can use bent coat-hanger wire to make sure the port runners are even.

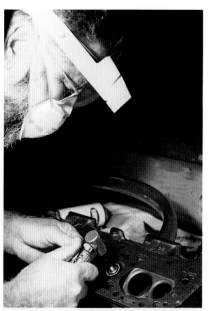
Abrasive sanding cylinders and bits are available at hardware stores and make pocket porting easier.

is actually quite sensitive and can feel differences as slight as a couple thousandths of an inch.

Small, ball-shaped stones and burrs are great for corner areas, and ball shapes are good for down in pocket areas. Use large sandpaper cylinders for long, round sections, and valve pocket work. Slightly rounded cone-shaped stones or burrs are good for the slight ramping on the bottom surfaces of the inlets to ports.

Cleaning up around the valve guides is a little tricky because you don't want to grind too much away and leave a knife-edge at the opening, but you do want to smooth and round off all the edges. Another thing John Jaroch taught me is to install long, Allen-head bolts through the guides and attach nuts on the bottom to hold the bolts in place. The Allen bolt heads help to preserve a little area around the valve guide. Be very careful in this area not to create deep grooves or take too much metal away. And check your work frequently, both visually and by using your fingertip.

POLISHING

Once a port is cleaned of slag, ridges, and roughness, switch to the sandpaper rolls and tapers. You could actually do a complete porting job with these on cast iron, but it would take quite a few of them. Even if you start out with burrs or stones, by all means use sandpaper disks to do your final smoothing and cleaning. Shoot a little WD-40 on them once in a while so they won't get clogged. Also, replace the sandpaper rolls when they get dull rather than trying to press harder.

Fine polishing of combustion chambers can be done by hand using #400 grit wet and dry sandpaper, or if you want to go for a truly shiny finish, you can use felt bobs and polishing compounds on your die grinder. Once again, the purpose of our efforts isn't to create a thing of beauty, but to make it as easy as possible for air to enter and exit the head.

When you have one port done, make templates of its inside dimensions using coat hanger wire. That way you can verify that each port is opened to the same size as the others. If the port sizes and combustion chamber volumes differ, your engine won't operate at its optimum performance level.

COMBUSTION CHAMBERS

After you have all the ports clean and smooth, place the head on your bench so its mating surface is up, shoot on a little machinist's bluing, then put a head gasket in place and scribe around the opening in the gasket for the combustion chamber. Slip a couple of old valves in place to protect the valve seats, then clean and smooth the combustion chamber area. Flat grinding disks are good for this, as are sanding disks and flapper disks of sandpaper.

You won't want to polish the combustion chambers if your engine is intended for the street, because doing

Use machinist's dye and the head gaskets you will be running in your engine to scribe around combustion chambers. Never enlarge the combustion chamber beyond the edge of the head gasket.

On the left is what a well-ported set of closed-chamber heads should look like.

so could cut swirl and actually lower performance. Just get the slag and roughness out, and chamfer any sharp edges, such as around spark plug openings and the edges of combustion chambers.

Also, be careful not to remove too much material because if you get too aggressive you could end up lowering your compression. If you are going to install 2.02" valves in a head that was equipped with 1.94" valves originally, you will need to de-shroud the area around the periphery of the valves in the side of the combustion chamber. Just don't go out beyond the gasket opening, which will result in gasket failure.

CHECKING COMBUSTION CHAMBER VOLUME

If your combustion chambers are different sizes, they will have different volumes, which means that your engine will have higher compression ratios in some cylinders than in others. If your engine is to function well, you won't want a difference of more than a couple of cubic centimeters between cylinders.

You will also want to take into account how much metal will have to come off the surface of the head to make it flat. Don't go over 9.75:1 on compression if you want to be able to run pump gas on the street. This figure will put

FIGURING COMPRESSION RATIOS

Compression ratio is simply the volume of the cylinder compared to the volume of the combustion chamber. To determine the volume of one cylinder in a Chevy small block (or any engine for that matter), you merely divide the displacement by the number of cylinders, which in our case is eight. For example, 350 divided by 8 is 43.75 cubic inches, which is also the amount of air the piston displaces when it moves from bottom dead center (BDC) to top dead center (TDC).

If we convert that figure into cubic centimeters we then get 716.94. Then, if we divide that figure by the size of the combustion chamber (let's assume it is 68 cc) we get 10.54, or nearly 11:1, which is a compression ratio that is too high for pump gas. However, if we use an open-combustion chamber head with a volume of 74 cc, then divide that into our cylinder volume of 716.94, we get a compression ratio of 9.8:1, which is more viable.

If we then use a 1/8-inch (.125") dished piston, we increase the size of the combustion chamber enough to get our compression ratio down to roughly 9.5:1, which is comfortable for street use. Of course, there are lots of other little variables that can come into the equation as well, such as how high the piston comes up in the cylinder and how far up the piston ring package rides. Quite simply, if you are taking .030" off the heads and another .040" off the block decks, you could be bumping the compression up dangerously.

MATCHING PORTS

Once you have opened your intake ports and smoothed them, you will want to clean up and open the intake manifold to match it—but not exactly. In the old days we used to go to extraordinary measures to line up the intake and exhaust manifolds with their ports exactly, but it has since been demonstrated that the intake manifold should be just a tiny bit smaller (.050" smaller at the port floor) at its mating surface, and the exhaust header openings should be a little bit larger all around by the same amount.

The reason is that, with the intake port just a tiny bit larger, a small amount of turbulence will be created in the incoming mixture that will help keep the fuel charge in suspension and mixed properly. On the exhaust side, a slight vacuum is created between exhaust pulses when the headers are slightly larger. This helps with scavenging and avoiding fuel mixture dilution.

It can easily take 30 hours or more to port a set of heads, so don't become impatient and try to hurry the process. If you are not the patient type, drop your heads off at a porting service and let them do the job. Otherwise you could ruin a good set of heads and cost yourself even more money.

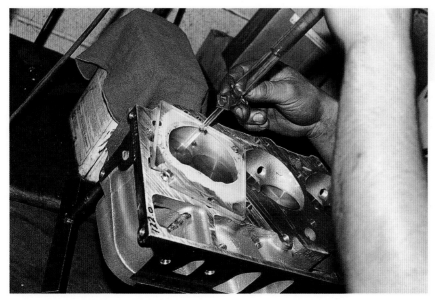

This is a professional rig, but you can determine combustion chamber volume using a graduated eyedropper from the drugstore and a piece of flat clear plastic.

you as close to detonation as you will want to go, and with that, ignition timing and fuel mixture will have to be pretty accurate to avoid problems.

The easiest and least expensive way to check the volumes of the combustion chambers is by using a sheet of clear plastic and an eyedropper or graduated beaker. The piece of clear plastic needs to be bigger than the diameter of the combustion chamber, and it needs a hole drilled into it to allow you to feed liquid into the combustion chamber with an eyedropper. You can pick up a graduated eyedropper, marked off in cubic centimeters, at most drug stores.

The mating surface for the head must be clean and the head must be propped up so it is absolutely horizontal. Use blocks of wood to support the head and use a carpenter's spirit level to adjust it to perfectly level. Lightly smear the valve seats with grease so they will seal, then install a couple of valves.

Mix up a little dish soap and water (you can add a little food coloring for higher visibility if you like) and slowly fill the combustion chamber, keeping careful track of the number of cubic centimeters it takes to fill the combustion chamber to the bottom of the piece of plastic. Repeat this process for each combustion chamber and note down the results. All of your figures should be within a couple of cubic centimeters of each other. Make fine adjustments as necessary.

If you find any significant difference, try juggling valves around in the heads. No matter how carefully made, your valves will vary in height slightly. Mixing and matching can often correct any difference in relative combustion chamber volumes. Only take more material out of a combustion chamber as a last resort to get volumes to agree.

CAMSHAFTS
Getting a Lift

COST 💲 LESS THAN $200

SKILL LEVEL

TIME 🕐 4 HOURS

Back in the 1960s, while I was filling up at a gas station on the way to Lions Drag Strip in Long Beach, California, a little 1941 Studebaker Champion two-door sedan pulled in. Its driver rolled to a stop in the street, then in a series of roaring jumps, got up next to the pumps and shut the engine off. He filled the tank with high-test, paid the bill, and then roared and jack-rabbitted the car back out to the street. As the traffic light changed, he took the engine up to about 3,000 rpm, slipped the clutch, bogged down a little, and then blasted away in a thunderous roar.

The fellow had no choice but to drive like that. The small-block Chevy in his Studebaker had such a radical cam in it that it could not get out of its own way until it got up into the higher-rpm ranges. But once it did, it went like stink. As I recall, later that night the guy turned 147 miles per hour. Of course, the car's gas mileage would have been awful, the engine wouldn't have lasted long in street use, and the car's heavy-duty clutch would have given the driver a sore leg in minutes, but those were, and still are to a great extent, the trade-offs.

Back then, when I was in my early twenties, I was just crazy enough to want to build myself a car like that. These days I want a machine that is a bit more streetable. I like a car with impressive performance and a sexy rumble, but I also want a clutch that doesn't require both feet to depress it, and I want to be able to get away from traffic signals without having to break the tires loose.

I tell this little story because it illustrates a very important point. You must decide what you want your engine to do, and what kind of vehicle you want to put it in before you choose a cam. Just going for the most radical cam you can find is a big mistake for street use, even if you build the engine around the cam. You could wind up with big flat spots in acceleration, short valve train life, and a car that is not particularly fast or even fun to drive.

CAM TERMS

BASE CIRCLE: This is the round part at the bottom of the cam lobe. Normally you don't need to think about it unless you are building a stroker engine, in which case you may need to run a small base-circle cam to avoid interference with the connecting rods. The base circle is also where the lifter should be riding when the valve lash is adjusted.

CAM PROFILE: The actual shape of the cam lobe. It varies greatly from cam to cam, and in some cases from intake to exhaust lobes.

CAM FOLLOWER: Device that rides on the cam and actuates pushrods and valves.

DURATION: The amount of time the valves are off their seats during the lifting cycles of the cam lobes.

HEEL: Same as the base circle

LIFTER: Same as the cam follower

LOBE: The eccentric part of the individual cam that opens the valve.

LOBE CENTER: The distance (measured in degrees) between the centerline of the intake lobe and the centerline of the exhaust lobe of the same cylinder.

NOSE: The highest portion of the lobe measuring from the base circle.

SPLIT OVERLAP: The point where both intake and exhaust valves are off their seats the same distance at the same time. At this point, the TDC mark on the vibration damper should be at the zero mark on the indicator.

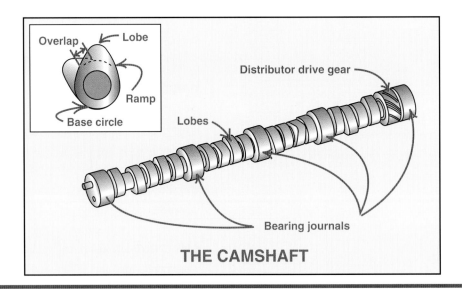

Overlap — Lobe
Ramp
Base circle

Distributor drive gear

Lobes

Bearing journals

THE CAMSHAFT

These days, with the advent of computers, the selection of cams is endless, so with a little thought and care, you can get whatever you want, if it is within reason. In the last 20 years, computer research has produced cams that can give you such awesome torque at low rpms that your Malibu will accelerate like a bullet from 0 to 60. You can also get cams that will give you awesome horsepower at high rpms, lower those E.T.s in the quarter mile, and shut down the competition. The stock cam is in between these extremes, though nearer the low-rpm end.

The people who developed your small block's original camshaft were no fools. They had a tough job to do. They needed to come up with valve timing that would provide a smooth idle, decent gas mileage, and low emissions. Yet it had to give you good performance at all rpm ranges and allow your engine to last for 100,000 miles and more without needing major work.

Quite simply, the camshaft in a conventional, four-cycle engine opens the intake and exhaust valves at just the right time so the fuel air mixture comes in on cue, is burned, and then the exhaust gasses are cleared from the combustion chamber in time for the next event. The cam also turns the distributor, which causes the spark plugs to ignite the mixture at precisely the right moment. It turns the oil pump and drives the mechanical fuel pump too. In a way, it is the brains of the engine.

The challenge for cam designers is that the optimum time for each combustion event varies with engine speed (rpm). Some cams do their best work at low rpm, others at high rpm, and others, like your engine's stock cam, are a compromise between the two. Many people would say, "Just give me the cam that makes the most horsepower."

But it isn't horsepower that makes it possible for a car to hit 200 miles per hour from a standing start in a quarter of a mile. It takes torque to do that.

A simplified explanation of torque versus horsepower is that torque is a measurement of the amount of work your engine can do, and horsepower is an indication of how quickly it can do it. An Indy Champ car engine can produce upwards of 900 horsepower, but you wouldn't want to put one in your 18-wheel Peterbilt because it wouldn't make enough torque to move the vehicle, even without a load in it.

On the other hand, a 600-ci Cummins diesel only puts out about 400 horsepower, but it can move 10 tons of cargo with ease all day long because it makes in the neighborhood of 1,200–1,400 foot-pounds of torque. The small 900-horsepower Indy car engine can do less work, but the work it does is done VERY quickly. A huge diesel engine can do an awesome amount of work, but it does it slowly. Of course, the cam is only one factor in the equation. Stroke, bore, displacement, and engine and vehicle weight, along with a number of other factors, are also involved.

A low-rpm engine makes the maximum possible power in the combustion chamber because the chamber has more time to fill with the fuel/air charge. A bigger charge means a greater force exerted on the piston when the charge is ignited. As rpms go up, there is less time for the cylinder to fill, and less time for the exhaust to be pumped out, so the amount of work the cylinders can do goes down. However, at high rpms, the total amount of work that gets done in a given interval of time goes up.

So, what's your choice? It really depends on your intentions. Do you want to move a lot of weight off the line in a hurry, perhaps sacrificing a little top-end performance, or do you want a little street rod to blow through the traps in the low nines?

Of course, there are other factors you need to consider as well. For example, you need to decide whether you will be running a standard transmission or an automatic, what your transmission and differential gearing will be, how many rpm your engine can handle, and how well-behaved you want your car to be on the street.

You can do all the homework yourself to determine what duration and lift you might need for your application, or you can simply call a reputable cam manufacturer with your requirements. For instance, recently when I was building a stroker motor for my 1958 Chevy pickup, I called Ron at Ed Iskenderian Racing Cams in Gardena, California, and gave him all the stats. Ron noted down the data I furnished and determined that their 270—280 dual-pattern Megacam would do just what I wanted.

I wanted impressive bottom-end acceleration and a fairly broad working rpm band, but reasonable gas mileage. I didn't care about screaming high-speed performance because my old hauler doesn't have the sophisticated suspension and steering required for a triple-digit top end.

I called Iskenderian because they are one of the oldest and largest racing and specialty cam makers in the world. There are lots of cam grinders, but Isky cams are tops, and they don't cost much more than no-name cams for most applications. Also, the folks at Isky are willing to answer your questions and help you with problems. And their catalog contains a section that tells you just about everything you need to know to install a cam and get it timed correctly.

HISTORY LESSON

Early automotive engines were designed with no overlap. That is to say, when the piston reached BDC on the induction stroke, the intake valve opened and let in the fuel/air mixture. The exhaust valve would be completely closed at this point. On the compression stroke, both valves would be closed. Then when the gas fired, the piston would come back down to BDC, the exhaust valve would open, then the gasses would be pushed out.

Early designers thought that if the valves were even partially open at the same time, there would be a loss of power. Later it was determined that a little overlap added to the engine's power because the slug of escaping exhaust gasses actually created a vacuum behind it that helped pull in the fuel/air mixture, thus providing a mild supercharging effect.

Ed Iskenderian started experimenting with the use of this effect back in the 1940s and developed overlapping cams that increased power dramatically. Isky referred to this overlap as the "fifth cycle" and set about developing cams to make the most of the effect. Then in the 1950s, he came up with his famous Isky Five Cycle cam that made awesome horsepower. The sound alone from an engine equipped with one of these was enough to intimidate the competition.

Of course, there is a limitation as to how creative you can get with valve timing on a single-cam engine. And there is a limit to how long a cam with conventional lifters and pushrods can hold a valve open. Dual-overhead cams permit much more flexibility. Also, a stock grind cam has rather pointed lobes so the valves stay fully open only for a short time.

To get the valves to stay open longer, the tips of the lobes must be made wider, but this can only go so far before it has a negative effect on valve timing. Also, the ramps on the sides of the lobes get so steep that it causes rapid cam and lifter wear unless you go to roller lifters, and even then there are limits. Finally, flat tappet lifter diameter is limited, so there is only so much area to work with before the valve starts to override the lifter.

There is also a limit to how much overlap a cam can stand. It is overlap that causes that rough idle with radical cams. At low rpm, some of the unburned intake gasses get passed into the exhaust manifold where they ignite, causing that popping, rumbling sound. At higher rpm, a more radical cam comes into its own and the engine can produce prodigious amounts of horsepower.

Most street rod applications are best set up with hydraulic lifter cams. Back in the early 1960s, hydraulic lifters could cause a dangerous situation called lifter pump-up at high rpms, but that is largely a thing of the past if your lifters and valve train are fresh and properly set up, and you keep your small block below 6,500 rpm. Also, the big advantage with hydraulic lifters is that the valves are kept in constant adjustment at zero lash, so they are much quieter in operation.

Disadvantages to radical hydraulic lifter cams are that they produce a rougher idle and they contribute to low intake manifold vacuum. The latter can be a problem in cars equipped with automatic transmissions and power brakes. A radical hydraulic lifter cam can actually cause you to lose your brakes unless you have an auxiliary vacuum booster tied into the power brake system.

Solid (mechanical) lifters can handle higher rpms and more radical cams, and they do produce a smoother idle, but the

Smear a little assembly lube on the cam bearings before installing the cam.

rockers must be adjusted frequently and carefully if your engine is to perform to specs. For most street applications, a hydraulic cam is the best choice, but if you really want radical performance for weekend bracket racing, go with a solid lifter cam.

MAKING IT BETTER THAN NEW

Once you have made your cam selection, buy new lifters, pushrods, and rockers to work with it. Try to buy all from the same manufacturer to ensure compatibility. Roller lifters and rocker arms cut down on valve train friction because they have rotating rollers riding on the cam and valves.

Roller lifters are great for any application, and they can allow you to run a more radical cam without durability problems. The only catch is cost. Roller rockers and lifters are many times more expensive than the stock ones. Of course, the latest generations of Chevy small-block V-8s already come with roller lifters.

Roller lifters are more expensive because they are made of steel rather than iron, and they are much more difficult to manufacture. If you can spring for roller lifters and rockers, by all means use them, but make sure the cam you buy is designed to work with them. Solid lifter cams work only with solid lifters, hydraulic lifter cams must have hydraulic lifters, and roller lifter cams only work with roller lifters, so don't try to switch them around.

INSTALLING A CAM

You can install a cam in a small block without tearing the engine down, and in most cases you can even install a cam without removing the engine from the car. However, the best way to put in a hotter cam is to do it when you have the

Screw in a long bolt at the front of the cam to use as a handle while installing the cam. Slip the cam in carefully, so you do not to smear the bearings or bark the cam lobes against them.

Notice the special crankshaft gear with three key-ways. One is straight up, one is 4 degrees advanced, and one is 4 degrees retarded to help degree in the cam.

Slip the timing chain around the crankshaft gear, then over the cam timing gear. Line up the timing marks, then attach the cam gear.

Timing marks must align straight across as shown here. If they are out by even one tooth on the gears, your engine will not run right.

engine down for overhaul. Cams (stock or hot) are not expensive, so even if you are just overhauling your stocker, replace its cam with a new one. Lobes wear flat and your engine will never be at its best with an old cam in it. Also, always install a new timing chain and new timing gears if they are notched or worn where the chain rides on the teeth of the gears.

To install your cam, find a long bolt with the same threads as the holes on the end of your cam and use it to help guide your new cam into place. Or you can attach the timing gear to the end of the cam to make handling it easier. Coat the cam bearings and journals lightly with a suitable assembly lube. I like Isky's Rev Lube for this task.

As you slip the cam in from the front of the engine, be careful not to bark the lobes against the block, and be very careful not to smear or mar the cam bearings. You can turn the cam slightly to work it through, but make sure you support it at both ends with your hands as you work. Once the cam is seated in the back bearing, try turning it. The cam should turn easily and shouldn't bind.

Smear each cam lobe with assembly lube. You should be able to reach the cam. Smear the lobes with lube before installation if you are only installing the new cam with the engine still in the car. This is a crucial step to avoid rapid lobe wear when the engine is in its first few minutes of running before the oil gets up into the galleries in quantity. Lifters are held against the cam under a lot of pressure by the valve springs, so without a good assembly lube, the cam lobes will self-destruct in minutes.

Turn the crankshaft until its gear's timing mark is straight up, or at 12 o'clock, pointing directly toward the cam. Slide on the cam timing gear and turn the cam until its timing mark is immediately opposite the crankshaft timing mark, or at 6 o'clock. Take the cam timing gear off again, smear the gears with assembly lube, dip the timing chain in clean motor oil, and slip it over the crankshaft timing gear and the cam timing gear.

Now hold the cam timing gear in place with your hand while you install its attaching bolts. The key-way in the crankshaft and the locator pin in the camshaft gear take the guesswork out of orienting the gears. Make sure you don't slip and get the timing marks out of orientation with each other, because if they are off even by one tooth, the engine will not run correctly.

What we have just described is the standard way to install a stock cam, and it will work fine for a performance cam most of the time. Since you are going to all this trouble, you might want to make sure your valve timing is spot-on. It is not unusual for cams to be out 1 to 4 degrees, and if they are, the cam won't perform to specs. That's why you should read the corresponding sidebar about degreeing in a cam before going any further.

You can use a magnetic base and a dial indicator to find top-dead-center (TDC) on the piston.

At TDC, zero out the dial indicator, then move your degree wheel to zero it out as well. You can tweak your pointer a little to align it precisely.

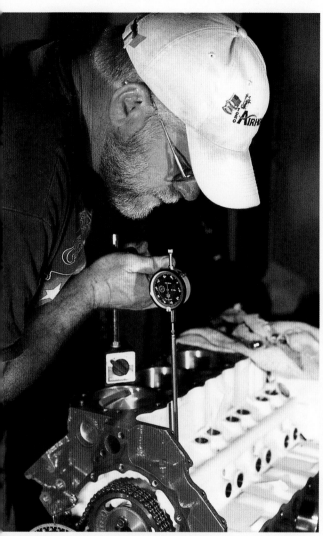

Install a lifter and then determine lobe center on the intake lobe first. Cams are correctly installed at perfect split overlap.

DEGREEING IN THE CAM

Most street cams can be installed as described in the text, but no matter how carefully each engine component was made, there is still the possibility of tolerance stacking. That is to say, your cam may well be machined right on the money, but the key-way in the crankshaft may be cut in the wrong place, the gears may not line up exactly as marked, and the timing chain may be a little tight or loose. All of these variables, added together, could make a difference to your engine's performance.

Cams also can be installed in the advanced or retarded position on purpose, to produce a little more power at the bottom end or more at the top. That goes for stock cams too. If you have to move a cam more than 4 degrees to get what you want, you are better off installing a different cam. If you advance the cam a little, you'll get a little more bottom-end power at the expense of the top end. If you retard the cam a little, you will get a little more top-end power, but lose at the bottom end.

Most cams are intended by the manufacturer to be installed at exactly split overlap, or right in the middle between the precise center of the intake and exhaust lobes, because that is where they will do the job they were designed to do. The trick is to find the exact center of each lobe, then split the difference to determine how the cam should be oriented. It is actually easier than it sounds. To do it, you need a degree wheel and a magnetic base. A positive piston stop is a good idea because it is more accurate than a dial indicator for determining TDC.

MAGNETIC BASE METHOD

To begin with, it helps to keep in mind that the camshaft in your small block turns at half the speed of the crankshaft, so the cam only does one revolution for every two of the crankshaft. Each cycle (induction, compression, ignition/power, exhaust) of the engine amounts to 180 degrees on your degree wheel.

Oil the number one piston lightly, and then slip it (without rings installed) and its rod assembly into its bore. Pop in a set of rod bearings, oil them, and attach the rod to the crankshaft. You don't need to torque the bolts to specs. Just snug them up. Rotate the crankshaft in the direction of engine rotation until the piston is at approximately TDC.

Set up your magnetic base and dial indicator so that the needle plunger on the dial indicator is compressed by about 1/2 inch on the center of the piston. It is important that the gauge needle be centered as close as possible to

Turn the engine to determine the exact lobe centers on the cam. Make sure there is no slop at the lifter.

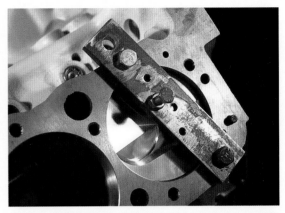

A more accurate way to determine TDC is to make yourself a piston stop out of steel strap and use that rather than a magnetic base and dial gauge.

Holes in cam drive gear can be drilled out and an eccentric wash (available from speed shops) can be installed on the locator pin t locate the cam exactly at split overlap.

Finally, secure the cam with a locking device like this. Just bend one tab on each bolt.

the piston's center because without rings on the piston, it can wobble and cause faulty readings if the dial indicator needle is nearer the edge.

Attach your degree wheel loosely to the crankshaft gear using a fine-threaded 3/8-inch bolt in the crankshaft snout. Next, make up a pointer out of coat hanger wire that reaches out to just in front of your degree wheel. You could use a stock, sheet-metal pointer, but a thin wire pointer can be bent into precise alignment rather than fussing with rotating the crankshaft to exactly the right spot. You'll see why this is important in a minute.

Slowly and smoothly turn the crankshaft until the dial indicator reaches its highest reading before starting to go back down. You don't need to be 100 percent on TDC because this method of degreeing in the cam compensates for any slight error. When you have determined the highest point the piston reaches to the best of your ability, set the dial indicator so it reads zero at that point. Now turn the degree wheel (but not the crankshaft) until it reads zero on your wire pointer.

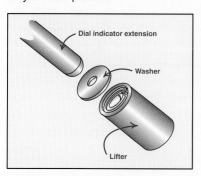

When degreeing in your cam, put a washer on top of the hydraulic lifter to support and center the dial indicator extension.

It is best to use solid lifters for this task, but if you don't have any, you can put a washer on top of a hydraulic lifter to keep it from compressing while you perform your measurements. Lightly oil a couple of lifters and put them in their bores. Press them against the cam gently with your thumb. Now place a pushrod in the intake lifter. Relocate your magnetic stand and place the needle of your dial indicator in the upper tip of the pushrod so it has about 1/2 inch of downward travel. Zero out the dial indicator.

Now turn the crankshaft in its normal rotation to exactly fifty thousandths as indicated on the dial indicator. Note the reading indicated on your degree wheel. You can turn the crank with a wrench using the bolt you put into the crankshaft snout, or you can move it with your hands.

Next, turn the crankshaft all the way around to fifty thousandths before zero on the dial indicator. Again, note that reading of your degree wheel. Add these numbers together and divide the result by two, which will give you

the exact split overlap figure. Assuming your cam is at exact split overlap at 108 degrees, you'll know whether it is installed in an advanced or retarded position. You should get a figure somewhere in the neighborhood of 104 to 112 degrees. The idea is to get it exactly in the middle.

To double-check yourself, check the exhaust lobe next. You'll know if you've measured accurately because, assuming, for instance, that the intake is opening at 104 degrees, the exhaust should then be opening at 112 on a cam that is at precisely split overlap at 108 degrees when installed correctly, indicating that the cam is 4 degrees advanced. If your figures from the intake and exhaust lobes don't result in the correct number at split overlap, you haven't got your dial indicator zeroed out at exactly TDC on the piston.

POSITIVE STOP METHOD

A more foolproof way to determine TDC is to install a piston stop. You can make one of these out of 1/4–inch-thick steel strap by drilling a couple of holes in it to coincide with head bolt-holes, then drilling and tapping a hole in the center and installing a bolt. The strap attaches to the deck of the block over a piston. The bolt is installed so the piston will bump against it before it reaches TDC. Then you turn the crankshaft until the piston just bumps the bolt on the positive stop and note the reading on the degree wheel.

Next turn the crankshaft back the other way once again until the piston just bumps the stop, and note your reading. Add these numbers and divide by two. This will give you exact TDC for the piston. From there you can accurately measure the lobe centers on your cam. If your cam is within specs plus or minus 1 degree, I would leave it alone, because cams are ground a little out to account for wear in the timing chain. If your cam is 2 to 5 degrees out, you should correct it.

You can do that by using a crankshaft gear that has extra key-ways cut in it 4 degrees (8 crank degrees) apart. Or you can drill out the holes in the cam timing gear to 11/32-inch and install an eccentric bushing to nudge the gear just a few degrees (no more than 3) in the right direction. Install the bushing with a little Lok-Tite, and swage it in so it won't fall out. Moving the cam in the direction of engine rotation retards the cam, and moving the cam against the engine advances the cam.

If you are degreeing in a cam for the first time, be patient, double-check your work and your figures, and get an experienced friend to help. As I said before, it sounds more complicated than it is. Gather the tools, follow the instructions step-by-step, and you'll soon get the hang of it. Your engine will run the way it was intended and perform at its maximum potential.

SHOT PEENING
Give It Your Best Shot

COST $30

SKILL LEVEL

TIME 5 HOURS

✔ YOU'LL NEED:

- ❏ Heavy-duty compressor with tank large enough to maintain sustained 100-pound pressure
- ❏ Sandblasting cabinet
- ❏ 1/8-inch-thick rubber mat for back of blast cabinet
- ❏ Bag of #230 cast steel shot.

What if I told you one simple, inexpensive process that you can do yourself at home can increase the cracking resistance of your small block's heads, connecting rods, bearing saddles, and crankshaft by between 10 and 45 percent? It's true. The process is called shot peening. It works something like media blasting, except the point of it is to relieve stresses and increase crack resistance in a component rather than remove material.

Shot peening is a form of cold working metal, similar to the way medieval sword makers used to hammer steel blades to make them more resilient. The difference is, instead of hammering, shot peening involves tiny spherical ball bearings that are blasted at a component using a special machine or even a home blasting cabinet. This relieves the item of tensile stress, which is bad, and adds residual stress, which is good.

Yet, if shot peening is such a great process, why didn't Chevrolet do it to their rods, heads, and crank in the first place? It wasn't necessary for their application. However, Chevrolet and other manufacturers do use shot peening to increase the resilience of their springs, gears, and suspension parts.

Chevrolets are designed and built to a price, just like any other production car. The bottom ends of Bow Tie V-8s have always been more than rugged enough to handle the punishment of normal service, and that was all that was required by General Motors. Chevy's engineers knew that the only time shot peening would be advantageous is if the engine were going to be pushed beyond its design envelope.

Peening takes time, and time is money, which becomes a lot of money when you build as many engines as Chevrolet does. But for street rodders it's a different story. We will be pushing our engines beyond their engineering parameters occasionally, and this relatively simple and inexpensive process can make the difference between a motor that can handle 7,000 rpm and one that might grenade a rod through the side of the block.

HOW IT WORKS

Most blasting media are sharp, jagged materials such as sand, aluminum oxide, or glass, but steel shot is perfectly round. It is made by dropping tiny blobs of molten steel from as high as 150 feet into water, which quenches the steel and shapes it into perfect little balls. This shape makes them ideal for hammering metal rather than abrading it the way most blast media does. Of course, even ordinary blast media will peen metal to some degree.

In the shot peening process, the surface of the part doesn't get as hard as the immediate subsurface, which becomes compressed, creating residual strength. Shot peening also closes the pores and tightens the grain of the metal, and that helps prevent cracks. Peening relaxes cast-in

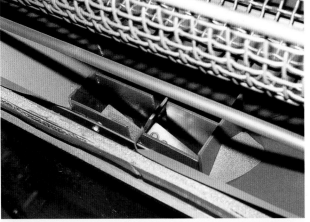
Professional peening machines use paddles to fling the shot at high velocity.

stresses that can cause rods and crankshafts to warp, too. It is especially beneficial for crankshafts because they are generally cast flat, then wrenched into shape while still hot and malleable, thus creating a great deal of cast-in stress.

Shot peening is so effective that there are big industries doing it all over the country. Many of them employ expensive and exacting techniques and make aerospace components such as rotor blades for jet engines. Shot peening makes it possible for these parts to spin at 45,000 rpm for 100,000 hours in diabolical heat without cracking.

When peening is done professionally, it is not blasted from nozzles, but flung by spinning flapper wheels. Special test strips called Almen gauges are even used in some cases to determine exactly how much peening is necessary to achieve specific results. These strips are sent to a lab to be analyzed before any work is done on the component. If we were building engines for NASCAR we might want to go this far, but for street use such exacting work is not necessary.

You can make considerable gains in resistance to cracking and corrosion just by using your blast cabinet at home to shot peen parts. In fact, you can peen your own engine components as well as most speed shops are able to do it because they generally just use a blast cabinet and fine shot too. Here is how to make your small block's engine components a whole lot tougher with very little effort:

CONNECTING RODS

Have your rods, crankshaft, and bearing saddles Magnaflux tested at a machine shop for cracks before you do anything with them. Shot peening won't help cracked parts. Also, have your rods straightened and trued. Your machinist will have a special jig for this. Only when you know you have a good set of straight rods, and before you have the rotating assembly balanced, should you move on to the next steps.

Contrary to what most people think, connecting rods don't usually break at their slimmest point, or necessarily in the area that takes the most stress. Instead, they often break at points where surfaces such as the rod bolt bosses intersect with the main casting. These areas form sharp angles that invite cracks. One reason such areas are so prone to fracture is that at extreme rpms, the rod journals take such a pounding that they stretch downward, pulling the big-end cap away from the rod.

Sharp corners should be carefully radiused, parting lines should be ground off, and casting roughness should be ground away. Don't remove those little numbers on the big ends of the rods that tell you which cylinder they fit into. After that, polish your rods to a satin finish using fine sand-

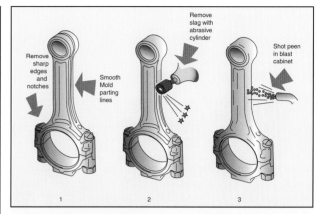

Shot peening can be done at home in your blast cabinet. Just follow these simple steps

paper or glass beads in a blast cabinet. Your connecting rods don't need to be shiny, but they should be smooth.

Next, clean your blast cabinet of abrasive media and wipe out any residue. Attach a square of 1/4–inch-thick rubber matting to the back wall of your blast cabinet to prevent damage to it. I just inserted a couple of screws at the top of my cabinet and pegged the rubber mat on them. Now put about a 3-pound coffee can of number 230 cast-steel shot into the hopper and push the suction tube down into it. Crank the pressure up on your compressor to at least 100 psi. Leave the old insert bearings in place when you shot peen rods, so those carefully machined journals won't be altered.

Shoot the surfaces of the rods from about 3 inches away and keep your blast nozzle at 90 degrees to the surface you are peening at all times. Work slowly and consistently until you have peened each rod surface for as close to the same amount of time as possible.

Grinding off mold lines and radiusing sharp angles helps prevent stress cracks.

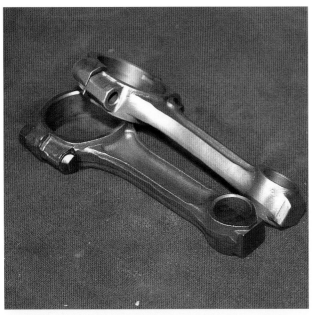

The rod on top is much stronger than the one on the bottom, even though they both came from the same engine. The reason: shot peening.

CRANKSHAFTS

Crankshafts should be cleaned of slag and roughness and shot peened before they are remachined. This can help cut down running friction and will strengthen the crankshaft considerably. Of course, once again you will want to radius any sharp edges, remove any slag, and grind away any roughness. The same shot you used for your rods will work just fine on your crank.

Shot peening your crankshaft is probably not necessary on crankshafts that won't be seeing tough duty such as bracket racing, but it certainly won't hurt anything. And because small block cranks are big and heavy, you may want to have yours peened professionally. Some shops will do the job in a blast cabinet, but the bigger shops will have a special machine that uses a paddle wheel to throw the shot.

Just make sure you do your shot peening before you have the crankshaft and other engine components reground and balanced. And don't forget to tell the machinist to radius around the oil holes in the bearing journals too. This will help avoid damage to the bearing shell and make the crankshaft a little stronger at the same time.

Parts are placed in a wire basket and tumbled during the peening process.

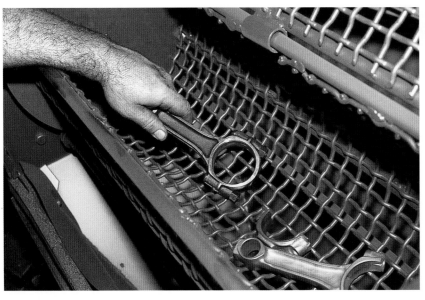

CYLINDER HEADS

Heads are especially prone to cracking, due to the stresses caused by heating and cooling and being clamped to the block. Have your machine shop bake your heads and Magnflux test them for existing cracks before going to the trouble of peening them. Give special attention to valve seats, bolt-holes, and exhaust ports. Of course, you will want to shot peen your heads before you have any machining done on them.

BEARING SADDLES

The sharp downward force exerted by combustion exerts a great deal of pressure on bearing saddles, and that can cause them to elongate and fail too. Sharp edges and irregularities invite fractures that can widen and lengthen, allowing the bearing journal to elongate and deform until the engine spins a bearing.

Cleaning up sharp edges and shot peening bearing saddles can help avoid this problem. Only remove what is required to smooth the bearing caps and radius the edges. A smooth, shot-peened surface will be much stronger than a rough surface that still harbors tensile stresses.

A few hours spent shot peening your parts can make a big difference to the durability of your engine, and this is especially true of high-revving motors. You may never push your street rod hard enough to stress it to a critical point, but the extra insurance may save you from having to rebuild an engine or even having to find a new block. Now when you redline your engine you can rest a little easier knowing that its rods, heads, and crankshaft are that extra bit stronger.

Here is a close-up showing before and after. Note that there are no sharp angles where the rod bolt attaches.

CRANK CALLS

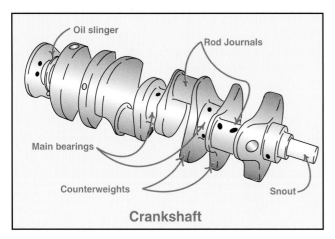

Crankshaft

- Oil slinger
- Rod Journals
- Main bearings
- Counterweights
- Snout

If the cam is the brain of your engine, the crankshaft is its brawn. That's why Chevy made it so strong. In fact, for street/performance use, the ductile iron crankshaft that your engine most likely came with is more than adequate, provided it is not badly worn or cracked. But if you are going to be revving the engine in the 7,000+ rpm range, especially for sustained periods such as with short-track racing, you will want a forged steel crankshaft because they are 35 percent stronger and they are more rigid, giving you an instant response.

In the 1950s, all Chevy small-block V-8s had forged steel crankshafts. Then, in 1963, Chevy switched to nodular cast-iron crankshafts. This was done mostly to save money, but iron crankshafts are by no means second-rate. And like every other component choice you need to make, it depends on what you want your engine to do. You only need to go to a forged or billet crankshaft if you are going to be building a radical engine for racing.

Which crankshaft you should choose for your engine depends on what you want the engine to do.

For street use in an engine under 400–450 horsepower, a ductile iron crankshaft is the best choice for several reasons. To begin with, a cast-iron crank can take more flexing than a forged steel crank without cracking. People who Magnaflux test crankshafts at machine shops will tell you that forged cranks are 10 times more likely to crack than cast cranks because of the forged crank's rigidity, despite the fact that they are 35 percent stronger. Also, cast crankshafts absorb inertial shocks better than forged, meaning that they require less damping.

For the purposes of this book, there is no reason to change over to a forged crankshaft, but I will cover the differences so you can make the most informed choice possible.

Worn crankshafts can be reground and polished, and bent crankshafts can be straightened, but cracked cranks should be discarded. So should grooved and ridged crankshafts. Grooved cranks are generally worn down through the hardened surface, and may have suffered from excessive heat, so they aren't worth the trouble either. If you can feel the grooves or ridges around the journal with your fingernail, get a new crank.

If you do have to replace your crankshaft, make sure you get the correct one for your application. There are dozens of possibilities, but only a few of them make sense for any particular engine. One of the most common mistakes is to unwittingly select a 305 crankshaft for a 350 motor. The 305 crankshaft looks identical to the 350, unless you really inspect it carefully, and many of them even have the same casting numbers.

The original crankshaft from your small block, provided it isn't cracked or worn out, is just fine for most street rod motors.

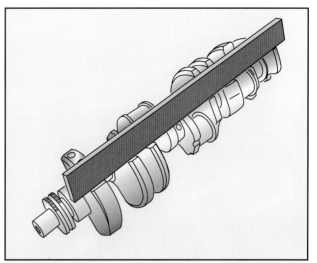

You can spot a 305 crankshaft by placing a straightedge across the five flats. If it sits evenly, you have a 305 crankshaft, which is not what you want for a 350.

LOOKS ARE DECEIVING

A 305 crankshaft will fit in a 350 motor, but it will not be counterweighted for the 350's larger rods and pistons. The whole rotating assembly would need an extensive balancing job. For performance purposes, a 305 crankshaft is not a consideration in anything but a 305 engine. However, in a 305, the standard crankshaft works great, and more and more street rodders are building 305s. Here's how to tell if you are looking at a 305 crankshaft or a crankshaft from a 350:

If you place a 305 crankshaft flat on a table, then lay a machinist's straightedge along the machined parts of the counterweights and throws from the flywheel hub to the front counterweight, it will lie flat. It won't on a 350 crankshaft because the 350 crank is shaped differently. A 305 crankshaft can be balanced out with stock 350 pistons and rods, but if you go to heavier, aftermarket components, the balancing job will be costly because the shop will have to add heavy metal to the 305 crank to get it to balance.

CHECK IT OUT

If you stay with your original crankshaft or go with a used replacement, you will want to make sure it is sound before you go to the expense of machining and balancing it. If you are buying a crankshaft from a wrecker, use the table in the appendix to determine which cranks will fit your engine. Once you have found a likely candidate, use a Spotcheck Jr. kit to check for cracks before you put your Visa card on the table.

With only the front and rear main bearings in place, check the crankshaft to make sure it is straight. You can do this using a feeler gauge, or better yet, a dial indicator and magnetic base.

And, even though you checked, you will still want to take any prospective used crank to a machine shop to have it Magnaflux tested. Doing a crack test is a must, especially with a used forged crankshaft. The test entails magnetizing the crankshaft and then spreading iron filings in a liquid solution on it. The iron filings are attracted to any gap, and under ultraviolet light they show up dramatically. Magnaflux testing is still the best crack test that is generally available for ferrous metals.

GOING FOR STROKE

One easy way to increase horsepower and torque in a 350 is to make your engine bigger by installing a crankshaft from a 400-ci Chevy small block, or by installing an aftermarket stroker crank. By doing so, you make the engine bigger by increasing its displacement because the sweep of the piston in the cylinder becomes greater. Thus, just by switching crankshafts (plus rods, flywheel, or flexplate and vibration damper) you end up with a 383- instead of a 350-ci-displacement engine.

The reason the flexplate and flywheel have to be changed out is that a 400-ci small block doesn't have the room inside its crankcase for all the counterweight that it needs in order to be balanced. As a result, there is additional balance weight on the flywheel and vibration damper. Also, the main bearing journals on the 400 crankshaft are larger than those in the 350, so they will have to be turned down to the 350 block. That's no big deal because you will probably want to have any used crank reground anyway.

Stroking a 350 is well worth doing and it will make a big difference in the performance potential of your engine. As we said before, it isn't horsepower that gives you neck-snapping acceleration. It takes torque to do that, and a longer-stroke engine is capable of a lot more torque than a short-stroke engine. Horsepower doesn't go up as dramatically in a stroker motor because the size of the combustion chamber doesn't get bigger in proportion.

If you are hot to do some serious racing, a used 400 crankshaft would not be the best choice. The 400 was never intended to be a performance engine, so all 400 cranks are ductile iron. That's fine for the street, but not so good for racing. For that you would need a cast-steel or forged crank, and those are much more expensive.

If money is not a consideration, but winning is, a billet crankshaft is the ultimate. Billet crankshafts are literally carved out of logs of steel. That's why they are so expensive. The machine work involved is extensive and time-consuming. It is truly the hard way to make a crankshaft. So why do it? Well, they do it because in a steel billet, all of the molecules of the steel are aligned for maximum strength. You will hear people talk about the "grain" of the metal. In a billet crankshaft the "grain" all runs lengthwise to the crank, making it very strong.

Forging also helps align and compress the grain of the metal to make the crankshaft stronger. But when a crankshaft is cast, the grain or molecular alignment is all mixed up, so the casting can't take as much twisting or torque. But how strong does it have to be? As we said at the outset, Chevy's stock, nodular iron crankshaft is more than adequate for street rod use. And Chevy's forged crankshafts are stronger yet.

For all-out racing where money is no object, a billet crankshaft is the ultimate choice. These are some billet crankshaft blanks.

When crankshafts are balanced, sometimes weight must be added to get them to balance, especially if you want to use a 305 crankshaft in a 350. Any crankshaft, new or used, should be balanced along with the rest of the rotating assembly.

CRANK I.D.

So how do you tell a forged crankshaft from a cast one? That's easy. Look for the parting line of the mold. If there is a narrow, distinct parting line, the crankshaft is cast. If there is a broad, raised die mark instead, the crankshaft is forged. The next question might be: How can you tell if a crankshaft is out of a 400-ci engine? Measure the mains using a dial caliper. A stock 350 crankshaft will have 2.45-inch main bearing journals (used ones will often be .010" undersize), but a crankshaft from a 400-ci engine will have 2.65-inch main bearings.

One other important thing to remember is that after 1986, Chevy equipped all of its small-block engines with a one-piece rear main seal. Crankshafts from later engines can only be used with later blocks. On the other hand, crankshafts from earlier engines that were equipped with two-piece rear mains will work in later engines if you use one of the adapters available from aftermarket sources.

AFTERMARKET ANSWERS

Lunati, Crower, and others make forged stroker crankshafts for Chevy small blocks, but my favorite is Scat's cast-steel stroker crank. It is a cast rather than forged crankshaft, but it is nearly as strong as a forged crankshaft without the shortcomings. And it sells for only a couple of hundred dollars more than a regrind on a stock crank.

Also, a Scat crankshaft costs quite a bit less than a new stock crank from Chevrolet. The casting is done in China to Scat's exacting metallurgical requirements, and then expertly machined at this end. This may sound a little scary in light of China's "Great leap forward" of 40 years ago, when poor-grade steel was pumped out in insane quantities.

Scat stroker cranks are an inexpensive way to build tons of torque into your engine.

These are Scat cast-steel crankshafts ready for machining.

Any crankshaft, new or used, should be balanced along with the rest of the rotating assembly.

Scat cast-steel stroker crankshafts come with generous fillet radii and chamfered oil holes, along with careful machining.

But China really has made a great leap forward since then, and now supplies steel and iron of consistently superb quality. The 80-60-06 cast-steel alloy (80,000 psi tensile and 60,000 yield with 6 percent elongation) used in Scat's cast crankshafts is superior to the O.E.M. cast-iron alloy from Chevrolet. In fact, DaimlerChrysler is having crankshafts made in China now too.

Scat's cast-steel crankshafts have been around for years and are race proven at local drag strips, so you do not need to worry about durability. I have not come across one that has failed yet, and I don't know of anyone who has. Of course, if you are building a 600-horsepower racing engine, you would want to go to one of Scat's, or another manufacturer's, forged or even billet cranks.

Another good feature of Scat's cast-steel stroker crankshafts is that they are designed to accommodate longer rods of 5.7 inches or even 6 inches, which means gentler cranking angles and more time for the piston at the top and bottom of the combustion cycles. This gives the fuel longer to burn at the top to produce more power, and it allows more exhaust to be expelled as the piston comes up on the exhaust stroke.

The only problem with 6-inch rods is that they put the ring pack very high in the piston and the wrist pin up into the ring pack, which makes for a more delicate piston. A better bet for a long-lived street machine is the 5.7-inch rod. They will give you a combination of great

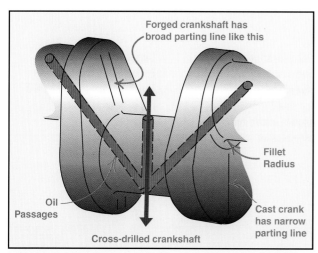

Forged crankshaft has broad parting line like this

Fillet Radius

Oil Passages

Cast crank has narrow parting line

Cross-drilled crankshaft

The blue arrow indicates where the crankshaft is cross-drilled for better lubrication. This is only recommended for very-high-revving engines in the 10,000-rpm range.

performance and durability as well. KB makes pistons for both applications that work very well and aren't costly.

MAKING IT BETTER THAN NEW

A new Scat crankshaft will come with generous fillet radii at the main and rod bearing journals to make it stronger. That's because when crankshafts crack and let go, they generally do so at the joints between the machined journals and the crankshaft throws. Scat cranks also come with the oil gallery holes in the journals chamfered to avoid damaging bearings and to help oiling.

If you decide to stick with a used crankshaft, unless it is within specs, have it turned .020" under and have the ends of the crank journals radiused. Believe it or not, the removal of this small amount of metal will not harm anything, and the generous fillet radii at the ends of the journals will make your crankshaft much more resistant to cracking. This, combined with shot peening, will give you a very stout crankshaft indeed.

Another trick that may make a difference at very high rpm is to have the machine shop cross-drill the main journals so they have two oil holes instead of one. The main journal hole is an inlet and the rod an outlet. This process is not really necessary for street rod use, but might make a difference at sustained high rpms and could also help if a crank gallery got clogged somehow. But if you are on a tight budget, the cost of cross-drilling might be better spent somewhere else.

CONNECTING RODS

For street rod use below 6,000 rpm, your stock connecting rods will do just fine. Make sure they are straight and crack-free, and then follow the advice in the shot-peening chapter to prepare them. After the rods are peened, have them carefully balanced with the rest of the rotating assembly.

Heavy-duty aluminum rods or special trick rods for racing are a must if you want to be reaching 8,000 rpm now and again. To do that, you will want an aftermarket or used forged crankshaft. Use the rods recommended by the crankshaft manufacturer. It is beyond the scope of this book to go into all the various forms of racing and what might be best in each application.

BEARINGS

I prefer Clevite 77s, as do many engine builders, but a number of manufacturers make crank bearings that are equally suitable. Clevites have never failed me, and are the choice of most high-performance street engine builders. They are fairly hard, thin bearings, and if you are going to be running in the dirt, you may want to go to thicker bearings with more embedability, which will permit grit to be trapped and covered by the bearing material. That way, if your engine does get a mouth full of dirt, it will be somewhat less likely to ruin the crankshaft.

HYGIENE
CLEANING UP THE MESS

COST  $20 - $30

SKILL LEVEL

TIME  2 HOURS

A few months ago, a young fellow across the street from my shop was overhauling the small-block engine out of his red 1969 Camaro. He was just finishing up when I walked over and had a cup of coffee with him. While we talked he went through the list of what he had done to the engine, and it included a rebore, new bearings throughout, a mild cam, forged pistons, headers, and a Holley double pumper. It sounded like a great combination. A couple of days later he had the engine in the car and it sounded sweet.

Then a week later I saw him with the Camaro's engine torn down on a stand again out in front of his garage. I strolled over and asked him what had gone wrong. He told me that he had neglected to clean out the oil galleries when he got the engine back from the machine shop, so metal shavings had been washed by the engine's oil right to the

Wash the block thoroughly when you get it home, and make sure to shoot solvent down in all the little oil galleries too. Then clean your engine again thoroughly after you have detailed and painted it.

crankshaft bearings and had scored the crank to the point where it had to be replaced. I told him not to be too hard on himself, because I had made the same mistake once and had suffered the same fate as a result.

That was a long time ago, but it was a costly lesson I never forgot. So in an effort to help others avoid the same calamity, I'd like to share the benefits of my expensive education. The number one thing to remember is to keep it clean. Dirt, grit, and machinist's metal shavings (swarf) are the enemies of engines. And dirt can be introduced at any stage of assembly.

In fact, the top racing engine builders assemble their engines in "clean rooms" where you could eat off the floor, and where there is a positive atmosphere at all times thanks to filtered air being pumped in. That way dust can't even drift into the room. You don't need to take it that far yourself, but you do need to make sure your engine, shop, tools, and hands are surgery-room clean.

Chase all threaded holes with the correct tap to remove dirt and metal filings.

Remove any slag around the oil drain holes using a die grinder and carbide bit.

Sweep and mop your shop before you even unwrap your engine parts. Just shooting a lot of compressed air around accomplishes nothing. Wipe down all your tools, and get rid of any sandblasting media, metal shavings, or other grit that could drift into your work area. Finally, keep your hands and clothes clean. Many top engine builders these days use disposable latex gloves while working to prevent oil and moisture on their fingers from attacking engine parts. I don't take it that far, but it isn't a bad idea.

Next, run a tap (make sure it is for the correct threads), down each bolt-hole in the block and heads, and chase the threads for any dirt, rust, or metal shavings. Use compressed air or a rifle cleaning brush to clean out the holes. Also, inspect the block and heads for any burrs or casting slag that might interfere with assembly. Often a burr is not easy to see, but if you run your fingertip along edges you can feel them. Remove burrs with a bearing scraper.

The oil return holes in the lifter valley often have a ridge of slag that should be removed with a die grinder or files. Any last-minute deburring, chamfering, or dressing should be done now. Be sure to do it before you clean the engine because you will not want metal filings blowing

An old-fashioned bearing scraper is great for deburring machined edges such as lifter bores and bearing journals.

around and scoring pistons, bearings, and crankshafts after your engine is clean.

As soon as you get your engine back from the machine shop, wash everything down with paint thinner. It's cheap, it doesn't leave an oily residue (though it does leave a thin protective film), and you can reuse it. Lacquer thinner is also good, though more volatile. If you wash your engine down with lacquer thinner, shoot it with a little WD-40, and then wipe it down afterward to prevent rust.

I like to use a big, clean plastic concrete-mixing tray to wash things in. For safety's sake don latex gloves and a face shield while you are doing your washing. Put the block on an engine stand and put the concrete mixing tray under it to catch the drippings. If you have a source of compressed air, hook up a solvent sprayer, set it at fairly low pressure, and shoot the paint thinner down into lifter bores, bolt-holes, oil galleries, and such.

Once your engine is clean, wipe it down with clean rags so the oily residue won't attract more dirt.

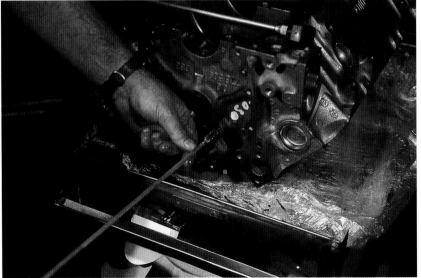

Clean out the cam-oil galleries, the galleries going to the main bearings, and the galleries in the crankshaft using a rifle bore cleaning kit. Keep working until a cotton swab comes out clean.

Bottle brushes, small scrub brushes, and clean rags are all necessary for the next task. With a small container of thinner, go around and scrub away any dirt or scale that is stuck in the nooks and crannies of the block. When you are finished, everything should be clean, bright metal. Be especially fussy about areas where oil flows through the engine, such as the lifter valley, the timing gear and chain compartment, and the tops of the heads.

Next, use a rifle cleaning kit to wash out all the little oil galleries in the block. Remove any plugs, then dip a rifle bore brush in paint thinner and work it back and forth in the galleries to loosen any residue and pull out any metal chips left over from machining. Just as you would with a rifle, keep working until you can shove a white cotton swab in the gallery and have it come out clean. Take out the pipe plugs you had installed at the ends of the cam galleries and clean them out too.

Don't forget to clean out all of the oil passageways in the crankshaft as well. Use a rifle bore brush of the appropriate size and keep working until you can push in a cotton swab and have it come back out clean. Any swarf in the crank will go right to the bearings in the first few minutes of operation and become embedded in them. They will then score the crankshaft, often to the point where it must be replaced. And that could be an expensive situation if you've just dropped in a new stroker crankshaft.

Finally, check everything one more time before moving on to the next step. Once you are sure everything is meticulously clean, wrap each component in a plastic bag, and set it aside where it won't get dropped or bumped. Store the crankshaft vertically so it won't warp. Strap it to a vertical garage stud or the leg of a workbench so it won't fall over and fracture your toes.

Blow air through your solvent sprayer until it runs clear of liquid. Pour the mineral spirits out of your concrete mixing tray back into a can using a funnel. You can use it again for washing parts, but if you don't, be sure to dispose

Don't forget to check the timing gears and other components for burrs too.

Mask off the gasket mating surfaces for the gaskets, or wipe them clean with lacquer thinner.

of it according to local environmental regulations. Wash out your concrete tray using dish soap and hot water, then use it under your engine during assembly to catch dropped parts.

PAINT YOUR PARTS

This step is not an absolute must, but it comes under the category of making things better than new. Professional engine builders paint the inside of the engine as well as the outside. Even though you don't see it, it makes a big difference. When you paint the lifter valley and the tops of the cylinder heads with epoxy paint, engine oil will run down out of these areas more easily, and there will be less tendency for the engine to build up sludge.

Painting the inside of the engine also makes it easier to clean up and work on too. Use only epoxy paint because ordinary spray enamel will just heat up, flake off, and become part of the sludge. Wash the areas you are going to paint with lacquer thinner to remove any oily residue. Mask off rocker studs, bolt-holes, and other items you don't want to paint, and use pieces of cardboard as masks while spraying. Put old spark plugs in the plug holes to protect their threads from paint. Don't use any primer because it will burn. Just shoot on a thin tack coat, let it get sticky, then shoot on a full wet coat of paint.

Now is a good time to paint the exterior of the block, heads, and any other items you want painted. Unless you are doing some custom color, you can just use engine

Mask off the areas you don't want painted, then shoot epoxy primer in the lifter valley, timing gear compartment, and rocker arm areas of the heads so oil will run back quickly and sludge won't build up in service.

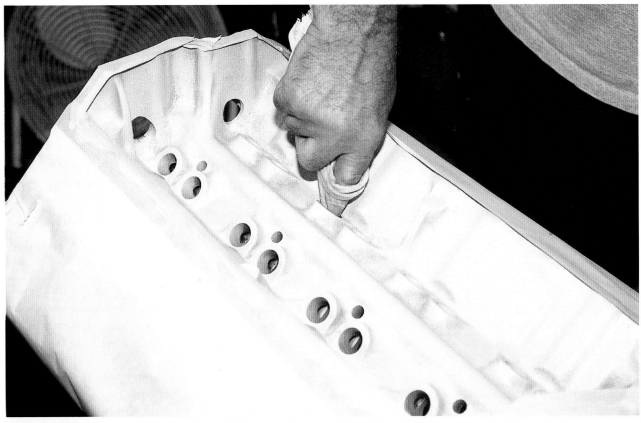

Use a rag dipped in lacquer thinner to clean out lifter bores. Nothing must interfere with smooth lifter operation.

enamel in aerosol cans that is mixed to match Chevy red. Again, don't prime, because it will cause the enamel to flake off. Just shoot on a tack coat, then shoot on a couple of full wet coats, and let the parts dry for a day or so before working on them. If you are doing a strictly correct restoration, you may want to paint the engine after it is assembled (just as they did at the factory), but I prefer not to paint over gaskets and such.

If you are going to paint your intake manifold, shoot on a little silver high-temp manifold paint, let it dry, then shoot on the orange enamel. That way the engine enamel won't burn off as it often does when applied directly on the intake manifold. Keep paint away from gasket surfaces, as it might not interact favorably with sealants. And while your paint is drying, now is a good time to polish any aluminum manifolds, water pumps, timing gear covers, and valve covers because you can't do the job once they are on the engine.

Finally, clean and wipe down your block, heads, and other components again and store them carefully. A dropped crankshaft or cam will most likely bend or even fracture, rendering it useless. Other components can gather dust, rust, and contaminants. Mop your shop every time you work on your engine, and keep your hands clean. Habits of care and precision are basic to proper engine building.

PREPARING FOR ASSEMBLY
BASIC TRAINING

Auto shop wasn't offered where I went to high school, so I learned to work on engines the hard way. When I was 16 years old, a grumpy mechanic named Dutch took me under his wing and taught me a few tricks. Rather than clutching me gently to his bosom, he usually slapped my cap off my head from behind when he wished to counsel me. Then, only after proceeding to tell me how worthless my entire generation was, he would point out what I had done wrong.

At first I helped him for free, just to learn. The fact that he didn't run me off was my only affirmation. The truth is, he may have been grumpy, but he had a good heart, and he took the time to teach me some things. Dutch is gone now, but for those of you who are novices, I'll share some of what he taught me. You'll have to come up with your own trick to help you remember things. Keep in mind that the sooner you make good techniques into habits, the better.

Putting an engine together is *not* like putting together a jigsaw puzzle, or at least it shouldn't be. By the time you are ready to assemble your engine, you should know where every piece goes and what it does. You can accomplish this by taking notes and photos when you take the engine apart, and by reading as much as you can about what each component does before you put your engine back together.

Putting together an engine is all about precision, such as getting tolerances right and making sure pistons are installed facing the right direction. Keep in mind that a couple of thousandths of an inch can make a huge difference, and that even particles of dust are that big, so you have to keep everything clean. Also, even if you aren't a novice, make notes of dimensions you have measured, what you have finished, and what you have left to do. When you come back to your engine later, you'll know exactly what you have to do next. Make sure you don't lose the card the machine shop gave you with all of their work listed on it.

IN THE BEGINNING

When assembling engines, use the right tool for the job. Most tasks are easy if you have the right tools, but are nearly impossible if you don't. For example, some beginners will use a crescent wrench for everything just because it is handy. This is a good way to round off bolts and nuts and damage your hands. A set of open- and box-end wrenches are basic necessities. A decent socket set is required too. And for anything beyond a tune-up, a quality torque wrench is imperative.

I prefer the type with a rotating handle and a scale to which you can adjust the wrench. The old-style, needle-and-arm-type wrench is pretty crude and hard to read precisely. If you buy one of the adjustable-type torque wrenches, be sure to set it back to zero after each use so the spring inside won't lose its tension. Open your wallet a little wider when you buy your torque wrench, and get the best one you can afford. It could make a difference in your engine's longevity.

Other specialty tools are also important for engine work, such as a ring compressor for installing pistons, vernier calipers, and micrometers for accurate measuring. An engine stand to make your work convenient and to save your back is a good idea too. Some tools, such as engine hoists, can be rented from tool rental yards, but you may have to purchase gear pullers and other specialty tools if you can't rent or borrow them. Nonessential tools that

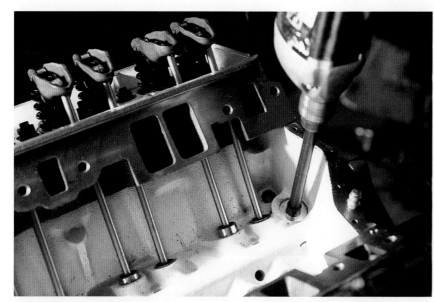

Taking the time to pump up the oil in the lifters using a priming tool is a useful professional tip.

Use a solvent sprayer and drip tray to make sure everything is clean.

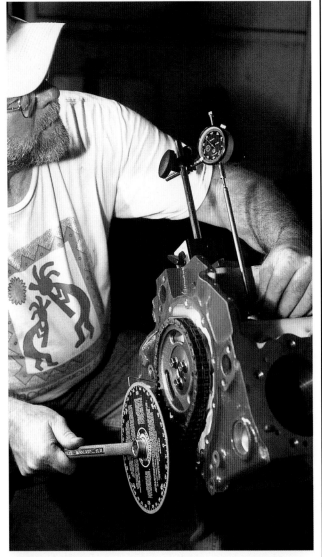

Habits of precision are critical to building a high-performance engine.

will make your life a whole lot easier include a parts-washing tank, an air compressor, and a solvent sprayer.

Swap meets and garage sales are great for picking up used tools, but make sure you buy quality items. Sears Craftsman automotive tools are top-notch and are not as costly as tools from some of the specialty companies. For specialized tools that will only be used now and then, cheap imports will work, but they are not generally as durable or precise as domestic, professional-quality tools.

And don't neglect the small stuff. Squeeze-type oil cans and plastic ketchup squeeze bottles make shooting on oil or cleaner easier. You will also want to buy some good hand cleaner, and collect a bundle of clean, lint-free rags. Before you start assembly, gather together assembly lube, cam lube, silicone sealant, Lok-Tite, anti-seize compound, and lacquer thinner as well as paint thinner for cleaning.

A CLEAN, WELL-LIGHTED PLACE

As we pointed out in chapter 14, cleanliness is critical. Grit in oil galleries or around a bearing shell can ruin the bearing and possibly your engine as well. Keep your engine and its components covered with plastic trash bags when you are not working on them. Sweep and mop your shop before you begin each work session, and wipe down your tools after you use them.

A dry garage with a concrete floor is a good place to work, but never work directly on the floor. You can also work outdoors on still days when there is no dust in the air. Make sure you have plenty of light where you choose to work. Fluorescent fixtures are available for a nominal price at home improvement centers and they require very little energy. Install several in your workspace, and keep a good trouble light handy too. Finally, a small flashlight is great for peering into dark crevices.

BREAK IT UP

When disassembling or assembling an engine, break the job into tasks. Then look over each task and think it out. Lay out the tools and other things you are going to need ahead of time. As you take things apart, place components on your bench in the order they came apart. You may think you'll remember, but unless you are quite exceptional, you probably won't.

If you are putting an assembly together, pause and think about what sequence the job will require. Lay out the components in order. You don't want to have to take things apart again just because you didn't remember to install something vital. If anything seems unfamiliar, read the chapter on that item again before going to the next step.

Resign yourself to the idea that you will most likely have to assemble some things two or even three times before you get everything right. Racing mechanics dry-assemble entire engines just to make sure everything fits and works together, and that they have the tolerances right before building the engine in earnest. If you are a novice, I highly recommend that you do the same thing. You don't need to put rings on the pistons during dry assembly, and you don't need to put a lot of lube or oil on things either because you will be taking everything apart again anyway.

IT'S ABOUT TIME

Seasoned mechanics with all the right tools can build performance engines in as little as a few hours, but it can take weeks for a novice to do the job correctly—especially if you are installing a cam from one manufacturer, a crankshaft from another, connecting rods from someone else, and pistons or heads from yet another company. All of these items are likely to be well-made and within specs, but they may not have been designed to work together. You can easily wind up with tolerance stacking and an engine that is too tight, too loose, or binding somewhere. Take the time to measure and find out before problems blossom.

If this is your first engine, it would pay to have the machine shop assemble the valve train for the heads before giving them back to you. They can do the job in a lot less time than you can, and they will have all the tools necessary. You may want to have the machine shop hang the pistons on the rods too. They can ream and fit them much more accurately than most of us can do at home.

Use the right tool for the job. This soft brass hammer will not damage steel components.

ALL ABOUT TORQUE WRENCHES

Quality torque wrenches have a micrometer-type adjustment built into their handle to adjust the applied torque. Just dial in the specified torque for the fastener, select the correct-sized socket, and tighten the fastener. This type of torque wrench will make a snapping sound when it reaches the selected torque. Do not tighten any more beyond the click, because doing so will overtorque the fastener and may cause it to fail. Never jerk or force the wrench abruptly. Just gently pull it to specs.

When you are given a value range, such as 85–100 foot-pounds for attaching the vibration damper, for example, tighten all of the fasteners evenly in three stages to the same value, whether it be 85, 95, or 100 foot-pounds of torque. When torquing larger items such as intake manifolds and heads, follow the proper sequence for that component.

When attaching cast-iron cylinder heads, follow the torque diagram in your shop manual or in chapter 26. Start in the middle of the head and run each fastener down in three stages. First, tighten all the fasteners to 50 foot-pounds. Then, starting in the center again, adjust the torque wrench to the setting for the second stage, or 60 foot-pounds. Then retorque the fasteners again. This time, start in the center, and torque them to the final spec of 65–72 foot-pounds.

If you do not tighten engine bolts and nuts to the specifications in your shop manual, they could work loose or become overtightened and break. Reputable hardware manufacturers have arrived at torque values for each type of fastener. This is usually stated in foot-pounds, or occasionally in inch-pounds (120 inch-pounds are the same as 10 foot-pounds). The assembly manual for your engine will have a torque specification section that will list the torque values for all of its fasteners, but here are the critical ones:

TORQUE LIMITS IN FOOT-POUNDS FOR A CHEVY SMALL BLOCK

Main bearing cap bolts 60–70

Damper to crankshaft 85–100

Connecting rod nuts 19–24

Oil pump to block 12–15

Flywheel to crankshaft 75–85

Valve rocker supports to head 30–35

Fuel pump to block 12–15

CYLINDER HEADS (IRON)

Stage 1 50
Stage 2 60
Stage 3 65–72

The scale on a torque wrench is in pounds and is at the base of the handle in most cases.

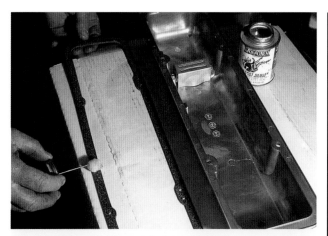

Use the right sealant for each task to avoid leaks and seal failure.

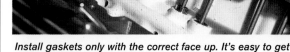

Install gaskets only with the correct face up. It's easy to get sloppy and create problems for yourself later.

KEEP RECORDS

When you check clearances, write them in a small spiral notebook. You'll be surprised how useful this kind of information can be as you go along. In addition, keep track of what you were doing before you quit for the day, to ensure that nothing is forgotten. For instance, you may have torqued the main bearings into place, but not the rods before you called it a day. If you don't take note of such things, you may come back and think you have done the rods too. Aside from avoiding catastrophe, such records also help refresh your memory if you have to work on your engine later.

There will always be more to learn no matter how long you play with engines, so don't try to master everything all at once. If any procedure seems daunting, practice putting together old parts until you get the picture. The main thing is not to get in a hurry and damage things. Also, don't be afraid to ask for advice from pros, or people who have more experience than you do. If you approach professionals with respect, they will usually be more than generous with their advice and aid.

Also be sure to use the correct lubricant for each task.

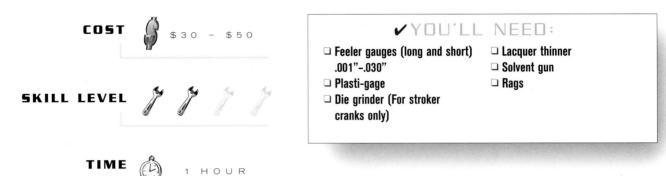

COST $30 - $50

SKILL LEVEL

TIME 1 HOUR

✔ YOU'LL NEED:

- ❑ Feeler gauges (long and short) .001"-.030"
- ❑ Plasti-gage
- ❑ Die grinder (For stroker cranks only)
- ❑ Lacquer thinner
- ❑ Solvent gun
- ❑ Rags

ears ago, I overhauled the 283 in my 1957 Chevrolet. I put it back in the car and lit it off hoping to enjoy a nice, smooth rumble. Instead I was treated to the irritating, intermittent click of piston slap. It wasn't bad and it was only in one bore, so I figured the rings just had not seated yet. But after a couple of weeks, the noise got more insistent. I took the head off, pulled the pistons, and measured them. They were all at least .010" smaller than specs. I took them down to the machine shop and had them knurled to bring them back out to tolerance.

This trick only worked for a short time before the noise returned. I finally ended up buying a new set of pistons and installing them. So why do I confess to this little fiasco? Well, I do so to offer an example of why it is important that you check all your engine's critical dimensions before beginning to assemble it. Good machine shops and piston makers rarely make mistakes, but nobody's perfect. And most machine shops will correct any errors they may have made, but they won't pay for your labor to extricate your engine and tear it down again if there is a problem.

If you are putting an engine together for the first time, the last thing you need is for some obscure mistake—not even of your own making—to throw a wrench in the works, so to speak. The machine shop is being asked to be accurate down to less than .001" in places, and that is impossible to do day in and day out without ever getting it wrong. Verifying that everything is right only takes an hour or so, and it can save you a lot of time and aggravation later. Here's how to do it:

PISTONS

First, make sure the pistons fit correctly in their bores. The correct tolerance will depend on which pistons you are installing, so follow the manufacturer's specifications exactly. Forged pistons usually require more clearance (.004" -.008"), but some manufacturers offer forged pistons that are correct with as little as .0015". Keith Black (KB) Hypereutectic–cast pistons only need .0015" -002", but racing pistons can have as much as .015" clearance. Such big gaps make for a rather noisy, oil-burning engine, but in the heat of competition, with the headers uncorked, who cares about a little piston slap?

How pistons should be measured in their cylinder bores is not uniform from manufacturer to manufacturer either. Most piston clearances are checked 90 degrees around from the wrist pin, but others are not. Also, very few pistons are made round from the factory. Most pistons are cam ground to an oval shape of between .020" and

.040" out of round, with the larger dimension at 90 degrees to the piston pin boss. This is done because the metals of the piston, the wrist pin and its keepers, and any steel struts in the piston expand at differing rates as they heat up.

Also, piston skirts are generally bigger around at the bottom than up by the ring lands. And to complicate matters further, some pistons are ground to a slight barrel shape when viewed from the side. But if you use a set of long feeler gauges and measure the piston along the area recommended by the piston maker, you will be fine.

Before you check the piston-to-bore clearances of your pistons, lightly wipe a very thin film of oil on the cylinder walls. To check piston-to-bore clearance, first slip a feeler gauge of the proper thickness into the bore and slip a piston without rings into the bore upside down until it is in all the way. Now pull the feeler gauge out slowly. It should slip out with gentle resistance. A spring-loaded scale

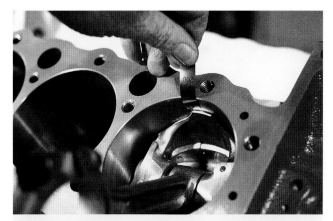

Use long feeler gauges to check piston clearances in bores.

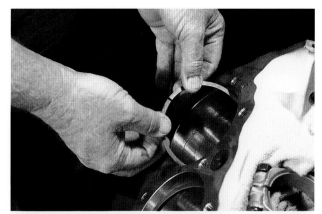

Pull the rings together at the gaps and then slide them into the cylinders to check end gaps.

Push a piston without rings on it upside down in the bore to square up rings for checking.

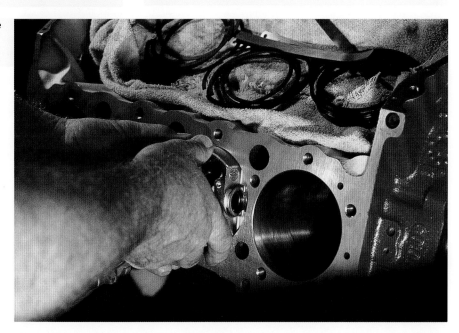

is good for checking the resistance if you have one. It should read about 10 pounds for just the right pull.

The next-thinner feeler gauge should pull out readily, and the next-size larger should not fit, or should not pull out at all. Check each piston to the bore in which you intend to install it. If any are slightly loose or tight, try switching them around to see if that helps, or to try to determine what the problem is. If a piston fits too tightly or too loosely in more than one bore, it is a little too big or too small. If, on the other hand, two or more pistons fit too tightly or are too loose in one particular hole, that cylinder may be too small and need a little more honing.

Chances are, all of your pistons will fit within specs, but it is well worth checking, nevertheless. If pistons are too tight in their bores, they will heat up and scuff, damaging

the pistons. They could even seize in their bores in extreme circumstances. If pistons are too loose, they will wobble in their bores and rattle as they did in my Chevy. Aside from the irritating noise, such pistons and their rings will wear out quickly and the engine will burn oil.

RINGS

Check each ring in its piston ring land using a feeler gauge. Follow the specs that come with your pistons or rings as to how thick the feeler gauge should be. If the ring land gap is too tight, the rings will seize and damage may occur. First, place the feeler gauge in the gap on the upper lip, then insert the ring into the groove. If the ring goes in sloppily, try the next-thicker feeler gauge. If the rings are too sloppy in their lands, ring flutter will be a major

109

problem. But if the rings won't fit with the correct feeler gauge in place, they will cause damage by sticking and scraping the cylinder. If your rings don't match specs, take them back where you got them and get new ones in the correct thickness.

Next, it is critical that each cylinder ring have a minimum gap between its two ends to prevent it from touching during heat expansion. As the engine comes up to temperature everything expands, and the pistons expand more than the rings because the pistons are made of aluminum. Rings are forced out against the cylinder walls as they and the pistons expand, so the ring gap diminishes. That is as it should be, but if the ring gap closes completely, the ring will score the cylinder walls and could even cause the piston to seize in its cylinder.

Again, follow the instructions with your rings and pistons. Many stock cast pistons require ring gaps in the .003" – .008" range for the first and second rings. But Keith

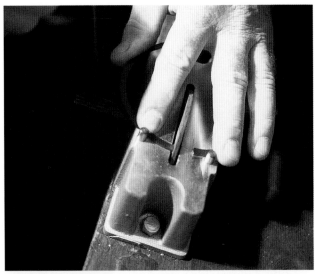

A ring grinder is the best way to open ring gaps. Hand-filing risks shattering or tweaking the ring.

Use feeler gauges to verify ring gaps. You can also use the same ring again in each bore to check bore diameter differences.

Black Signature Series–cast pistons need a top ring gap of .025" because the tops of the pistons get so hot and the ring grooves are very high on these pistons. At any rate, most quality ring sets do require some adjustments to their ring gaps, so check the manufacturer's specifications and adjust the gaps accordingly.

You can just put each ring in a vise with a couple of pieces of soft wood to cushion it, then file the ends of the rings to the correct dimension, but that takes quite a while because it is a trial-and-error process. You have to put the ring in the vise, file it a bit, take it out and put it in a cylinder, and check it with a feeler gauge, and then put it back in the vise and file some more. With a ring-grinding tool, the process goes much faster. These little tools aren't cheap ($65 at this writing), but they are worth it.

Also, a ring-grinding tool does a cleaner, more accurate job. You just gently press the ring against the stops and turn the crank. Count the number of turns it takes to get a ring to the fit with the correct gap, then do the same minus three or four turns on each succeeding ring and trial fit it. Before you install the rings on the pistons, deburr the inside corners of the gaps and the new edges you've made to prevent scratches on the pistons.

MAIN AND ROD BEARINGS

Ideally, your rod and main bearings will fit exactly within specs. But the world is sometimes less than ideal, so it pays to check. The task is simple. Just pick up a few strips of Plasti-gage at your local auto parts store. I like to get several different ranges and keep the stuff on hand.

To check your rods and mains, you will need to put your main bearing shells in and install the crankshaft. Thoroughly clean the backs of the bearings and the journals in which they ride with lacquer thinner and a lint-free rag. You do not want oil behind a thin-shell bearing, and you certainly don't want any grit or dirt. Even a tiny bit of grit will change the bearing clearance, and oil on the backs of the bearing shells could cause the engine to spin a bearing under certain circumstances.

Put in the bearing shells, being careful to make sure they are facing the right way. (Notch-to-notch is standard.) Again, don't apply any lubricant. Just gently lay the crankshaft in place. Now put pieces of the round Plasti-gage strip on the main journals and torque the bearing-end caps in place according to specs.

Tighten the bolts evenly in three stages from the center mains out to the ends. Main bearings are normally torqued to 65 foot-pounds but check the specs for your particular

Rings must also have the proper clearance in their lands in order to function properly.

Use a piece of Plasti-gage on each main-bearing journal to verify clearances.

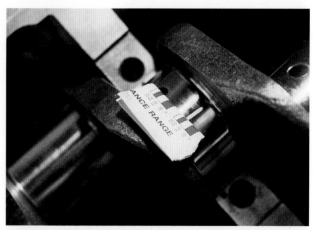
Check the Plasti-gage reading with the packet it came in. The stuff is surprisingly accurate.

Use Plasti-gage to check each rod bearing clearance too. Moisten it with a little saliva to get it to hold still.

Use the graduated scale on the Plasti-gage packet to confirm clearances.

engine in your shop manual. Never turn the crankshaft in its bearings with the Plasti-gage in place because it will smear the plastic and spoil your readings.

Loosen the main bearing caps evenly and pull them off. The round Plasti-gage will be squished into a flat strip. Use the measurements on the paper jacket the Plasti-gage came in to verify the bearing clearance. If the main bearings are too tight, they will not get enough oil and will smear and gall. If the mains are too loose, they will not hold oil pressure.

Should your bearings be too tight, take your crankshaft back to the machine shop and have it polished to specs. If the bearings are too loose, that is a bigger problem. The crankshaft will have to be reground and the next-oversize bearing will have to be installed. In any case, don't be tempted to just put the engine together and hope for the best. If you do that, you can expect the worst.

Using Plasti-gage, check each connecting rod bearing too. These are probably the most critical bearings in an engine. They take a lot of shock and punishment in service,

BUILDING A 383 STROKER

If you are building a stroker motor, the rod bolts must be installed at the machine shop and ground on a bevel to clear the camshaft. This should be done at the machine shop because it is important to do it before the rotating assembly is balanced. The bottoms of the cylinder bores at the pan rails must also be ground a little to accommodate the bottoms of the rods.

The easiest way to figure out where to relieve the block is to install the rods one at a time and snug them up, oil the crank and bearings to prevent damage, then mark where each rod's big end contacts the block. Mark the area with a felt marker, then take the rod back out. When you have the block marked for each rod clearance, use a die grinder or round crosscut file to take off what is necessary to allow the crankshaft to turn. You want about .020" clearance to allow for heat expansion. Take the crankshaft and bearings back out and clean the block thoroughly before reinstalling the crank and pistons.

When installing a 400 crank in a 350, you will need to grind the block slightly in these areas in order to get the rod bolts to clear.

and they get thrown around a lot. It is absolutely necessary to thoroughly inspect the connecting rod bearings because when they go bad it is usually catastrophic. Again, make sure the bearing journals are clean, oil-free, and dry. Do not turn the crankshaft during the test. Connecting rods should normally be torqued into place at 45 foot-pounds, but verify this in your shop manual or with the bolt manufacturer.

If you are installing a stroker crank, due to the increased stroke you need to make sure the rod bolts clear the cam and the sides of the lower cylinder bores and drip rails. If you choose to install a high-lift cam, it will need to have a small base circle in order to clear the rod bolts, and you will need to have the rod bolts ground down to clear the cam lobes. If the cam is standard lift, you do not need a small base circle cam, but the rod bolts will still need to be ground to clear.

This is not a job you can do yourself because grinding down rod bolts will affect the balance of your engine's rotating assembly. When installing a stroker crank, whether it be one from a 400-ci engine or an aftermarket Scat crank, make it clear to your machinist up front what you are doing and explain the situation about the rod bolts. That way they can be ground evenly and balanced properly.

Another problem when installing 400 cranks is block clearance. Down at the base of each bore, near the drip rail for the pan, the bottoms of the rod bolts will touch. The best way to determine exactly where, and how much needs cutting away is to install a piston in each bank and mark the area where the rod bolt touches with a marker pen.

Remove the rod, crankshaft, and crank bearings and grind away the area on the block that is interfering. I like the gap to be at least .020," just to make sure nothing can wobble or expand to close the gap. A die grinder such as you would use in head porting will do the job quickly, or you can use a half-round, crosscut hand file to do the job.

After you grind away the material, clean up the block using a solvent gun, and then make sure the rods clear before beginning final assembly. It doesn't pay to get hasty when building a hot engine. All of your money and effort could go up in blue smoke if you make a costly mistake. There are other checks and verifications that you will need to make as you assemble your engine, but we have thoroughly covered the preliminary checks that will help you avoid problems before you get rolling.

FINAL MEASUREMENTS

113

COST  LESS THAN $100

SKILL LEVEL

TIME 4 HOURS

BOTTOM-END ASSEMBLY

✔ YOU'LL NEED:

- Gasket set
- Assembly lube
- Silicone sealer
- Anaerobic sealer
- Clean, lint-free rags
- Quality torque wrench
- Socket set
- Ring compressor
- Soft hammer (brass or copper are good)
- Squirt can and oil
- ARP bolt-stretch gauge (optional)
- Plastic tubing for rod bolts
- Feeler gauges
- Homemade vibration damper installer (optional)
- Cam lube
- Large screwdriver
- Felt marker
- Die grinder
- Laquer thinner
- Small file
- Propane torch
- Leather gloves

Get a selection of slick stuff such as Isky's Rev Lube, silicone sealers, anaerobic sealer, and medium-thread locker.

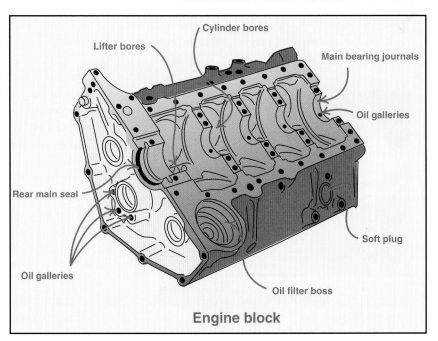

Engine block

(Labels: Lifter bores, Cylinder bores, Main bearing journals, Oil galleries, Soft plug, Oil filter boss, Oil galleries, Rear main seal)

Now for the fun part: putting all of those gleaming, clean, beautiful new parts together to make a magnificent small-block engine.

Before you begin work on the bottom end, install the camshaft. It is much easier to do with the crankshaft out of the block. Smear a little assembly lube on the cam bearings and, using a long bolt in the front end as a handle, slip the cam into place. Be very careful not to bump the cam's lobes against its bearings. The cam should seat against the plug line up in its bearings and should turn freely. Smear the cam lobes with Iskenderian's Rev Lube or another quality cam lube. See chapter 11 for details on how to time the cam properly once you get the crankshaft installed.

INSTALLING THE CRANKSHAFT

Unless your original timing gear is nearly new, with no ridges or wear, you will need to install a fresh one. Line the gear up with its key-way and use a large socket and a brass mallet to tap it into place. Keep tapping until you feel the gear seat against the crankshaft. Don't just pound directly on the gear to install it, because you could damage or distort it. Next, install the top half of the rear main seal. Coat its lip generously with oil and slip it into place. If you are working on an older engine that takes a rope seal, leave it out for now.

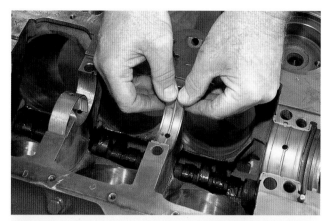

Clean the saddles with lacquer thinner, then press in the main bearing shells.

Pop the main shells in end caps and smear a little assembly lube on each one, but don't mix them up.

Use a long bolt or screwdriver in one of the bolt-holes for the flywheel to set the crankshaft in place.

Clean the main bearing saddles with lacquer thinner, and wipe down the backs of the bearing shells too. There should be no trace of dirt or oil on them. Oil could play a part in spinning a bearing, and dirt will cause the bearing to deform and wear unevenly. This may sound fanatical, but it is important because bearing shells have a very tight, crush fit, so any small bit of grit can cause the bearing to deform inward, and that could generate heat and cause excessive wear.

The main bearing saddles are notched, as are the bearing shells, so you can't install them incorrectly. Just push them into place with your thumbs. You may notice that the bearing shells stick up just a tiny bit from their saddles. If so, all is well. That's the way they should be for the proper crush fit. Coat the crankshaft bearing shells with assembly lube and gently set the crankshaft in place.

CHECKING END FLOAT

Next, lever the crankshaft back toward the rear of the engine using a large screwdriver and check the gap between the rear thrust surface of the rear main bearing and the corresponding flange on the crankshaft using a feeler gauge. The dimension should be between .002" and .007".

If it isn't, you need to determine why. If you replaced the crankshaft bearings, a problem with end-float would

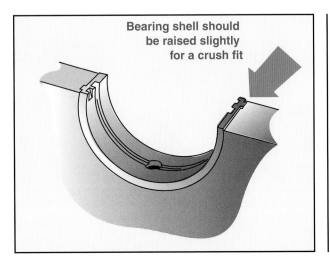

Bearing shell should be raised slightly for a crush fit

be unlikely, but with an old main bearing shell in place, a misadjusted clutch could have caused unusual wear on the thrust surface of the rear main. If the difference is .020" or greater—which is unlikely, but possible—you will have no choice but to replace the crankshaft.

If the end float checks out, place the lower halves of the bearing shells in the main bearing caps and coat them with a little assembly lube. Be very careful not to get the bearing caps mixed up in the process. If you followed the instructions in the disassembly chapter, you marked them with a punch so you know which one goes where, and which way it faces.

Lightly oil the rear main seal, and then press it into place. The main bearing caps, like the block journals, have notches in them to orient the bearing shells. Install the main bearing caps notch-to-notch with the bearing saddles in the block. Align the caps carefully, then tap each one with a rubber mallet or a small brass hammer to make sure it seats properly.

If you are going to be demanding the max from your engine, I recommend replacing all rod and main bearing bolts with new ones. When bolts are used in the engine for years on end, they become stretched. Although they will do in a pinch if you have nothing else, if you are going to be doing any racing or pushing the design envelope of your engine at all, you should replace them with quality engine fasteners such as those manufactured by ARP.

Coat the bolt threads with a little oil before installing them. Torque the main bearings into place evenly in three stages, using a quality torque wrench. Just snug them up for the first go around. Then, starting from the middle mains and working out, take the bolts down to 45 foot-pounds. Finally, torque the main bearing bolts on a small block with two-bolt mains to 70 foot-pounds. If

Check the crankshaft end float by moving the crankshaft to the rear using a screwdriver, then check at the rear main with a feeler gauge.

Install main caps loosely, then tap with a brass hammer to make sure they seat properly.

REPLACING OLD-STYLE ROPE-TYPE REAR MAIN SEALS

Soak the rope-type rear main seal in oil overnight. When it is completely saturated, press it into place in the block, then work it well into the groove using a dowel or small socket. Cut the ends off about 1/32 inch above the surrounding lip at each end of the bearing journal for a slight crush fit. Follow the same process for the bearing cap.

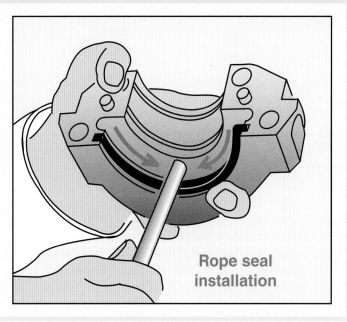

Rope seal installation

Take the main bearings down evenly in three passes, and then torque them to specs.

you are building up a four-bolt block, tighten the inner bolts to 70 foot-pounds, and tighten the outer ones to 65 foot-pounds of torque. And if you are lucky enough to be working with an aluminum four-bolt main block, tighten both the inner and the outer bolts to 70 foot-pounds.

MAKING IT BETTER THAN NEW

If you really want the last word in strong bottom ends, use ARP studs and nuts instead of bolts for your main bearings. Studs have superior clamping ability, and they don't twist and clamp at the same time the way bolts do, so the torque is more consistent and even. Studs cost a little more, but are well worth it if you are building a performance engine.

HANGING RODS

If you are going to hang your own rods, be sure to install them on the pistons facing the right direction. Chevy small-block rod beams are offset slightly from the middle of the big and small ends. Such rods should be put in with the offset toward the center of the crankshaft throw.

Stock pistons have four equal valve reliefs in them so they can be installed on either side of the block facing either direction, but others, such as Keith Black Signature Series flat-tops, have the valve reliefs cut so they must only be installed with the valve reliefs up toward the top of the block. Also, these kinds of pistons are both left- and right-hand to accommodate the placement of the intake and exhaust valves in the heads. Make sure you hang them on

Oil the ring grooves using a squirt can before installing the rings.

I prefer to spiral rings into place, but if you have sensitive thumbs, use a ring expander to install them.

the rods alternating from front to rear ,with the intake relief to the rear on the number one piston, and so on.

Of course, unless you purchased pistons with full-floating wrist pins, you will want to have the pistons hung on the rods at the machine shop in order to make sure the fit is absolutely correct. With full-floating wrist pins, you can merely oil the wrist pins and push them into the bushings cold, then install the spiral clips to hold them in place. Check each clip to make sure it is properly seated, and make sure each piston moves freely on its wrist pin, but with no slop or wobble.

FITTING RINGS

If you haven't already, read the previous chapter on final checks to make sure your rings have the correct gaps and clearances for the pistons, and make sure the pistons have the correct fit in the cylinders. Oil the ring grooves, and then carefully spiral the flat bottom section of the oil ring into place. Be careful not to score or gouge the piston. Next, install the bottom ring's corrugated center section, making sure it does not overlap, and that you install it with the right side up. Finally, spiral on the top piece of the oil ring, or use a ring expander if you prefer.

I find that I have fewer problems and less chance of ring damage if I spiral rings on than if I use a ring expander. It is easy to stretch and damage rings with an expander, but if you have soft thumbs, you may need to use one. Next, install the middle ring. Make sure it is right-side up (there is usually a dot to indicate the ring top), oil it, and then spiral it into its groove.

Finally, install the top compression ring and rotate all of the rings so their gaps are staggered, as shown in the diagram on the next page. This step is important because if the ring grooves line up, you will have combustion gasses blowing down into the crankcase in service, especially when the engine is cold and the gaps are wider, and this can damage your engine and contaminate its oil.

INSTALLING PISTONS

Next, install new rod bolts. Again, I prefer ARP for maximum durability. There is nothing quite as nasty as a rod letting loose at redline. Clean the bearing saddles in the

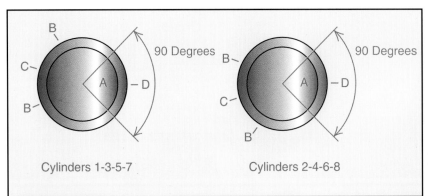

Rotate rings according to the diagram so you won't have blow-by problems. Place the oil ring spacer gap within the 90 degree arc labeled "A." The spots marked "B" are where the oil ring rail gaps should be positioned. Rotate the lower compression ring gap to "C" and place the top compression ring gap at "D."

Cylinders 1-3-5-7   Cylinders 2-4-6-8

Slip pieces of rubber or plastic hose on the rod bolts to avoid nicking the crankshaft during installation.

rods as well as the backs of the bearing shells with lacquer thinner, and then pop the shells into place on the rods. Do the same for the rod caps. With the bearings in place, smear a little assembly lube on each shell.

To protect the crankshaft, install short lengths of plastic tubing on the rod bolts or use the little plastic boots sold specifically to protect crankshaft bearing journals during piston and rod installation. Or, if you have nothing else, you can wrap the rod bolts with masking tape to cover their threads. Turn the crankshaft until the crankshaft journal on which you are going to install a rod is at approximately bottom dead center (BDC). Now shoot a little oil on the cylinder barrel and wipe it around.

Oil the top of the piston and the rings, either by dunking the piston in a can of clean, fresh oil or by shooting on oil with a squirt can. Make sure the piston is facing the right direction, then slip the number one (driver's-side front) rod and piston assembly into place down to the rings. The bolts in the big end of the rod need to clear the crankshaft journal. Slip a ring compressor over the top of the piston and tighten it to compress the rings flush to the piston.

Using a brass or copper hammer, tap the top of the ring compressor all the way around to make sure it is seated on the block. Now, with the end of a wood hammer handle, tap the piston down into its bore. If it hangs up, don't try to pound it into place. Instead, readjust your ring compressor and try again. The piston should slip into place with a fairly gentle tap. This process can take a bit of getting used to, so be patient, and above all, don't try to bully the pistons in.

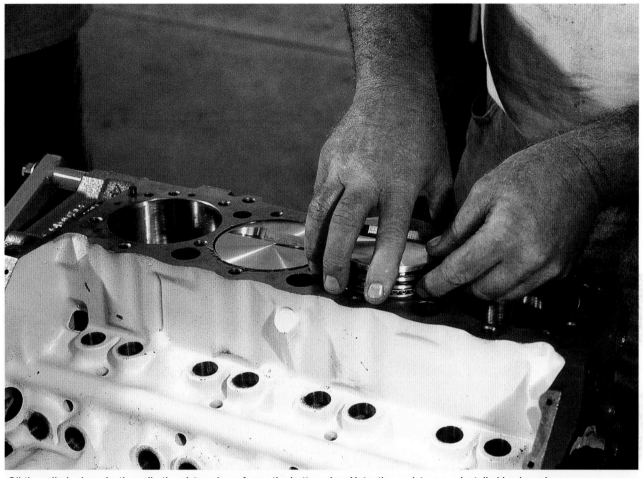

Oil the cylinder barrels, then slip the pistons in as far as the bottom ring. Note: these pistons are installed backwards.

Guide each rod onto the crankshaft with the crank at bottom-dead-center (BDC).

The wooden handle of a hammer can be used to gently tap pistons into their bores. If the piston hangs up on a ring, don't try to force it. Start over and make sure the ring compressor is on correctly and tightened securely.

This timing gear has three notches to allow for different cam timing. Tap on the timing gear using a piece of soft wood and a rubber mallet, if necessary.

As soon as the piston pops in, pull it down onto the crankshaft and attach its bearing cap. Lightly snug up the nuts required to hold the cap in place for now. Proceed to install the rest of the pistons, making sure they are facing in the right direction and that the crankshaft is near BDC for each one.

CHECK THE ROD GAPS

Before you torque the rod bearing caps into place, check the clearance between the rods on each bearing journal. They do need a little breathing room and will bind when they warm up if they are pressed tightly against each other. Push the rod bearings apart, and with a feeler gauge, determine the clearance. It should be between .005" and .0014". If it is too tight, the sides of the big end journals will need to be dressed at the machine shop to make them fit properly. If the fit is over .020" (a very unlikely scenario) there is no easy remedy. Slightly wider rods or a different crankshaft are the only options.

Turn the engine bottoms up and torque the rod bolts to the correct specifications (usually 45–50 foot-pounds, but follow the specs supplied with aftermarket rods, bolts, and so on), or if you really want to do the job as accurately as possible, use a stretch gauge from ARP to verify rod bolt stretch, which should be .005"-.006". Take them down in three even passes. First, snug them up. For the second pass, take the rod bolts up to 30 foot-pounds, and finally, torque them to 45–50 foot-pounds (35 foot-pounds for pre-1967 engines).

ATTACH THE OIL PUMP

Put the oil pump in a vise, being careful not to overtighten it and deform anything. Coat the pipe for the oil pick-up basket with a little sealer, then tap the oil basket into place.

Fill the pump with oil by pouring it in through the main orifice while rotating the gears. I do this to keep the pump from developing a bubble and cavitating in it during the first few minutes of running, which could be disastrous.

My friend John Jaroch uses a special tool he devised out of all-thread, nuts, washers, and a very large socket to install the vibration damper.

Now, locate the oil pump on its cast mount in the block. Tighten the attaching bolts evenly into place.

PUT ON THE TIMING GEAR COVER

Before you install the timing gear cover, use a small file or bearing scraper to remove any burrs or sharp edges on the crankshaft snout and its key-way and key. A slight chamfer on the forward edge of the key will help the vibration damper go on more easily. Oil the timing gears and chain liberally. Wipe the gasket mating surfaces clean with a little lacquer thinner.

Coat the mating surface on the block for the timing gear cover with a thin layer of silicone sealer, and then coat the gasket. Let this skin over (about five minutes), and then press the gasket into place. Coat the outer face of the gasket with sealer, then coat the timing gear cover. Press the timing gear cover in place using the locator pins. Install the bolts that hold the pan in place but leave them loose.

INSTALL THE VIBRATION DAMPER

Vibration dampers are a press fit and can be a little tricky if you've never done one before. With a bearing scraper or small file, clean any burrs from the key-way of the damper. Coat the crank snout and inside the vibration damper with a little oil. Evenly heat the vibration damper's center cast hub with a propane torch until the oil in it starts to smoke. Just don't get carried away and heat the damper until the rubber starts to separate inside it.

Using leather gloves, push the vibration damper onto the crankshaft snout as far as you can by hand. Don't cock the damper; it must go on straight. Next, screw a home-made vibration damper install tool, made with a 7" piece of all-thread from the hardware store plus a few washers and a couple of nuts, into the crankshaft snout and install a large socket on the all-thread against the damper. Tighten the nut down onto the washers against the socket to push on the damper. Tap around the vibration damper near its

123

Put the side rail cork gaskets in place with a little silicone sealer, then seal the joints for the rear and front main seals using a small blob of anaerobic sealer.

Use a feeler gauge to make sure you have installed the correct front seal.

center every few turns to keep it from becoming cocked. It should slide home without too much trouble.

If you don't care to make the tool shown on page 123, you can use the standard block of 2x4 and a hammer to drive the damper on, but this is a caveman way to do the job. Never beat on the outside ring of the damper or tap around the periphery of the damper, because you can ruin the rubber inside it. Now torque down the timing gear cover nuts to 7–9 foot-pounds.

POP ON THE PAN

Check out your bottom-end assembly one more time, and check to make sure you torqued the rod and main bolts or studs to the correct specs. Wipe everything down with a clean, lint-free rag, then shoot and wipe a little oil on the rods, cylinder bores, and pistons.

Wipe the pan rails clean of oil using a little lacquer thinner, then apply them with a small bead of silicone sealer. You don't want the excess to come off and cover the oil pick-up screen. Coat the cork gaskets with silicone and let the silicone skin over. Press the gasket evenly into place on the block rails.

Coat the front and rear main bearing pan seals with a little oil and press them into place. Your gasket set may come with two front pan seals (one thin and one thick), so be sure to use the one designed for your block. Now, wipe the ends of the seals clean with a little lacquer thinner and squirt about a 1/8-inch gob of anaerobic sealer right at the joint where the seal meets the cork gasket.

Coat the outer surface of the cork gasket with a little sealer, then coat the pan rails. Let the sealer skin over, and then press the pan carefully into place. Install the pan screws (the bigger ones go at the corners) and torque them down to 7–9 foot-pounds. Don't over-tighten the pan bolts because if you do, the cork gasket will just squeeze out and you will distort the pan rails and cause leaks.

COST APPROXIMATELY $150

SKILL LEVEL

TIME 6 – 8 HOURS

✔ YOU'LL NEED:

- ❑ Gasket set
- ❑ Assembly lube
- ❑ Silicone sealer
- ❑ Gasgacinch
- ❑ Anaerobic sealer
- ❑ Clean, lint-free rags
- ❑ Quality torque wrench
- ❑ Socket set
- ❑ Soft hammer (brass or copper)
- ❑ Squirt can of oil
- ❑ Wire brush
- ❑ Laquer thinner

- ❑ Modeling clay
- ❑ Dull putty knife
- ❑ Feeler gauge
- ❑ Dial caliper
- ❑ Motor oil
- ❑ Oil pump priming tool
- ❑ Magic marker
- ❑ Permatex silver anti-seize
- ❑ Permatex Ultra Copper High-Temp Sealant
- ❑ Lube grease

W e're almost done. Now is not the time to get impatient. These last steps are just as important as all the others. Lay out your tools, gather the required sealants and assembly lube, and prop open this book to the torque specifications in the appendix so you can tighten each item correctly.

Turn your engine right-side up on its stand, and wipe everything down with a clean rag to make sure no dirt or dust has drifted into the top of the block while you were doing the bottom end. If you are going to be using your original head bolts, clean their threads thoroughly using a wire brush, or chase them with a die. Rust, dirt, and damaged threads can cause your head bolt torque readings to be very inaccurate, and they can cause undue twisting action, heat, and damage to both the bolts and the block.

If you did not need to have the block or heads cleaned and resurfaced, scrub them carefully and make sure there is no rust or old gasket bits on them. Any irregularity could contribute to a bad seal or leaking head gasket. Roughness, gouges, and pitting in the head or deck can all present problems. Wipe these surfaces down with a little lacquer thinner before installing the heads.

Cover the lifter valley with a clean cloth. Use a couple of bolts in the accessory holes as handles to set the heads in place.

TOP-END ASSEMBLY

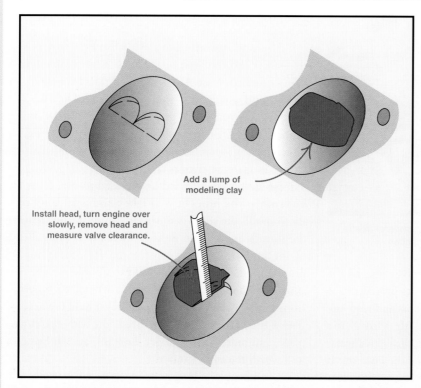

Install head, turn engine over slowly, remove head and measure valve clearance.

Add a lump of modeling clay

Use modeling clay to check valve clearance.

MEASURE THE MODIFICATIONS

If you have gone to high-lift rockers, installed different types of pistons, or removed a significant amount of material from the heads or decks (significant being in the neighborhood of 30-60 thousandths) be sure to check the valve head clearance with the pistons. The easiest way to do this is to spread a lump of children's modeling clay on the top of the number one piston and then install and torque the head, assuming the valves and springs have already been installed at the machine shop.

To do this test, you'll need a couple of solid lifters. Oil them and place them in their openings. Install a couple of pushrods of the correct length for your cam, then install the necessary rocker arms, tighten them into place, and adjust them according to specs. Now slowly and gently turn the engine over by hand a few times. If it starts to bind at all, stop immediately. A valve may actually be coming into contact with the piston.

If there is no resistance, turn the engine over through all four cycles (two complete revolutions). Remove the head. There will be two impressions in the clay, made by the opening valves. With a dull putty knife or other object that will not scratch the top of the piston, cut through each impression and measure the clearance where the valve comes closest to the piston.

The intake valve requires at least .090" and you need 0.100" for the exhaust. This may sound like a lot, but remember that as an engine warms up everything expands, and besides, at high rpm the valves can actually "loft" a little from all that motion in the valve train. If there isn't enough clearance, you may need to have the pistons relieved a little or have the valves recessed in their seats. Of course, both of these measures are last resorts, but are sometimes necessary with high-lift cams, high-lift rockers, and milled heads.

Another problem caused by changes in valve train geometry is spring lock. This is when the valve springs actually compress to the point where their coils touch. Valve springs do a whole lot of rapid flexing and generate a fair amount of heat as a result. If they bind, they certainly can't compress any further, and the valve they control can't open any further either.

To check for spring lock, turn the engine over slowly and watch the valve springs on one cylinder. Check both the intake and the exhaust using a feeler gauge. If there is less than .012" clearance between spring coils, you will need different rocker arms, shorter pushrods if the rocker arms require it, or different springs.

The final valve train check is to make sure the pivot point on the rocker arm is centered on the valve and does not move off the top of the valve in operation. Roller rockers are easier on valves and last longer, but even they can exert great side loads on valves and bend them, or cause damaging valve guide wear if they override the tips of the valves. Problems can develop when a high-lift cam or high-lift rockers are used, especially in combination with pushrods that are not the correct length.

Studs are much better than bolts for mounting cylinder heads because they exert more consistent clamping action.

Install the head gaskets with the numbers up and the metal O-ring seals down. (This is the proper procedure for most common head gaskets, but check yours and read any accompanying instructions before installing them.) You can use a couple small gobs of Gasgacinch or silicone sealer to hold the gasket in place while you place the head on. If you are using head studs, no sealer is necessary with most common head gaskets, unless you are going with the metallic gaskets (copper is the most common), which are only really necessary or advisable for radical racing engines.

Also—just in case you become concerned—the large holes opening into the water jackets on your heads have only small holes corresponding to them in the head gasket. The large holes in the head were put there mainly to pour sand out of the head casting during manufacture. The small holes in the gasket help regulate water flow and pressure and should not be opened up.

MAKING IT BETTER THAN NEW

Most racing engine heads are installed with studs and nuts. There are a couple of good reasons for this. First, the clamping action of studs is much more even, because as bolts are being torqued down, they are twisting as well as pulling. A stud just exerts straight up-and-down force because it remains stationary as the head is being torqued into place. Obviously, proper head bolts are more than adequate

under normal circumstances, but I'm a man who wears a belt and suspenders.

A second reason I like studs is because they position the gasket and the head properly as these components are being installed. I use ARP studs and nuts because of their known and guaranteed superior quality. They are a bit pricey, but if you can afford them they are well worth the money. They help prevent cracked heads, warping, and blown head gaskets, all of which can be terminal to your engine in extreme circumstances.

Assuming you cleaned and chased all the head bolt-holes when you brought your block home, all you need to do to install the studs is to smear a little silicone sealer on the threads and tighten them in by hand. It isn't called for in the instructions that come with ARP studs, but after putting them in finger tight, I like to double-nut them and snug them another half turn with a wrench to keep them from turning when I install the nuts that hold the heads on. It is a little tricky to get the heads on with the studs in place, and more trouble to get them off later, but studs are well worth the extra trouble.

Use a couple of long bolts in the accessory holes at the ends of the heads as handles when you set the heads on. Make sure you set each head on straight. If they hang up a little on a long stud or two, apply gentle pressure on the studs to push them out of the way by a thousandth or so. The heads should drop into place easily once you get them properly started.

Coat studs, nuts, and washers with moly lube and put them in place finger-tight.

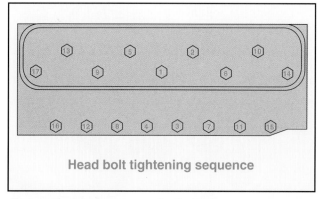

Head bolt tightening sequence

Here are the torque sequences for the heads.

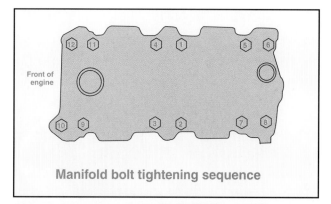

Manifold bolt tightening sequence

Here are the torque sequences for the intake manifold.

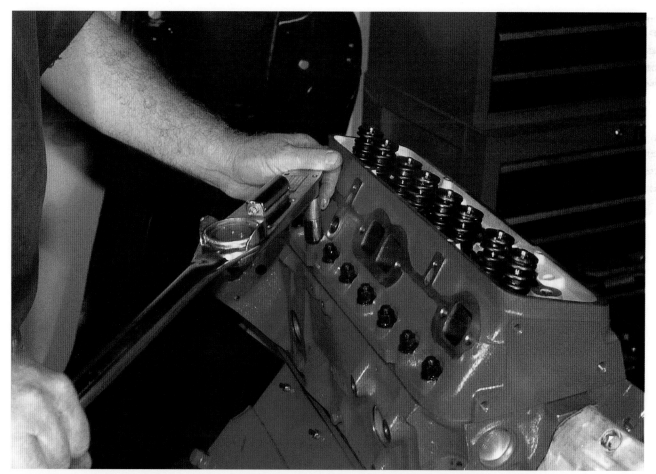

Use a good torque wrench and take the head bolts down in three stages, following the diagram above.

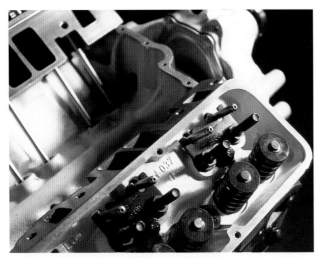

Pushrod guides are a good idea for hot street engines. Coat the tips with assembly lube and slip pushrods into place.

Check to make sure that the pushrods rotate as you adjust the rockers into place.

Coat the pivot balls with assembly lube, slip them into place, then install the locking nuts.

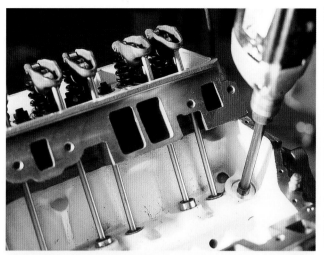
Pump up the lifters using a 3/8-inch drill and pump-priming tool.

Oil the washers and nuts with a little assembly lube before installing them on the studs. Without assembly lube, the washers can get slightly cockeyed, hang up on the studs, and cause your torque readings to be erroneous.

Next, torque the heads down in three even stages, working in a circular fashion from the centers of the heads out, following the diagram earlier in this chapter. First, take the nuts or bolts down evenly to about 20 foot-pounds, then go to 45 foot-pounds. Finish at 70 foot-pounds.

INSTALL THE VALVE TRAIN

Solid lifters need only a light oiling before installing them. Submerge hydraulic lifters in a container of clean motor oil and push their plungers down using an old pushrod to expel as much air as possible. Wipe off any excess oil and install them, making sure they are flat-end down and dished-end up. Next, put a dab of assembly lube on the ends of the pushrods and slide them into place through the heads.

Check the stud slots of the rocker arms for burrs, coat the inside bearing surfaces and valve contact tips with a little assembly lube, and then place them on the studs. Smear on a little assembly lube and then slip the half-round pivot balls onto the rocker studs. Install the adjusting nuts, making sure the beveled side is up and the flat side is down. Now just take the nuts down until there is about 1/8 inch of clearance between the rocker arms at the valves and pushrods.

If you can't spring for ARPs, buy new head bolts of the correct hardness or, if your old head bolts are sound and not stretched to their elastic limit, you can still use them. Compare them with a new bolt using a dial caliper. If they are stretched, replace them. Even if they are not stretched to the limit, they lose about 15 percent of their strength each time you use them, so keep that in mind when working on older engines.

Smear the head bolt threads with a little silicone sealer and install them, then snug them down with a small wrench. The short ones go along the bottom, outside the valve cover, and the two medium-length bolts go at the ends. The long bolts go in the rest of the holes.

PREADJUSTING HYDRAULIC LIFTERS

Fill a new oil filter with oil and spin it up on its mounting plate. Pour a couple of quarts of oil into the sump. Now, grab an old distributor drive or an oil pump priming tool (good ones are available from TD Performance Products, listed in the Resources chapter), chucked into a 3/8-inch drill.

Insert the tool into the distributor drive hole until it engages with the oil pump drive. Run the drill to get the oil circulating. The engine will burp a little air and spurt a little oil out of the rockers as you work, but keep the drill spinning until the lifters are pumped up to operating pressure. Spin up the oil pump until oil comes up through all the pushrods. The lifters should be totally firm when you try to depress the pushrods into them.

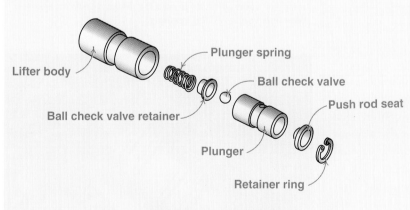

Hydraulic valve lifter

Hydraulic lifters can be cleaned and rebuilt. Keep everything clean, and lubricate parts with 10 wt oil. Wrap them in plastic until they are ready to be reinstalled.

Use a pry bar and a couple of bolts screwed well into the vibration damper or the flywheel to turn the engine to get the number one piston up to TDC on the ignition stroke. Use your "0" timing mark on the vibration damper as a reference. You'll know when the piston is on its ignition stroke because the valves for that cylinder will be even and won't move at that point.

Slowly and carefully tighten the rocker arm, adjusting nuts until there is no lash between the rocker arms and the pushrods and valve tips. Check the pushrod as you tighten to make sure you don't overtighten it. The pushrod should turn easily, but there should be no gap. Now take the adjuster nuts down one more turn so the lifter plungers are in the center of their travel. The pushrods should not readily turn at this point.

Next, you can carefully mark off the vibration damper into quadrants to make adjusting the valves easier. Just draw a line with a magic marker directly and precisely across the center of the damper to the other edge, then draw another line exactly 90 degrees to that one across the center of the damper to divide it equally. Turn the damper to the next quadrant line and prime the lifters again. Adjust the valves on the next cylinder that comes up on the power stroke, and continue on around twice until you have all of the valves adjusted. Ideally, adjust the valves according to the cylinder firing order: 1-8-4-3-6-5-7-2.

Later, when the engine is running, we'll readjust the valves to get them just right. Many people wouldn't go to the trouble of pumping up the lifters, but doing so avoids getting the valves adjusted incorrectly. The process pumps the lifters up so they won't clatter when the engine is first started. I like this preadjustment method because it is a little safer than just trying to adjust hydraulic lifters by feel.

SOLID LIFTERS

You don't need to pump up oil pressure to adjust solid lifters. Just bring the number one cylinder up to TDC on the power stroke and set the valves to the recommended cold setting in the cam instructions, or set them about .002" looser than the hot setting. Work your way around to each cylinder in turn, as previously outlined. With an extra .002" you won't run the risk of having the lifter clearance too tight, which could cause an exhaust valve to burn. Be sure to set the lifters again after the 20-minute run-in period, too, because the engine will settle in and expand, so the clearances are apt to change.

Coat valve cover gaskets and the mating surfaces for the valve covers with a little Gasgacinch, let it get tacky, then

Coat the valve cover gaskets with a little Gasgacinch on one side and anti-seize compound on the other before installing valve covers.

Use a few spots of sealer to hold the intake manifold gaskets in place until you install the manifold.

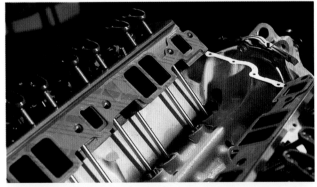

Note that the front seal for the intake manifold, lying up in front of the engine ready to be located, has been coated only sparingly with sealer.

carefully press the gaskets into place on the valve covers. Now coat the exposed parts of the valve cover gaskets with a thin coat of Permatex silver anti-seize and install the valve covers. Tighten the screws just enough to snug them up, but not enough to deform the cork gasket.

The reason for just coating the gaskets with sealer on one side is so you can go back in and adjust the valves after the engine is run in without damaging the gaskets. The valve cover area is not under a lot of pressure, so they won't leak if the seals are good and they are evenly tightened into place.

INSTALL THE INTAKE MANIFOLD

Make sure the mating surfaces are perfectly clean. Old gasket bits, rust, gouges, and dirt can all conspire to cause a vacuum leak that will make your engine run lean and could cause poor idle and burned valves, among other things. I like to use a little Gascacinch on the front and rear neoprene seals just for extra protection. Give the seals and the metal contact surfaces on the block and manifold a light coat and let it get tacky. Then press the seals into place. Use a small gob of silicone sealer at the ends where the neoprene seals join with the manifold gaskets to seal the joints.

Fel Pro head and manifold gaskets (as well as most other types sold today) are self-sealing, so they don't need any sealant applied to them. Just use a couple small blobs of silicone sealer to locate them and hold them into place while you install the intake manifold. Place the manifold evenly on the gaskets, making sure the water inlet (the bigger hole) is at the front of the engine and the distributor hole is at the back.

Put a little silicone sealer at the corners where the neoprene seals mate with the manifold gaskets.

Place the intake manifold on the seals and be careful not to disturb them.

Install the intake manifold bolts finger-tight, then torque them into place evenly to 25–35 foot-pounds in three stages according to the diagram Intake manifold installation on a Chevy small block needs to be done carefully because the manifold also acts as a cover for the lifter valley. Any leaks can result in poor performance due to vacuum loss, as well as oil leaks. After the engine is run in, retorque the intake manifold bolts to specs.

I like to use studs to attach the carburetor, but the original bolts are fine too. Don't use any sealer on the carburetor gasket. Just press it into place on the intake manifold, install the carburetor, and then torque the bolts or nuts evenly to 12–15 foot-pounds. The start-up chapter will cover how to check for leaks.

EXHAUSTING PROBLEMS

If you are staying with stock exhaust manifolds, it will probably be easier to put them on now rather than waiting until the engine is in the car. But if you are installing a set of tuned headers, you will want to wait until you have the engine in the chassis before installing them so you can make sure everything clears properly.

If you are staying with stock manifolds, I recommend studs and nuts rather than bolts to hold the manifolds on. If you have studs in place, manifolds are much easier to locate and center exactly after porting and matching than they would be with bolts. When using aftermarket headers, it's a different story. If you install studs, you may not have the clearance in the engine bay

134

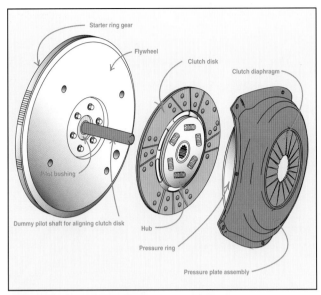

This is the sequence to follow when installing a clutch. Be sure to use an old transmission clutch shaft or alignment tool to avoid damage to components.

to pull the headers back far enough to slip them over studs once the engine is in the car.

Whether you install stock manifolds or headers now, or after the engine is in the car, here's how to do it: If you are installing stock manifolds and if you have had them surfaced at the machine shop so they are perfectly flat, you don't need any sealant on their gaskets. Just attach them and torque them into place starting from the middle and working out. Take them down evenly in three steps. The inner bolts should be torqued to 25–30 foot-pounds and the end bolts should be 15–20 foot-pounds.

Aftermarket headers require a little more care. Smear the gaskets with Permatex Ultra Copper, High Temp Sealant (Part Number 101BR) on both sides to help smooth out any unevenness, then push the headers up into place and install the bolts finger-tight. Take the bolts down evenly from the centers of the headers to the outer primary tube bolts. Chances are the headers will be a little bowed so their ends are further away from the block, but they should draw down easily.

Tighten the header bolts evenly, and then torque the ones you can reach with a torque wrench to 25–35 foot-pounds. Tighten the bolts your torque wrench can't reach to the same feel as the torqued bolts. Developing a feel for torque specs is one of the things mechanics do over time because of just such situations. The most important thing

to remember is that you don't want to overdo it. It is better to be a little loose than to smash and deform the gasket.

Once the engine is thoroughly warmed up after starting it for the first time, torque the header attaching bolts down again, and then check them after a week or so, and also every time you change your oil after that. Headers are generally longer and heavier than stock manifolds and tend to vibrate loose a little more easily as a result.

WATER PUMP AND FUEL PUMP INSTALLATION

Coat both sides of the gaskets and then the mating surfaces for the water pump with sealant and attach the pump to the engine. Its bolts should be taken down evenly to 25–35 foot-pounds. Slip the fuel pump actuating rod into place. Holding the rod up with a finger, and have an assistant turn the engine over until the rod is at the bottom of its stroke (moving up toward the cam). This makes putting the fuel pump on much easier. Slip in the front motor-mount bolt that goes all the way through and tighten it against the actuating rod enough to hold it in place while you mount the fuel pump. Coat the fuel pump gasket with sealant on both sides, and coat the mating surfaces as well. Let this skin over, and then install the fuel pump. Remove the motor-mount bolt.

At this point we're ready to take the engine off its stand and install the flywheel, or flexplate. You can do this with the engine on a cradle, or once the engine is situated in the car. In any case, you will need to mount the bell housing before installing the engine.

If you are converting an engine from automatic to standard, be sure to install a pilot bushing in the end of the crankshaft. If your engine was set up for a stick shift originally, it might be a good idea to install a fresh pilot bushing. You can drive the old bushing out by filling the bearing with lube grease, and then driving a drift the diameter of the clutch shaft into it. The bushing will pop out due to hydraulic pressure. Carefully drive in the new bushing with a wooden or soft metal dowel the diameter of the pilot bearing.

Install the bell housing, and then the flywheel or flexplate using new bolts especially made for the job such as those made by ARP. Never use ordinary hardware store bolts because they are not strong enough. And if the flywheel lets loose, it could be a very dangerous situation, not only for your car but for you as well. Flywheels have been known to blow up like hand grenades under such circumstances. Use new locking devices and torque the flywheel bolts to 55–65 foot-pounds.

CARBURETORS
HIGH ASPIRATIONS

Want out-of-the-box horsepower? Go with a Holley. They're the easiest to tune.

Probably the most poorly understood aspect of engine tuning is the carburetor. Many novice street rodders think that the bigger their carburetor is, the better their engine will perform. Not true. In fact, the most common reason for customer unhappiness with high-performance carbs can be traced to overcarburetion.

People often buy a big 850-cfm carb when 600–750 cfm is ideal for their engine. Then when they install it and put their foot in it, their engine stumbles and sags before finally coming to life. They return the carb thinking it's faulty, when in fact it is their thinking that is faulty. The problem is that the big carb gets a weak signal because of the lack of air velocity—it doesn't come on when it needs to for good midrange acceleration.

Think three carbs are better than one? Not necessarily. The linkage is more complex, and a properly sized four-barrel will work better for most street applications.

You see, a carburetor's job is to vaporize gasoline and mix it with air. Bigger carbs can mix more fuel into more air, but that is only useful if you have a bigger engine. Actually, for routine driving with a stock Chevy small block up to about 3,500 rpm, a stock two-barrel works fine.

It's only when you jump on the gas and take the rpm up past where most people routinely drive that two more throats will do you some good. In fact, if your carburetor is too big, your engine will not get enough fuel at low rpm because of inadequate air velocity. When you install a jug the size of a hot tub on your small block, air can take its time getting to where it is going, so the drop in pressure from piston suction isn't enough to pull much fuel into the slow air stream of a too-large carb.

In fact, a small carb gives great performance until the engine gets up into the higher-rev ranges, where it will then starve for air. Coming up with a good compromise between low-end oomph and high-end horsepower is the key to a great street rod engine, and it's actually harder to accomplish than setting up a constant throttle racer. So how do you determine which carburetor your small block needs? It's simple. We'll get to that in a minute, but first, let's look at how a carburetor works:

DEEP BREATHING

Did you ever fool around with your mother's old-fashioned squeeze-bulb perfume sprayers when you were a kid? Well, they are nothing more than a primitive type of carburetor. Perfume sprayers and carburetors both take advantage of the Bernoulli effect. Daniel Bernoulli was an eighteenth-century Swiss mathematician who was probably goofing around with his own mother's spray bottles when he came up with his principle. What he found out was this: As the velocity of a liquid or gas increases, its pressure decreases.

That's why air sucked at high speed past a fuel tube inserted into the side of an air horn will draw the fuel out

A tunnel-ram manifold looks dramatic and smooths airflow while maintaining velocity, but it's definitely not for the street because of its limited power range.

into the rushing air. And this effect can be increased dramatically by narrowing the air inlet just at the point where the fuel tube enters it.

That's called the Venturi effect and it's named after an Italian physicist who first figured out this little trick a couple hundred years ago. When you narrow the tube, the incoming air must speed up to get through the narrow spot, where it loses more pressure, thus creating an even greater pull on the fuel tube.

Of course, there is a lot more to a modern carburetor than just the Venturi effect, but it almost all works on the same principle. For instance, there is an accelerator pump that shoots extra fuel into the carb when you tromp on the gas suddenly, and there is a choke to increase the air vacuum and draw out a rich fuel mixture for cold starts, and then there are jets that determine how much fuel is released into the air through the carb.

In addition, there are float bowls (that operate much like toilet tanks) that provide your carb with an adequate fuel supply at all times. And there is a needle valve that shuts the fuel off when the float bowl is full. Each of these systems is simple enough in itself, but when you put them all together, the result is several hundred small parts that add up to a fairly complex device.

If you decide you want to rebuild or custom-tailor your own carburetor, even though you'll find some of the basics in this chapter, I strongly recommend that you pick up a book on your particular brand and model of carb and study it before you start tinkering.

And if you can afford it and want the ultimate in performance, I recommend sending even a new carb to a place like the Carb Shop in Ontario, California, to have them adapt it and jet it to your engine's needs. They build carbs for winning race cars and will put your carb on a Dyno to make sure it will do what it is supposed to do before they send it back to you. It is important that you provide them with all pertinent information such as engine size, cam duration, and header type, plus what kind of car the engine will be going into, and what kind of racing you might want to try.

On most Holley four-barrels you can check the float level through the sight glass without removing the float bowl cover.

HOLLEY

Rochester Quadra-Jets, Carter AFBs, and Holley four-barrel carburetors will all give good performance, but the easiest carbs to set up are Holleys. And you can buy them in just about any cubic-foot-per-minute (cfm) rating, so you can have exactly what you need for your application. They are inexpensive when compared with the new knock-offs of the old Quadra-Jets and Carters being sold under other names and will provide equal or better performance. And Holley sells literally everything you might need or want to tune your carb yourself.

If you need to change the float level, you can adjust it right on top of the carb.

Idle mixture screws are conveniently located so you can get at them without contorting yourself.

Here is a Holley float. The chamber comes off the end of the carb with four screws.

Everything you need to install and tailor a Holley comes with the carb.

Because Holleys are modular and because they have been designed to be easily custom tuned, they are certainly the best choice for the novice street rodder. You can determine the float level in a Holley just by using the sight glass in the side of the float bowl, and you can make any necessary adjustments without even removing the float bowl cover. You can also easily get at the jets and the accelerator pump(s). Every new Holley also comes with the springs and other items you need to fine-tune it.

If you want great out-of-the box street performance with no fuss, I recommend a four-barrel Holley matched to your engine (according to the formula above), and a Holley Weiand dual-plane intake manifold to go under it. The Holley company has been around for as long as the automobile, and has been making racing carbs longer than anyone, so you can take advantage of their millions of dollars and thousands of hours of research. And you can rely on their quality because each carb is tested and tuned before the company sends it out the door.

ROCHESTER QUADRA-JET

The old Rochester Quadra-Jet was superbly engineered and is one of the best small-block carbs ever. They flow 750–800 cfm in stock form and can be set up for just about any street or strip application. The only problem is that they don't make them any more. And yes, new Quadra-Jet knock-offs are available, but they are expensive. You can have the same thing for less by buying a reworked Rochester or, if you already have a Q-Jet on your engine, you can send it out and have it rebuilt and super-tuned to your needs.

HOW MUCH IS ENOUGH?

Use this formula to determine what size carburetor your small block needs:

Engine size in cubic inches x maximum rpm/3456 = cfm

This formula assumes 100 percent volumetric efficiency. Most street rod engines will be running at around 85–90 percent volumetric efficiency, so the formula provides a more than adequate size of carburetor.

Q-Jets will provide race-winning performance with a little tweaking and tuning. Of course, the least expensive way to go with a Q-Jet is to rebuild and rejet it yourself if you have the experience and skill to do it. If you don't, send it to a shop where it can be custom tailored and rebuilt by experts. The accompanying photos in this chapter show some of what the Carb Shop does with each Q-Jet they rework.

CARTER AFB

These are great carbs, too, and can be made to run with the best of them. There are modern knock-offs of the old Carters available, too, but once again, you can save money by having your old one rebuilt and tested. Carters aren't as easy to work on as Holleys, but one point in their favor is you can change the metering rods in them without removing the float bowl lid. If you have a good Carter already, don't toss it out. Rebuild it and run it. They're hard to beat.

MANIFOLD DESTINY

There are three common types of intake manifolds. The most popular one used for the street on Chevy small blocks is the dual-plane type. It helps provide better low- and midrange power, but sacrifices a little at the top end of your engine's rpm range.

The second common type of intake manifold is the single-plane configuration. Inline six- and four-cylinder engines generally have single-plane manifolds because they are simple and efficient, but V-8 engines suffer to a degree when using single-plane manifolds under certain circumstances because of the fact that adjacent cylinders (5 and 7)

continued on page 146

Otis Bretzing is the Carb Shop's Rochester expert and he believes Q-Jets are the best all-around carb there is. He can go through one in half the time most people can.

To disconnect the accelerator pump, Otis taps out the pivot pin rather than disassembling the lever mechanism.

CARBURETORS

continued on page 142

141

Unscrew the top of the carb to get to its inner workings. Keep everything in order as you take things apart.

Remove the idle mixture needle next. Clean and inspect it. If it is damaged or pitted, replace it.

This is the fuel inlet filter. Be sure to replace it, and only run without one if you have a top-quality in-line filter in the system.

Shown here are the metering rods in the Quadra-Jet. Changing these is one way of tailoring the carb to individual engines.

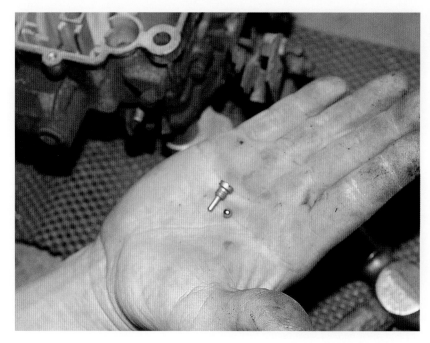

This is the pump check-ball and its retainer. No spring is used on the Rochester.

continued on page 144

Otis at the Carb Shop can put everything in a pile because he knows these carbs inside and out, but most of us have to lay everything out in order to do the job right.

Fuel chamber plugs are driven in and surrounding metal is peened over them. Remove the metal, pull out the plugs, and when replacing them, use epoxy to hold them in place.

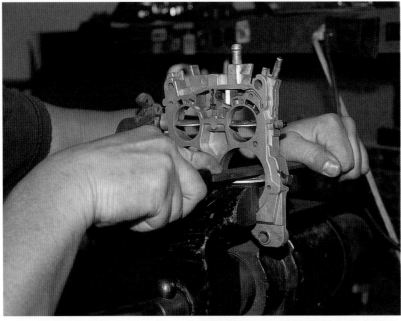

Throttle butterfly screws are swaged in place and must be filed flush before they will unscrew. Use new screws and swage them in place when rebuilding the carb so they can't come loose.

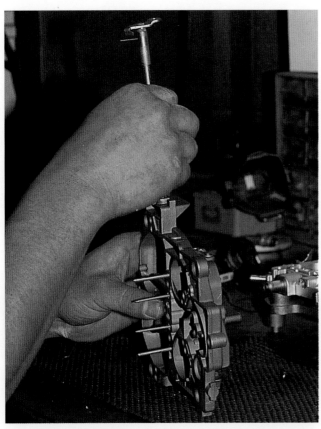

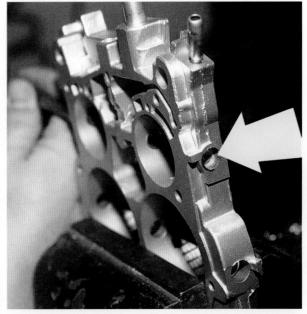

Air leaks around the throttle butterfly shaft are a common problem on old carbs.

The throttle body must be drilled oversize with brass bushings installed to fix leaks.

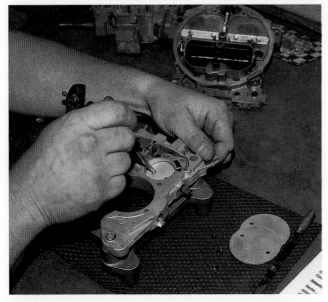

Getting butterfly valves aligned properly and facing the right way is critical to good performance.

A single-plane intake manifold gives great performance in the higher-rpm ranges, but can be a little soggy on the bottom end.

This is a Performance Products dual-plane manifold. It outperforms many name brands.

Continued from page 140

can have open valves at the same time, allowing the fuel mixture to become diluted at low rpm.

Also, because fuel/air velocity is low at low rpm in an open-plenum single-plane manifold, fuel can actually condense and puddle out on the manifold floor, especially in cold weather. On the plus side, single-plane manifolds have shorter, straighter port runners, so at high rpm they really come into their own. They have an edge over dual-plane manifolds up around 7,500 rpm and beyond. So what it comes down to is this: If you want maximum top-end horsepower and don't mind going from rather sedate acceleration at lower rpm to sudden, tire-smoking torque as the engine comes up on its cam, go for a single-plane manifold.

But if you want neck-snapping launches from idle when you hit the gas, and steady power up through to the power peak on your street engine, go with a dual-plane manifold. Single-plane, manifold-equipped cars are harder to drive, though they have an edge in straight-line acceleration at peak power. Most street rodders prefer a good dual-plane manifold because they make their car more user-friendly. Cornering can be a real problem if the power comes on abruptly in midcorner, as it can do with a single-plane manifold.

On single-plane manifolds, all of the barrels of the carb dump into a large, common plenum that feeds short, straight runners. The loss of gas velocity at low rpm because of the open plenum is the single-plane

manifold's biggest shortcoming, but its straight port runners are its virtue. As we said in the chapter on head porting, air doesn't like to turn corners, especially when it's moving fast.

Dual-plane manifolds are set up so that each side of the carb feeds one side of the engine, and it does so through different-length, rather curvy runners. These are marginally less efficient than straight runners, but they do keep the gas velocity higher at low rpm, giving the carb much clearer signals. The chances of bogging down at low rpm are diminished, unless you have installed a carb that is too large for the engine.

The third type of manifold you sometimes see is the tunnel ram. Some of these use a plenum chamber on top to even out the vacuum pulses, and others use individual port runners right from the carb. Either way, the point of a tunnel ram manifold is to iron out those abrupt turns the air/fuel mixture has to make when it leaves the carburetor and enters the intake manifold. The long port runners help maintain gas velocity into the engine, and that helps fill the combustion chambers to the max.

There are a couple of big disadvantages to tunnel ram manifolds for street use. The first is hood clearance. The usual solution to hood clearance is a big scoop that blocks your vision to the right of you. The other problem with tunnel ram manifolds is that they only provide an advantage in a limited, high-rpm range. They look impressive, but they aren't very practical for street use.

CARBURETORS

When it comes to air filters, bigger is better. Taller is also good. This one from TD Performance Products will do a great job if the element is changed periodically.

The ultimate air filter is a K&N. They're washable and actually increase performance over what can be had by running with no filter at all!

AIR FILTERS

This is one situation where bigger is always better. The more filter area you have, the less restrictive the filter will be. Air filters can be especially restrictive if their tops are too close to the carb. The top of the filter should be at least 3 inches above the carb, and 4 to 6 inches are better. The diameter of the filter should be as big as your wallet can accommodate. It has always seemed crazy to me to see street machines with top-quality, Holley double-pumper carbs topped with tiny air filters.

If you can afford it, a K&N filter is the way to go. Standard paper filters work well and offer very little restriction if they are kept refreshed. But K&N filters offer virtually no restriction and are designed to be washed out and reused. In fact, engines often run more efficiently with a K&N filter on them than they do with no filtration at all! The reason is, without some kind of filter, turbulence can develop at the carb throat that will cause less efficient breathing. K&N air filters cost more, but you only have to pay for them once, and they are the least restrictive filters available.

Paper filters work because they have millions of tiny holes in them that are too small for dust particles to pass through. However, the dust gets drawn in to all those tiny holes and slowly clogs them. K&N air filters somehow trap the dirt without clogging. Of course, in dusty situations, they will eventually start restricting air, but it takes a much longer time for that to happen. Dirt-track and off-road racers favor K&N reusable filters overwhelmingly just for this reason. Baja 1000 drivers have even been known to breathe through them.

HEADERS AND EXHAUST

PIPED-IN POWER

When I was a young lad, I used to love shoving my Chevy into second gear and backing off the throttle, just to hear that sexy rumble as I blasted through a local tunnel. It was music to my ears. Unfortunately, not everybody shared my tastes in music. One set of 17-inch glass packs only lasted a week before the local constabulary wrote me up. But the craziest part of the whole thing was that my loud exhaust system probably actually hurt my Chevy's acceleration and top end.

As we have said several times in this book, knowing what you want your engine to do, then selecting the right mix of cam, heads, manifold, and carb, along with the right exhaust headers, are all keys to getting more usable horsepower and torque out of your Bow Tie small block.

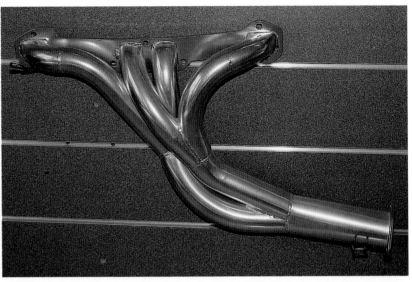

These graceful tri-Y, four-into-two-into-one headers with fairly short primaries would be great for fairly high-revving radical street machines.

Putting together a winning combination requires thought and planning, but the results can be dramatic. On the other hand, carelessly mixing together even the best components could easily result in an engine that is less dependable, less enjoyable, and less powerful than the stock one you started with.

Begin by asking yourself how often you will actually be driving around in the 6,000–8,000 rpm range. Are you

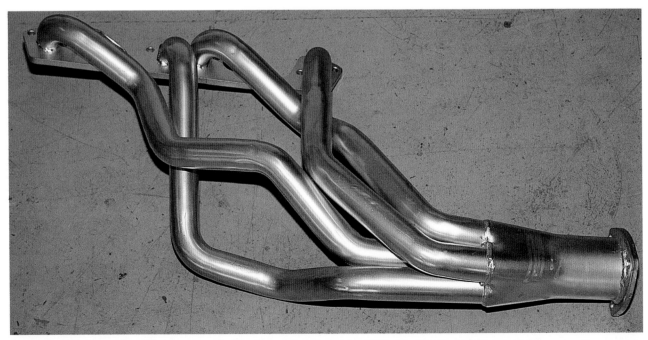

Long primary tubes such as this keep gas velocities high and produce lots of torque in the low- to mid-rpm range.

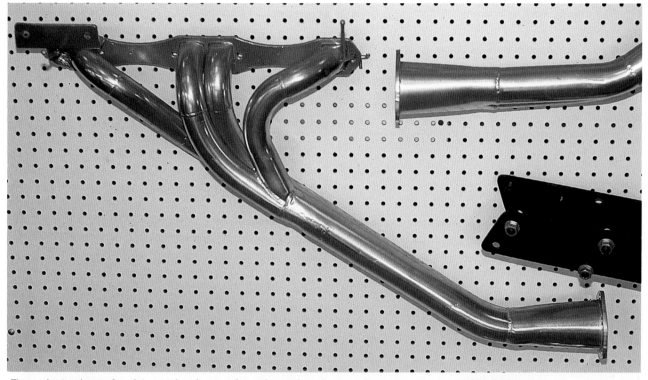

These short, primary, four-into-one headers are for racing and produce maximum horsepower at 7,000–8,000 rpm.

building a racer that you only want to be able to coax to the strip and don't mind back-shifting constantly to get it there? Do you care that the car will not climb hills worth beans and will have a big flat spot in its acceleration just at the rpm range you are used to driving in around town?

Or are you building a hot machine intended for the street that you would like to run through the traps occasionally just to see what it will do, but will be driving back and forth to work occasionally? In short, do you prefer a car that has impressive performance but is well-behaved, or do you want a wild bronco? Unfortunately, you can't have both in one car.

A radical cam with lots of overlap needs one kind of exhaust headers and a street rod needs another. If you choose a cam designed to produce midrange grunt, you will want an exhaust system designed to complement it. The same is true for a cam designed to produce awesome high-end horsepower.

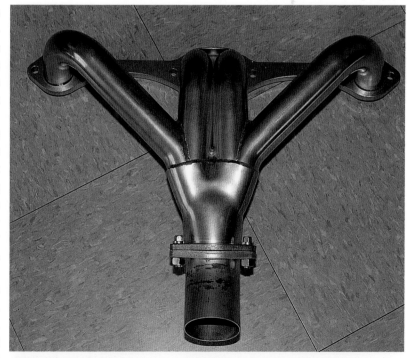

A nice step up from stock ram's-horn manifolds is this set of tight-clearance headers from Doug's.

At a casual glance, you might think an engine would develop maximum power if it had large-diameter short stacks right off the heads. They certainly looked cool on the old slingshot dragsters. But they don't work so well because the diameter of the header pipes determines the velocity of the exhaust gasses and the intensity of the resulting negative pressure wave. If the primary pipes are too short, no beneficial scavenging effect takes place, or if it does, it is at a very high and very limited rpm range.

It all has to do with taking maximum advantage of that "fifth cycle"—the overlap between intake and exhaust valve opening and closing—and how much overlap your engine can tolerate. Timing the overlap and exhaust pulses correctly can actually suck the last of the exhaust gasses out of a cylinder and can even help pull in the fresh fuel/air mixture.

STICKING WITH STOCK

The stock exhaust systems on classic Chevy engines were developed to be completely adequate for normal driving, and they were designed to be quiet and durable. They were also designed to fit in crowded engine compartments. In fact, lots of two-barrel–equipped, standard-performance, V-8–powered Chevys only come with one exhaust pipe and muffler, which is all they really need.

Such systems are quieter, less expensive, and they don't rust out as quickly as dual systems. Of course, high-performance, four-barrel–equipped Chevys came with twin exhaust systems with one pipe for each bank of cylinders. This setup is generally adequate for normal street use, except in rev ranges near the redline of the engine.

Your Bow Tie mouse motor probably came with cast-iron log manifolds. These are very restrictive in

A set of old-style ram's horns can be made to work well at lower rpms, and are the best choice among the stock manifolds.

performance situations. The next step up in efficiency would be to find a set of original Corvette ram's-horn, cast-iron manifolds with the center exhaust dump going straight down, or canted slightly to the rear of the car. They are less restrictive than log manifolds, less expensive than headers, and will still fit nicely in most engine compartments.

The big problem with stock systems at high rpms is that your engine starts developing what is called back pressure. The exhaust gasses being pushed out of the system by the pistons are under so much pressure that they can actually back up into the incoming fuel/air mixture of adjacent cylinders and dilute it, especially when all the exhaust ports dump into a log manifold instead of being separated. The effect is used intentionally to some degree in later, smog-controlled engines to develop a leaner, cleaner-burning mixture, but it cuts performance dramatically in the process.

Stock ram's horns can actually be opened and port-matched to produce almost as much power as cheap headers. If you use the exhaust gasket you will be running in your engine as a template and open and smooth the cast headers as far up into them as you can go with your die grinder and abrasive rolls, you can actually develop about 65 percent of the performance improvement that a set of conventional headers will make. All it will cost is a little labor, and your exhaust system will be quiet and long-lived.

Stock, ram's-horn cast-manifold dual exhaust systems don't develop harmful back pressure in normal service, but they aren't very good for pedal-to-the-metal performance either because they don't do anything to help the engine perform better. That takes tuning. And by tuning, we mean using the high- and low-pressure waves through the exhaust system to increase performance dramatically.

With tuned, tubular headers, when the exhaust valve opens, a burst of high-pressure hot gasses moves down its individual primary tube at very high velocity. This creates a high-pressure wave that sends a low-pressure wave back up the exhaust system. The gas particles don't actually change direction. It works sort of like when you throw a stone into still water. Behind the high-pressure waves are low-pressure troughs pulling the next wave along, though the water keeps moving in the same direction.

These low-pressure counter-waves can help create more torque at certain rpm ranges, depending on primary pipe length, pipe diameter, and valve overlap. Incidentally, there used to be a lot of fuss about having equal-length primary tubes, but this has not turned out to be as important as once thought, even for constant-throttle racing motors. That's because equal-length pipes, though they might theoretically produce the ultimate torque, can only do it at a very spiky, narrow rpm range. With primary pipes that vary in length by as much as a foot, the benefits are spread over a range of 3,000 to 4,000 rpm.

WHY TRI-Y?

For street use, tri-Y, or four-into-two-into-one headers are superior to four-into-one headers that just dump straight into a collector, or secondary tube. By pairing two primary tubes before having them go into the collectors, you get much more usable, midrange torque, and your engine will pull well over a broader range.

These headers don't look quite as cool as the four-into-one headers so popular today, but they don't give you a large flat spot at lower rpm ranges like the four-into-one headers do either. Four-into-one headers are great for racing, but they're not so great for street use. Tri Y, two-into-one headers help time the negative pressure waves much better by having that extra step, which makes them work well at more street-usable rpm ranges.

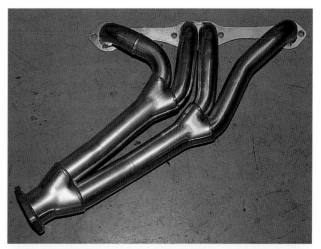

Doug's makes tri-Ys for tight spots too. These will give you great performance and still not get in the way.

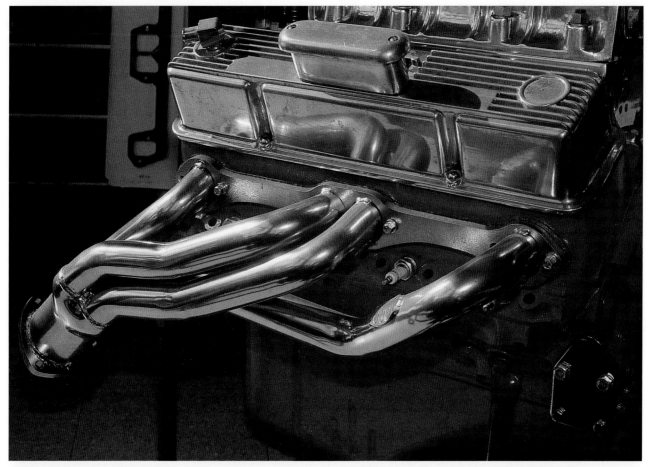

These four-into-one headers will produce prodigious amounts of power, but do so within a narrower rpm range than tri-Ys.

PIPE DIAMETER MATTERS

As a rule of thumb, a Chevy small-block primary pipe inside diameter should be about 1.16 times the exhaust valve open area. If you go bigger, you will slow down the exhaust gasses and hurt bottom-end performance. If you go too small, the pipes will be restrictive and you will lose velocity due to friction loss. Also, you will make the system susceptible to back pressure.

So how does that translate into usable numbers? Well, a Chevy small block that is intended to produce 200 to 400 horsepower will work well with industry standard 1-5/8-inch inside diameter primary pipes. From 400–600 horsepower, 1.75-inch I.D. pipes are what you want. On a Chevy small block, anything above 1.75-inch I.D. won't fit without an adapter anyway.

For secondary, or collector tubes, 2.5 inches to 3 inches is about right. Slightly larger collectors may be required for very-high-performance street engines. Short collector lengths of 18–24 inches are right for a 7,500-rpm, radical-cam racing engine, but longer collectors will get you launched quicker and are better for street use. The same is true for primary pipes. Longer primaries in the range of 24 inches to 36 inches help bottom-end power.

MAKING CHOICES

Choose your headers carefully because not every manufacturer makes headers for every application, and quality isn't always consistent. I like Doug's Headers because the quality is consistently high, and Doug Thorley has been developing and manufacturing winning headers for many years. Check any headers you buy for flatness at the mounting flange and for good clean welds at the joints.

When you order a set of headers, make sure to tell the vendor the make and model of your vehicle, the year, and which transmission and accessories your car has. You will also want to specify whether you want plain pipe, chrome, stainless, or a special coating such as Jet Hot. Plain pipe must be kept painted to prevent rust. I like black barbecue paint for this job.

Chrome looks oh-so-nice until it blues, but it can contribute to hydrogen embrittlement, which weakens the pipe. Jet Hot coatings coat the pipes inside and out to prevent corrosion, and are very durable. Stainless (if available) is quite durable, but it does expand and contract more than mild steel, so it is more prone to leaks and loosening.

INSTALLATION

Installing headers isn't as easy as it might seem on a fully assembled car. Some must come in from the top; others must be installed from the bottom. Talk to the manufacturer, get a guarantee that they will fit your application, and read and follow the instructions that come with the headers. You may have to remove certain accessories to get the things in, and you may have to dimple the headers in a few cases to get them to clear everything.

Finally, you will want to install a cross-over pipe or X pipes to help even out the exhaust pulses and quiet the system. A cross-over tube will also cut vibration noticeably, and with headers, ringing and vibration can get irritating. To figure out where to place the cross-over tube, shoot a little cheap aerosol paint down the sides of exhaust pipes, run the engine for about 20 minutes, then determine just where the paint stopped burning off. That's where to put the cross-over, if possible.

Thick, 3/8-inch plates are important to prevent warping due to high heat at the mating surfaces with the heads. Don't settle for thinner brackets.

On some later cars with lots of accessories, it is necessary to custom build headers to clear everything.

These vintage megaphone headers look good and sound outrageous, but they don't produce the torque or horsepower of later, tuned headers.

MUFFLER MYTHOLOGY

Many old-timers still think that a straight-through glass pack is less restrictive than a reverse flow. Not true. Unless the straight-through muffler has a very large inside diameter (which will be much too noisy), it will actually restrict flow through it. Those cheap glass packs on my aforementioned Chevy of years ago sounded cool, but slowed me down considerably. And some of the new reverse-flow mufflers offer no more restriction than open pipes!

Place your mufflers as far from the engine as possible, and run the exhaust pipes all the way to the rear of the car. Shorter exhaust pipes don't help performance, and you run the risk of dangerous fumes getting into your car.

Also, running the pipes to the rear helps cut noise in the cockpit. Longer pipes behind the muffler don't make any difference to performance, so there is no advantage to cutting them short.

FINAL THOUGHTS

If you install a set of headers on an engine that has been performing well, it will probably run a bit lean afterward. In that case, you may have to rejet the carb. Retune and retime your engine to make maximum use of your new exhaust system. If you've gone a bit radical, watch those back shifts through tunnels. The local cops may not like your taste in music, either.

SHOCKING DISCOVERIES

COST  &100–$500 (DEPENDING ON THE SYSTEM INSTALLED)

SKILL LEVEL

TIME 1 HOUR

In late 1974 General Motors introduced HEI (High Energy Ignition), making the old, tried-and-true breaker-point ignition system obsolete. HEI ignition systems deliver a hotter spark every time, with no miss at high rpm and no routine maintenance required to keep them in adjustment. It was a major breakthrough. Then in 1981, HEI was replaced, too, with a computerized ignition that was even better.

As a result, these days there are any number of ways an engine builder can go with ignition. But for most of us, simplicity is an important factor. A complex, expensive, distributorless, computerized system that needs reprogramming to get it to do what you want it to do is not every street rodder's idea of the ultimate ignition system, if he has to install it himself.

And you don't need the latest system. An HEI distributor equipped with a hot coil and a spark timing box can

My choice for the ultimate street rod ignition is an MSD Street Pro Billet distributor and a 6AL Ignition Control Box.

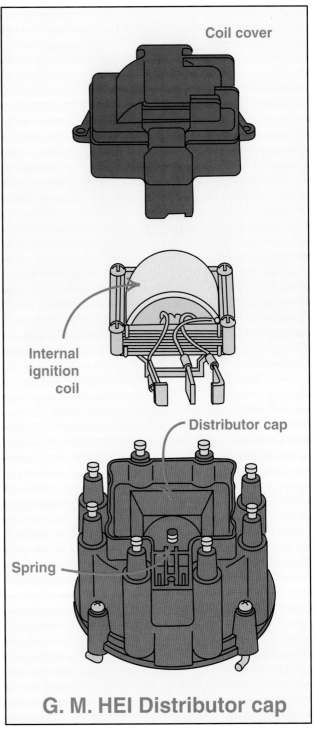

Coil cover

Internal ignition coil

Distributor cap

Spring

G. M. HEI Distributor cap

Shown here are components of a GM-type HEI ignition system.

If you want to stick with a breaker points–type ignition system, dual points are the way to go. This distributor is for a six-cylinder engine, but you get the point.

ignition system will work fine. If you are most comfortable and familiar with points-type ignition systems and don't want to spend the money for a more current system, you don't really need to. There are things you can do that will make your old system perform well.

To begin with, if your old distributor has any slop in its bearings, rebuild or replace it. If you can wiggle the shaft back and forth at all on the cam end, it will be impossible to keep the points gapped properly. And while you are rebuilding your old system, it's a good idea to replace the distributor cap, too, because minute cracks in it can develop carbon tracks in them and cause misfiring.

Finally, make sure that you put in a new set of points and gap them precisely before reinstalling the distributor. And keep in mind that if you have built your engine for high performance, you can count on having to replace points and plugs at least every 10,000 miles. Also keep in mind that frequent checks for timing and points wear and burning are very important to good performance with breaker points.

produce awesome results and is much easier to install. And even breaker-point systems still have their place and can be made to perform very well, depending on the level of performance you desire.

More than 60 years of development helped make breaker-point ignition systems dependable. They function well up to around 5,000 rpm, provided everything in the system is in good shape. But a major drawback with them is that they require frequent maintenance. Points burn and go out of adjustment and rubbing blocks wear down.

But for street rod engines, the biggest problem with breaker-point ignition systems is that at high rpm the points don't allow the voltage to build up enough in the coil before the plugs are fired. Dual-point distributors can help increase the duration of the spark, but only a small amount, unless you also use two coils. Then there is the problem of "point lofting." That's a situation where the rubbing block on the movable point starts to bounce off the lobes of the distributor cam at high rpm. There is no good way to correct for this problem. Points that can handle 8,000 rpm plus are available, but they don't last long.

If you are building a vintage engine and don't plan to rev it over approximately 5,000 rpm, a breaker-point

An MSD distributor has the mechanical advance on top where you can get at the little springs to tailor the advance.

MAKING IT BETTER THAN NEW

New breaker-point distributors set up with advance curves tailored to race-tuned engines are available, as are dual-point distributors if the traditional approach is what you are comfortable with. Combining one of these with a hotter coil can make your old system work very well within its limitations, and you will still have a stock-looking car if you are restoring a classic.

Another thing you can do that will make your breaker-point ignition system last much longer between tune-ups and run much better at higher rpm is to install a capacitive discharge system. You can buy aftermarket systems from MSD that hook up to your old points-type distributor that will bypass the points, so they only carry light current and act as a switch. MSD ignition control boxes are easy to wire in. Just make sure that you mount the box where it will remain cool and won't get wet.

GOING FOR MORE ENERGY

The next step up is to go to a GM HEI system. Ignition coils can produce very high voltage (in the neighborhood of 60,000), but breaker-points can only handle about 20,000 volts. But with an HEI system, the ignition is triggered by a stationary permanent magnet tripped by a small spinning wheel in place of the points. High voltage is not carried through the magnet, so it does not burn out.

You get a much hotter, longer spark to the plugs with an HEI distributor. The voltage to the plugs is so much higher that the terminals on the distributor cap are located about 1/2 inch apart just to avoid cross-firing. And as a result of the higher voltage, the gaps in the spark plugs can be greater

For street use you also need a vacuum advance. Without one, your gas mileage will be terrible.

(.040" to .060") so even marginal plugs will continue to fire, and good plugs will provide a very healthy, hot spark.

GM–type HEI ignition systems are easy to install and require no routine maintenance, but they do have one drawback. When they fail, they are difficult to troubleshoot. Luckily, such systems seldom fail. But if you are only familiar with the old points-type system, you may have a hard time figuring out what is wrong without a set of instructions and an ohmmeter. One other consideration when swapping engines equipped with GMC's large HEI is whether the distributor will fit in the engine bay. In some older cars, the firewall will be in the way.

GM's HEI distributor is so big because everything is built into it. The coil is mounted in the cap, so the only thing you need to do to hook up the system when replacing an old breaker-point distributor is eliminate the ballast resistor and attach a couple of wires. On mid-1950s Chevys the ballast resistor is that porcelain block with two wire connections mounted on the firewall. On later Chevys, the resistor is nothing more than a piece of stainless-steel wire. Either way, the resistor isn't needed with an HEI ignition because there are no points, and there is no need to drop the voltage to the coil to keep from burning them.

On the contrary, electronic ignition needs a full 12 volts at all times to work properly, so you don't want a ballast resistor that drops the voltage down to 9.3 volts to the coil during operation. Even running your car with a partially discharged battery will affect performance with H.E.I ignition. In fact, if you have hooked up a lot of aftermarket accessories that your car didn't come with, you will want to install a heavy-duty alternator to keep the battery topped up.

GM's stock HEI system works well and can be used as is, but of course the advance curve on the distributor is also stock, which means it is set up to meet E.P.A. requirements. That's an advantage if your car must meet smog laws, but if it doesn't, you can play with the advance curve on your stock HEI system, or better yet, buy an aftermarket HEI unit from MSD. It will come with all the springs and extras to tailor it to your engine and it will be well-made and beautifully designed.

MAKING IT A LOT BETTER THAN NEW

An even better setup is to go with an MSD magnetic pick-up distributor and add an MSD 6AL ignition control box and hot coil. Not only will this configuration give you a hot spark and an advance curve to fit your driving needs, but it will also give you a multiple, long-duration spark (20 degrees of crankshaft rotation at all rpm) that will allow a more complete burn and more power as a result. These spark boxes also come with adjustable rev limiters, so if you miss a shift or have a lead-footed teenage stepson, the engine won't grenade.

SPARK PLUGS

The reasons for running hot or cold plugs in your engine are the opposite of what many would imagine. A low-performance, low-stress, stock street engine needs to run hot plugs, and a high-performance, high-stress, four-barrel–equipped engine needs cold plugs. It seems strange until you know the reason why.

Whether a plug runs hot or cold has nothing to do with the amount of electricity going through it. That remains the same no matter which type you use. The terms "hot" or "cold" actually refer to how much heat is carried away from the combustion chamber through the spark plug. In a high-performance engine, combustion chamber temperatures are higher because the engine is burning more fuel and air, so a cold plug is necessary to avoid a glowing plug causing preignition, which will lead to a devastating detonation of the compressed mixture.

A cold spark plug transfers heat rapidly from its firing tip to the engine block, its porcelain insulator, and the cooling system. On the other hand, a hot spark plug transfers heat more slowly. In an understressed engine, losing heat through the spark plugs amounts to losing power. Hot plugs have longer firing tips that extend farther into the combustion chamber. Cold plugs are almost flush with the end of the plug. For a modified small-block street engine, you will want to install somewhat colder plugs.

Keep in mind that different years of engines have different plug configurations too. For instance, before 1971, small-block spark plugs had flat seats and used copper compression washers under them. After 1971, GM went to a tapered seat plug with no washer under it. Never try to switch them around. The threads are different on the plugs, though you can force a fit.

Plugs used with breaker-point ignition are generally gapped at .025"-.030", but later plugs for high-energy systems are generally gapped from .040"- .060" because they are designed to take advantage of a much hotter spark. Hotter sparks and bigger plug gaps mean that plugs last a lot longer, though for your street engine to run its best you'll want to replace the old plugs when the electrode starts to become rounded and eroded. That's because spark plugs work much better when the spark jumps from a fine point or edge to another fine point, rather than a broad, rounded surface.

WIRING

A lot of performance can be lost through marginal-quality spark plug wires. Even if they exhibit no obvious problems, the high-voltage current that runs through spark plug wires will always take the path of least resistance, and that may be to the engine block or to an adjacent wire, causing a cross-fire or misfire situation. When I was a young lad I worked the night shift at a gas station. While checking oil, I would often be treated to a light show when I opened the hoods on cars that had not had their spark plug wires changed in years, or that had cheap wires installed.

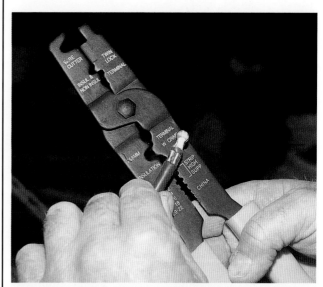

If you buy a universal ignition wiring set, make sure you tuck under about 1/2 inch of wire and double-crimp on the connectors using a crimping tool.

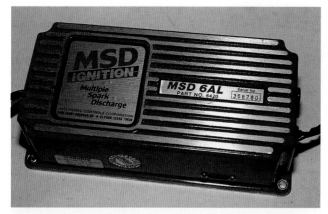

The best way to make old-style ignition points last is to hook up an MSD Spark Control Box.

Use aftermarket wire separators, available from auto supply stores, to keep wires from arcing and to make the engine room tidy.

I bent the metal tabs to hold the separators so ignition wires don't make contact with the block and make only minimal contact with one another.

That was also before HEI ignition systems. Ignition wiring has improved vastly since those days. And while the cost of a set of high-quality MSD 8.5-mm silicone-coated ignition wires may seem high when compared with old-style wires, they are a necessity for good, lasting performance. MSD wires are helically wound around a glass core and triple-insulated, so they offer minimum resistance and maximum insulation to curb electromagnetic interference.

No matter which type you use, proper separation and routing are important with ignition wires. They should never be placed on or near hot surfaces, or any metal surface for that matter, and they should be spaced 1/2 inch apart as much as possible. Aftermarket wire organizers with rubber or plastic clips are the best way to keep your wires separated, and they make your engine bay look neater too. I also like to add the little white plastic numbers that slip on to the ignition wires to avoid mixing them up.

INSTALLING AN HEI DISTRIBUTOR

Your engine should have its number one piston (driver's-side front) at TDC on its power stroke before you start. If for some reason you have disturbed the piston's position, or didn't establish it in the first place, you can bring it up again by putting your thumb over the number one spark plug hole and cranking the engine by just bumping the starter. Be sure to ground the coil high-tension wire to prevent sparks.

When air starts to push past your thumb, you know the piston is coming up on the power stroke with both valves closed. Now just turn the engine over a little farther at the vibration damper bolt until the timing mark on the plate at the front of the timing cover lines up with the "0" timing mark on the vibration damper.

Now look up the static timing figure for your engine in the shop manual or on the specs for your cam. It could be anything from 12 degrees before BTDC to 0, but most likely it will be around 8 degrees BTDC. If you don't know the static timing figure, 8 degrees BTDC will get your engine running. Then you can hook up a timing light and fine-tune the setting.

The distributor slips in with the vacuum advance canister facing out to the passenger side of the engine at a 45 degree angle, or pointing roughly between cylinders four and six. Number one cylinder on the distributor cap is at the front on the driver's side as shown in the photo. Mark it with a bit of masking tape so you won't get confused and mark it on the base of the distributor also.

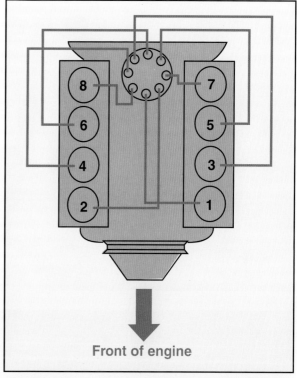

The firing order for the Chevy small block is 1-8-4-3-6-5-7-2, as shown here.

Mark the number one distributor terminal using tape, then mark the distributor base as well.

Put a little Gasgacinch on the seal and slip it onto the distributor. You don't need to put sealant against the intake manifold.

Put a little assembly lube on the distributor bevel drive gear. Turn the rotor counterclockwise approximately 2-1/4 inches on a GM–type HEI distributor from the number one nipple on the distributor. (Rotate a conventional distributor about 1-7/8 inches counterclockwise to get it to line up properly.) Now have a look at the position of the drive spline in the bottom of the distributor. Use a large screwdriver to turn the drive spline on the oil pump down in the engine so it will line up with the distributor spline.

Slip the distributor into place. You may have to jockey it around a little to get it to seat, but it should drop into place with the rotor lined up on the number one you have marked. If it doesn't, you could be one tooth off on the drive gear, and your timing will be off. In that situation, you'll need to pull the distributor up a little and seat it again. Finally, turn the distributor base slightly to line up the pick-up with a contact on the

continued on page 161

IGNITION

159

Remove the distributor cap using a screwdriver.

When installing GM-type HEI distributors, turn the rotor 2-1/4 inches counterclockwise from number one before installing it. This way, it will line up with the number one terminal when the distributor gear is engaged.

segmented rotating timing wheel. The distributor should still have its vacuum-advance canister facing to the left at a 45 degree angle. If it doesn't, your distributor is most likely installed one tooth off.

Plug in your ignition wires. The firing order for Generation I and II engines is 1-8-4-3-6-5-7-2 with number one being the front cylinder on the driver's side. Hook up the wires in order, starting at number one and working clockwise around the distributor. If you are installing new wires, be careful to route them so the wires from adjacent firing cylinders don't come near each other. Even good ignition wires can arc across under certain circumstances because electromagnetic energy from one wire can energize an adjacent wire.

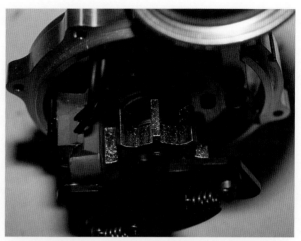

Turn the distributor slightly so that the nearest paddle on the little segmented wheel in the center lines up with the magnetic pick-up after the distributor is in place.

Once you have number one up on its compression stroke, bring the timing marker on the vibration damper to the "0" mark in the timing tab by bumping the starter.

The easiest way to make sure cylinder number one is ready to fire is to ground the coil high-tension lead, then take out the plug. Hold your thumb over the hole and bump the starter until you feel air escaping. Number one is nearing the top of the compression stroke.

Here's my recipe: It makes 420-450 horsepower, buckets of torque, and it's built to last. Blend ingredients carefully, then jump in and hang on.

When I refer to a recipe for speed I'm not talking about a concoction you would use to give yourself a chemical lobotomy. I'm talking about the old definition of the word. I'm talking about going fast. Very fast. There are lots of good ways to do it—just as there are a lot of ways to make good chili. Ever been to a chili cook-off?

Chili cook-offs (more accurately called chili eat-offs) are like elementary school fights. The first guy to cry loses. Some chili is just too mild to be taken seriously. Extreme chili will make you scream in agony and cry like a baby. The best chili is hot enough for you to prove your manhood, yet still enjoy your afternoon.

Good street rod engines are like that too. They're hot, but still fun to drive. They'll leave your opponent crying, but you can still drive home on city streets. They are a careful balance between a well-tuned, basically stock motor and a Funny Car engine that only functions well at the track.

There are as many good recipes for chili as for street rod engines. And while I don't have a good recipe for chili, I do have great one for a Chevy small block that will leave your opponent cursing (if not weeping) in your dust. I've told you how to go about making it in this book, but here is the abridged ingredient list:

BLOCK

Start with a good 350 carcass. Any of the Chevy small blocks can be built to the hilt, but there are piles of good speed equipment available at reasonable prices to fit the standard 350. Make sure the block is sound and that it has been crack-tested, sonic-tested, and cleaned before you start. Also make sure its cylinders will clean up at .030" over. Yes, most of the small blocks will go bigger, but you could wind up with structural and heating problems if you punch them out too much.

CRANKSHAFT

A stock crankshaft that isn't cracked badly, scored, or bent can be turned down and polished to work for the street. Chevy cranks are tough. But if you want truly awesome torque, go for a Scat stroker crank. They're virtually indestructible and will give you a real edge in competition. You can't wind them up quite as high as an aftermarket forged crank, but they are actually less likely to crack, and a stroker crank will give you such an off-the-line launch advantage that you will break your opponent's spirit right out of the hole. Scat stroker cranks are a bargain too.

Holley-stamped aluminum roller rockers lighten the valve train and cut friction and wear.

A Scat stroker crank turns a 350 into a bigger engine without making it a heavier engine. It's also the secret behind all that torque.

CAM

Camshafts are cheap, so why not buy the best? I like Iskendarian's 270–280 split-duration Megacams or a straight 280 Megacam with hydraulic lifters and stamped, standard-lift rockers.—nothing fancy or radical. The 280 will give you lots of midrange kick and sounds wonderful. Isky's 270–280 runs a little smoother, but it gives you lots of bottom end. I prefer hydraulic lifter cams because they require no routine valve adjustments, yet still provide impressive performance.

RODS

If you go with a Scat crank, use the 5.7-inch forged rods with full-floating wrist pins. These rods are a bit longer than stock and that makes the pistons linger a little longer near the top so

you can take better advantage of maximum cylinder pressure at higher revs, and they linger a little longer at the bottom, too, allowing more exhaust scavenging. Rods longer than 5.7 inches are available, but they push the wrist pins up into the ring package, making such pistons a little frail. Also, unless you are building a high revver, standard H beam rods are fine. Just make sure you use them with decent big-end bearings, such as Clevite 77s.

PISTONS

There are lots of good pistons available, but I like Keith Black (KB) Signature Series hypereutectic cast-aluminum pistons. They are manufactured using special technology that makes them almost as tough as forged pistons for a lot less money. You can get KBs in the size you need, and you can get the domed, flat, or recessed types. Avoid domed pistons if possible because they mess up the turbulence and flame pattern needed for maximum burn and power. Be sure to use good moly-compression rings and three-piece oil rings: Childs & Albert are my favorites.

HEADS

The 1960s Chevy 68-cc closed-combustion chamber heads were designed beautifully but are now extremely rare and expensive. They will also push your compression too high, given the rest of this recipe. They are wonderful for racing, but you can't run them on the street on pump gas unless you go to dished pistons, which is just another way to open up the combustion chambers.

A TD Performance Hamburger 7-quart pan can actually add a few horsepower thanks to its windage tray, and it will increase durability in a big way.

Open-chamber 74–76-cc heads are still common and can be made to perform well with a pocket-porting job. These are also what most of us can afford these days. Don't turn down a set of double-humpers if you can get them for a good price. Keep in mind that the later, 1980s-era heads are thin and prone to cracking.

If you can afford it, a set of World Products Sportsman II cast-iron heads will really wake up your small block. They are a bit more expensive than stock heads, but not that much more after you have your stockers rebuilt. World Products offers 72-cc combustion chambers so you can run flat-top pistons for maximum power without risking detonation. World's castings are much more precise than stock heads and will produce appreciable gains in horsepower right out of the box.

A little careful pocket porting and cleaning up of the port runners will do wonders with Sportsman II heads as well. And if you can spring for them, World Products aluminum heads work even better because they will allow you to run slightly higher compression, due to their superior ability to dissipate heat. Since heads are where most of the horsepower is, it would pay to put as much money as you can into good ones.

OIL PAN

If you have the ground clearance and can spring for one, a Hamburger 7-quart oil pan from TD Performance products is a great way to go. The increased oil volume helps keep your engine's vital moving parts cooler by keeping the engine's oil cooler. A Hamburger pan will also make sure the

Doug's headers are tried and true. They are beautifully made and really help pump out the ponies.

If you are a relative novice, get a Holley. For this recipe, a 670-cfm Street Avenger is ideal, and it is easy to set up and fine-tune. Parts are readily available to make Holleys do anything you want, and to fit any engine you might want to build. Everything you need to tinker with is right out where you can get to it, and Holley carbs are tested at the factory before you ever get them, so they are essentially trouble-free.

A Rochester Quadra-Jet will do a great job too. In stock form, they flow 750 cfm, which is more than enough for most street small blocks. If you have a little carb tuning experience or take the time to send your Q-Jet to a place like the Carb Shop in Ontario, California, you can make these carbs perform as well or better than any of them. They are more complex to work on than the Holleys, and you need to know how to tweak them, but they are great carbs. Although they don't make them anymore, new knock-offs are available. But it is a lot less costly to redo an original.

engine has a healthy supply of oil in hard cornering and hard acceleration because it has one-way trap doors that keep the oil where it needs to be. Finally, it is surprising how much drag is created at high rpms by a crankshaft spinning through a sump full of oil. Hamburger pans have windage trays built in that wipe the crank clean of excess oil and cut down drag.

HEADERS

Four-into-one headers look cool, and if your exhaust system is going to be exposed down the side of a T-bucket you might want to sacrifice some midrange just to have them. But tri-Y, four-into-two-into-one headers are better for street use because they give you a broader power band. They won't quite give you as much top-end power, but the difference is not noticeable unless you are building a dragster. Doug's headers are my choice because I know they are top-quality, well-designed, and tested. Go with the ceramic-coated types for durability and ease of maintenance.

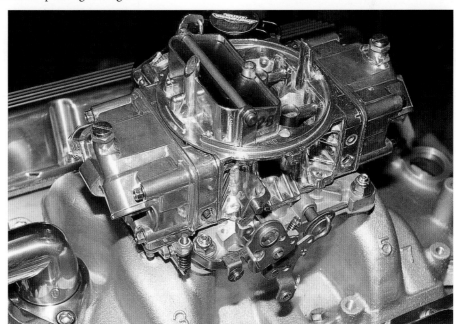

This is a Holley 670-cfm Street Avenger four-barrel. It's just right for our torquer motor and looks as good as it performs.

A K&N washable air filter is the best there is, and actually makes your carb breathe better because it does not restrict flow, but makes it more consistent.

An MSD capacitive discharge ignition system gives you hot spark through 20 degrees of crank rotation at any rpm.

INTAKE MANIFOLD

Most street rodders are more comfortable with a dual-plane manifold. A single plane gives you a rather hard-to-manage and soggy bottom end, though they really come on strong in the higher-rpm range. My favorite intake manifold for the street (when using a Holley carb) is the Weiand dual plane. The manifolds are beautifully made and have been flow bench proven.

A Performance Products dual-plane manifold is an inexpensive alternative that flows better than many of the big name brands.

If I had less to spend, I'd go for a Performance Products dual-plane intake manifold. They are less expensive than most performance manifolds and have been shown in tests to flow as well as many of the big name brands. They're cheap because they are made in China, but the quality is excellent. If you do a little port matching and top one of these with a well-tuned Q-Jet, you'll easily be able to play with the big kids.

IGNITION

The GM HEI system works well and can be used basically as-is, but of course, the advance curve on an O.E.M. distributor is set up to meet EPA demands, which is good if your car must meet smog laws. If not, you can play with the advance curve on your stock HEI system, or better yet, buy an aftermarket HEI unit from MSD. It will come with all the springs and extras to tailor it to your engine, and it will be beautifully designed.

It's even better to go with an MSD magnetic pick-up distributor and add an MSD 6AL spark box and a hot coil. Not only will this configuration give you a hot spark and an advance curve to fit your driving needs, but it will give you a multiple spark that will allow a more complete burn, and more power as a result. Once you have such a system dialed in, you can forget regular tune-ups, too.

START-UP
LIGHTING IT OFF

Lightning flashes; thunder crashes. The platform is slowly lowered from the opening in the roof of the laboratory. Dr. Frankenstein rushes over, looks down, and sees his creation twitch its pinkie. IT'S ALIIIIIIIIIIIIIIIVE! screams the doc in maniacal glee as he dances a hideous gavotte. I know the feeling. In fact, I've been known to shout the same line after starting an engine that I have just built. For a motorhead, there is nothing quite like hearing what has been a 600-pound paperweight cough and roar to life.

All that care and hard work finally pays off. It is the singular most exciting moment for a street rodder. Of course, it can also be the single most disheartening one, too, if you haven't prepared for the event by checking everything out carefully before you start your new engine. That's because in its first critical moments of life, things have to settle in. Parts that have never been introduced to each other before now have to work together as a team.

Hook up the temperature gauge and oil pressure sending unit. Make sure all of the vital fluids are topped up. Good quality 10W-30 motor oil is all that is required to break in your engine. However, if you plan to run your motor only on synthetic oil, you will need a special synthetic break-in oil. Otherwise, the piston rings will take quite a long time to seat properly.

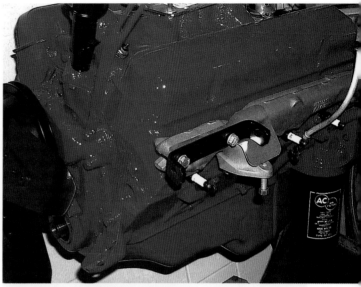

Attach the brackets and be sure to fill the oil filter and install old plugs to keep dirt out before putting your engine in the car.

✔ START-UP CHECKLIST

❏ Check the oil. Use a good grade of 10W-30 detergent oil and make sure you fill the oil filter before installing it. (A special break-in oil is strongly recommended for synthetic oils.)

❏ Use only water as coolant for the initial run-in. It makes fixing any leaks much easier and you can just dump it out. Afterward, put in the correct amount of 50/50 coolant-to-water mixture.

❏ Check the ignition static timing, and make sure that you have the distributor wires in the correct order in the distributor cap.

❏ Make sure the valves are adjusted to the cold setting indicated in your shop manual or to the specifications provided by your cam manufacturer.

❏ Verify that the fuel lines are connected properly and tightened securely, and that you have fresh gas in the tank. Gasoline has a shelf life of six months. If the gas in the lines has been sitting for longer than that, drain it out.

❏ Make sure the throttle linkage works without binding, and that the throttle butterflies are fully open when the throttle is wide open.

❏ Make sure the throttle return spring is properly connected at the carburetor.

❏ If your car has an automatic transmission, make sure it is in "Park." If your car is equipped with a standard transmission, make sure it is in neutral before starting the engine.

❏ Check to see that all accessory belts are tight, but not too tight. They should flex about 3/4 inch in either direction when pressed in the middle using your thumb.

❏ Make sure no tools, electrical cords, or other items are left in the engine bay where they could fall into the fan or cause other problems.

Fill your engine with oil. A good-quality 10W-30 will do just fine unless you will be running synthetic oil, in which case you will need special synthetic break-in oil.

couple of years ago where a fellow started his van, which was backed into his attached garage, to warm it up before the family left for church. Sadly, he left the door to the kitchen open. The fumes filled the house and killed the entire family. It sounds incredible, but it's true. And even if you hook up a hose to the exhaust system to take the gasses outdoors, leaks from manifolds, headers, or mufflers can be deadly.

Hook up a remote starter and an engine tachometer, or have a friend stand by and watch while you start the engine. Electric fuel pumps are nice in this situation because they will fill the float bowl quickly without you having to crank the engine and further discharge the battery. A fresh engine with an empty carb will have to turn over several times to fill the carb float bowl before it will fire. Priming the carb can be dangerous, but if you choose to do so, use an oil squirt can and a small amount of fuel.

If the engine doesn't start after several revolutions, go around and recheck everything on the checklist earlier in this chapter to make sure you haven't missed anything. You may have forgotten something obvious in your excitement. Once the engine fires, take it slowly up to about 2,000 rpm, and then run it up slowly to 2,500 rpm and back down to 2,000 rpm for about 20 minutes. But don't let the rpm fall below 2,000.

The valve train components (cam, lifters, pushrods, and rockers) need to seat and wear in together. If the rpm is left at idle, these parts, as well as the cylinder bores, may not get enough oil to sustain them for these first critical moments. Of course, if there are any strange sounds or roughness, shut the engine off immediately and find the problem. Also, keep an eye out for oil, fuel, and coolant leaks. A helper to cycle the engine while you check these things out is a must.

Trapped air in the water jacket can be dangerous, so if your engine took less coolant than is called for, make sure you top up the coolant as soon as possible after the engine gets going. In fact, a good way to avoid this problem is to leave the thermostat out of the engine for the first 20 minutes of running. That way the coolant begins circulating immediately and trapped air can't heat up, cause steam, and damage the engine.

Slip an oil pump priming tool (TD Performance Products makes a good one) into the hole where the distributor goes and pump the oil pressure up until it reads on your dash pressure gauge if your car has one. Otherwise, just spin up the pump for at least one full minute so oil will fill all of the little galleries and top up the lifters. Then reinstall the distributor.

GENTLEMEN, START YOUR ENGINES

Be sure to start your new engine *outdoors* where there is plenty of ventilation. Carbon monoxide is insidious, odorless, and deadly. I remember a tragic accident that happened locally a

This handy device, available from tool stores, makes engine installation easier and safer.

If you spot a leak, slowly lower the rpm to idle, then shut the engine off and make the necessary repairs. Keep an eye on your temperature gauge at all times too. If the needle drifts up very far past normal, ease back on the throttle and shut the engine off. Check to see that your engine still has enough coolant. If the radiator is low on coolant after the engine has been run for a few minutes, it's probably because trapped air has finally escaped.

As soon as the engine has warmed up for 20 minutes, fine-tune the timing and the carb. If your engine has mechanical (solid) lifters, adjust them now. Be sure to wear heavy gloves that come up your arms so you won't get burned by hot oil. With mechanical lifters the valves must be hot, with the engine running at a fast idle before you adjust them. Set them to the cam grinder's specs. You will need to adjust them again every 6,000 miles for your engine to run its best.

If your engine has hydraulic lifters, now is the time to fine-tune them too. Just take each adjuster in (or out) until you can barely notice the clicking, take it down to no click, then take it down 1/2 turn further. No further adjustment should be necessary, but check them every 20,000 miles or every 24 months. Just change your oil regularly and use a good quality of detergent oil to keep the lifters healthy.

EXTRA CARE

If you do not experience any problems, keep your engine between 2,000 and 3,000 rpm for a full 20 minutes, then back the throttle down slowly, and shut it off. Let it cool for an hour or so, then check the torque of the head and manifold bolts. Many of the head gasket makers these days say you need not re-torque the heads, and if that is the case with the head

Make sure you fill the cooling system with the correct coolant and water mixture. Also, make sure your pressure cap is the correct one and in good repair.

Use a timing light to adjust the timing of your new engine. Move the distributor a few degrees at a time until you get it just right, and then tighten the distributor clamp.

After your engine is thoroughly warmed up, then allowed to cool, retorque the heads, intake manifold, and headers.

gaskets you purchased, defer to the instructions with the gaskets. I still check the head and manifold bolt torque just to make sure I didn't get a false torque reading due to a burr or something else during my first reading. I would also recheck these items with the first real oil change. Gaskets can compress with the cycling of hot to cold.

Also, change the oil and take a look at what comes out of the pan. You should see nothing at all in the oil and certainly not feel anything in it. If there are bits you can see, you will certainly want to drop the pan and check the bearings. However, if you cleaned the engine thoroughly before assembly and checked all the clearances, this should not happen.

SHAKEDOWN CRUISE

If everything checks out and there is no overheating, take your car around the block. Keep an eye on the gauges and listen carefully for untoward noises. When you get back home, check your spark plugs. They should be dry, with a little soot on them. If any are wet with oil or coolant, pull the head and find out why. This would normally be accompanied by steam or blue oil smoke at the tailpipe. If everything functions fine, congratulations!

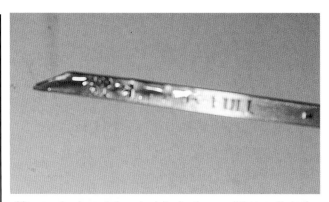

After running in and changing oil, check your oil frequently in the first few thousand miles to make sure you don't have a leak or another problem.

170

Be sure to adjust rockers with the engine running and hot. Hydraulic lifters only require that you take them down until they stop ticking, then 1/2 turn further.

ROUTINE MAINTENANCE

Be sure to change the oil and filter after 1,000 miles, and don't push the engine while you are letting it settle in. Also, check the coolant, and take another look at the spark plugs.

It is also a good idea to take your car to a shop that has a chassis dyno and let them dial it in and make sure it is in proper tune. Dyno tuning can get the carb mixture and, more important, the ignition advance curve spot-on. And don't forget to keep an eye out for oil and coolant leaks. Chances are you will only need to tighten a bolt or two a little to fix them. Good luck and happy hunting at the bracket races.

DYNAMOMETER TESTING
GIVE YOUR ENGINE A PHYSICAL

COST APPROXIMATELY $450 FOR ENGINE DYNO; $150 FOR CHASSIS DYNO

SKILL LEVEL

TIME 6–8 HOURS 1–2 HOURS FOR CHASSIS DYNO

✔ YOU'LL NEED:

- ❑ Gasket set
- ❑ Torque wrench
- ❑ Socket set
- ❑ Screwdrivers
- ❑ Carburetor parts including jets, metering rods, needles, squirt can of gasoline
- ❑ Spark plugs, distributor cap, rotor
- ❑ Alternate components such as carbs, manifolds, headers
- ❑ Leather welding gloves (for changing hot components)
- ❑ Gasket scraper
- ❑ Spark plug socket
- ❑ Oil and drain pan
- ❑ Ear plugs

George at Vrbancic Brothers Racing in Ontario, California, watches the monitor as he runs up the engine.

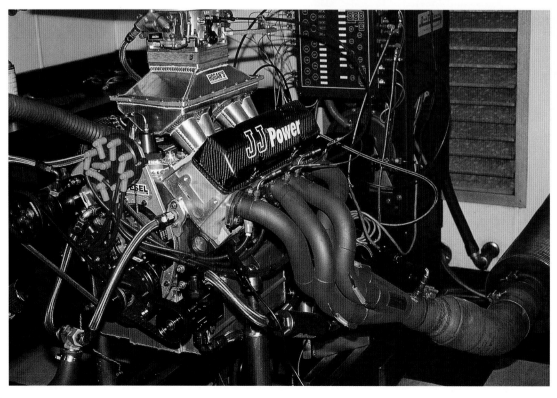

How about 900+ horsepower out of this normally aspirated Chevy small block? Dyno tuning can help do that.

DYNAMOMETER TESTING

Nine hundred horsepower! That's how much the small block was making on the Vrbancic Brothers' engine dyno. I read the computer myself so I knew it was true. Of course, this engine didn't produce such unbelievable power when they first hooked it up earlier that morning. It took some tweaking and changing out of components to get everything just right. They also fixed a couple of minor oil leaks. But there it was—close to 1,000 horsepower out of a Bow Tie mouse motor.

Of course, this monster mill was built for the strip. It would never grace a street machine. And it was well worth the owner's money to have this mighty mouse dialed to perfection because doing so could mean the difference between taking home a trophy and going home broke. But what about the street rodder building a milder motor? Is putting it on an engine dynamometer worth the trouble? The answer is yes. Like many aspects of engine building, if you can afford to get your engine dynoed, it's well worth the $450 a day it costs to have it done.

The engine is set in a test jig and its flywheel is bolted to a device that looks a lot like a pair of heavy-duty torque converters. Attached to them is a torque arm and strain gauge that measures torque. Horsepower is extrapolated from the torque figures. The engine attempts to overcome resistance in the stators. Water under pressure is used to create the resistance. There are also dynos that use your car's engine to drive a big electric generator, but they are less common.

A REAL EYE-OPENER

Most people think of engine dynamometer testing solely as a method of establishing horsepower, but it can do much more than that. Putting a fresh engine on a dynamometer before installing it is a prudent safety measure because it allows you to break it in correctly, fix any oil leaks, and most important, get the timing and carburetion set up exactly as they need to be. And yes, you can do all of that with the engine in the car, but it is much more difficult.

Besides, the first few minutes of any engine's life are critical to its longevity. Lifters can eat up a cam in a hurry if they don't get a healthy oil supply. And poor ignition timing and a lean mixture can damage a piston in no time, if undetected. Lack of oil pressure to bearings and oil leaks from mating surfaces can be dangerous, too, and are hard to spot on an engine installed in a crowded engine bay.

The guys try some different component combinations and check for oil leaks between pulls.

This is an oxygen sensor. It indicates whether an engine is burning its fuel correctly.

shifting errors, ambient temperature, cold tires, and all of the other variables that can render your performance figures invalid.

On a dyno, the first moments of life for your new motor will be presided over by trained technicians who have had lots of experience breaking in engines so their cam lobes don't get galled and their lifters damaged. They will also make sure that oil pressure is where it needs to be before they even start the engine, and that the operating temperature is kept within strict parameters once it is running. In the unlikely event that anything breaks on the dyno, it most likely would have broken anyway. Fixing an engine out of the car is much easier than trying to deal with it once it is installed in the chassis.

Then there are the bragging rights. At the end of the day, you'll have a printout proving exactly what your carefully

All of these problems are easily remedied on an engine dyno because you can get to everything easily, and you can hook the engine up to sensors that can monitor everything including exhaust gas temperature, rpm, fuel/air mixture, and ignition timing. Lambda (oxygen) sensors can also be tied into primary exhaust tubes and tell you which cylinders are running leaner and hotter. And they can be fitted farther down near the collector tubes to let you know how the engine is performing overall.

TRY IT, YOU'LL LIKE IT

You can also try various components, such as intake manifolds, carbs, headers, and even camshafts to see which ones perform best for your needs. For example, you can see first-hand what kind of torque and horsepower a dual-plane manifold makes versus a single plane at any given rpm, and what kind of power your engine puts out with tri-Y headers versus four-into-one collectors or stock, cast-iron manifolds.

A day on the dyno will allow you to tune your engine to its utmost before putting it in your car. That way you won't have to wait in long lines to make those runs at the strip and then somehow factor in

If anything, such as an oil leak, shows up on an engine dyno, it's easy to fix.

DYNAMOMETER TESTING

crafted powerplant can produce. And you'll be able to tailor your engine's performance to your particular ride too. When you set it in the car, you'll know everything is as it should be, and that the engine will perform as you intended it to.

COME PREPARED

If you are interested in testing different cams, an engine dyno is really the way to go, because changing cams with the engine in the car is time-consuming and difficult to get right. Of course, you'll be expected to bring along any components you want to try, and you will also need to bring your own tools. It is unprofessional—not to mention uncool—to borrow tools from the dynamometer shop. Besides, when it comes to custom components, the shop is not likely to have them on hand for you to try.

The ultimate setup for tuning is to have a set of headers with an exhaust gas temperature sensor or an oxygen sensor in them as well, unless the dynamometer shop has headers to fit your engine. The Chevy small block is easily the most popular engine to race-tune, so they might just have what you need. Exhaust gas temperature can be important because engines make the most power when running very lean just before they melt down. It is very important that internal temperatures don't get too high, or too low.

It may be possible for your dyno shop to hook up lambda (oxygen) sensors at each exhaust port to really get an accurate picture. These tests aren't critical unless you are a serious racer, because you aren't going to be seeking ragged-edge performance. But if you're the type that likes to take things to the max, this is one good way to do it. For the street, as long as your ignition timing is right all through the advance curve, your carb is set up properly for the secondaries to kick in when they should, and the mixture is optimum through the rpm range, you'll be fine.

CHASSIS DYNAMOMETERS

An engine dyno will tell you what an engine can do in terms of brake horsepower with no accessories hooked up to it. That means no clutch, transmission, driveshaft, or differential. But it won't tell you what your *car* can do out in the real world because an engine dyno only tests one component. To test what an entire car can do, you need a chassis dynamometer. A session on one of these is less expen-

sive than an engine dyno, depending on how much time you spend on it. The average session runs about $100 plus labor for an hour, and can do many of the things an engine dyno can do.

There are two kinds of horsepower figures commonly quoted. The first is brake horsepower, which is what a totally unfettered engine can produce on an engine dyno, and the second is rear-wheel horsepower, which is less impressive, but

A chassis dyno tells you horsepower at the wheels, and that can be a real eye-opener.

Newer chassis dynos can tell you much more, and everything is displayed on a computer monitor or printout.

more critical to your success on the strip. Accessories such as fans, pulleys, and air-conditioning compressors eat up more horsepower than you might think. And then there is all that heavy driveline to turn in addition to the weight and diameter of your tires and wheels.

Not only can you figure rear-wheel horsepower, but you can easily determine what rpm you'll be turning at your favorite cruising speed if you don't have a tachometer, and even calculate your likely mileage. You can do most of the engine corrections that you can do on an engine dyno, though the corrections may not be as accurate. Of course, fixing things can be a lot more trouble with the engine in the car.

Chassis dynos are less expensive and more commonly available, so I recommend that if you are building a small block for the street, have the engine checked out before you put your foot in it at the local drag strip. All of those expensive components and your hard work could come to a tragic end if something isn't right.

Here is an old-style chassis dyno. It shows rpm, vacuum, dwell, amps, volts, and exhaust gas composition.

Randy at Don and Harold's in Long Beach, California, runs up a 1955 Nomad with a 327 in it for its annual physical.

Type of transmission, tire size, and rear-end gears determine rpm at cruising speed.

Also, if you've built a bottom-end torque engine for a big, heavy car, you will most likely want a differential with slightly taller gears than you would want if you had a high-rpm screamer in it. Gearing is as important to speed as the engine is, and your stock gearing may be all wrong for the engine you've built. Check it out on a chassis dyno.

Larger-than-stock-diameter tires have the same effect as higher gearing; smaller-diameter tires mean that your engine has to spin faster to go the same distance in the same amount of time. Also, fat, heavy tires create more rolling friction and eat up more torque, so you will want to work with various combinations here too. And if you are running an automatic transmission, you will want to establish its stall speed and its shift points. Setting your car up based on data from a chassis dyno can make all the difference to its real-world performance.

TURBOS AND SUPERCHARGERS
BLOWN AWAY

A neatly done turbocharger installation gives this tri-five Chevy classic 900 horsepower to play with.

When a normally aspirated internal combustion engine is running, air enters each time a piston is pulled down inside its cylinder on the intake stroke because as the piston recedes, it enlarges the chamber, causing a vacuum. This vacuum is filled by air rushing in through the carburetor, which charges it with atomized fuel on the way. The fuel and air mixture is in turn compressed by the rising piston. Then, at just the right moment, the mixture is ignited, which superheats the air, causing it to expand and push down on the piston. The hot air is then released through the exhaust system. That, in a nutshell, is how a reciprocating engine works.

Atmospheric pressure is about 14 pounds per square inch at sea level, and that is what causes the cylinders to fill with air. So it stands to reason that if you increase the air pressure beyond atmospheric by forcing more air into the intake system, you will have a denser mixture, a bigger explosion in the cylinder, and more power as a result. It's called supercharging. In fact, supercharging is another form of upping the compression ratio.

It's not a new idea. The French were supercharging race cars as far back as 1909 with dramatic results. Nothing else you can do to an engine will add as much power. Some people may assume that nitrous oxide injection is a better option, but let me point out that nitrous is just a chemical form of supercharging, albeit a temporary one. In fact, horsepower gains of between 30 and 75 percent are possible just by adding a supercharger. Small-block Chevys can easily crank out 600 horsepower with a blower attached.

The major catch for most of us is cost. Installing any of the superchargers or turbochargers can set you back $3,000 to $5,000 at this writing, and that is more than most of us will spend on the entire engine. There are a few other drawbacks for the hobbyist working at home, too, such as installation, plumbing, and setting up the ignition. Also, blowers work best with fuel injection, and there's more to learn about setting up the system and tuning it. If you are serious about supercharging, there are several good books on the subject. I suggest you start with the *Supercharging, Turbocharging, and Nitrous Oxide Performance Handbook,* published by Motorbooks International.

Of course, there are limits as to how much of an increase in pressure you can put into a Chevy small block or any other engine. That's because as you compress air, it gets hotter. And as the air in a supercharger gets hotter it becomes less dense, so the power gains start to diminish. Also, if the air/fuel mixture coming into the engine becomes too lean or too hot, it may explode on its own and cause detonation, which will ruin your engine in short order.

Too much boost, a high compression ratio, or a combination of the two will cause detonation in a supercharged engine. Detonation occurs when the combustion pressure goes so high that the inlet charge explodes before the spark plug arcs. When this happens, combustion takes place while the piston is still moving up in the cylinder and that causes a tremendous shock to the pistons, rods, and crankshaft.

The flame speed across a cylinder under normal circumstances is somewhere between 120 and 200 miles an hour. But when fuel detonates—exploding under pressure before the spark plug even fires—the flame speed goes up as high as 2,000 miles an hour and the shock destroys your ring lands and pistons. A richer mixture (one with more fuel in suspension), or one that is less compressed is cooler, so it is less likely to detonate. Also, there are devices called intercoolers that cool the compressed air before it goes into the engine and they help prevent detonation too.

But even when you can get a cool, dense mixture into an engine under high pressure, you need to take into account whether your engine's bottom end can handle the all the extra

The big Roots-type blower on this Corvette is enough to intimidate the competition, but is gross overkill for street use.

power. Four to seven pounds' increase in boost is maximum for the street, and if you want a reliable car for daily use, keep it down around four or five, max. That's enough to give you good midrange torque, yet keep you from running over your own engine parts.

ROOTS-TYPE BLOWERS

Most rodders and engine builders are familiar with the Roots-type blower, which has been around for a very long time. Those big, polished blowers you see sitting atop dragster engines are generally the GMC type 6-71. The basic design actually goes back to the late nineteenth century and was developed to pump air into mines. Inside that big housing on top of the engine are two sort of figure-eight-shaped metal vanes that rotate in close tolerance with one another to move air.

And since the device can move air much faster than an engine can consume it, the air in the intake manifold becomes compressed. The blowers you see most commonly at the drags were originally developed by GMC for big, two-cycle diesel truck engines. Hot rodders were quick to see their advantages

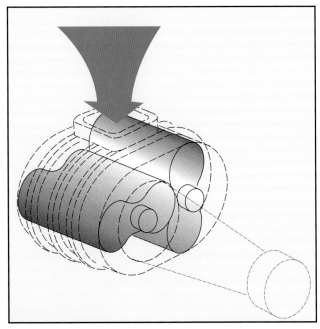

Here's how a Roots-type blower works: Air is pumped into the intake manifold by twin internal vanes.

and adapted them to their engines many years ago. These old-style, crankshaft-driven blowers can give you more boost than you'll ever need, look impressive, and make a lot of exciting noise, but they are not the best choice for street use.

Big blowers require a fair amount of power just to turn them over, and they don't fit under the hoods of most street vehicles. They also give you poor mileage if you run them with carburetors instead of fuel injection because the fuel/air mixture must be kept rich to avoid detonation. Of course you can mitigate this by driving conservatively, but then, why would you want a blower? For a dragster there is nothing better than a honking big blower, but on the street they're sort of like using a sledgehammer when a ball peen hammer would do the job.

A better choice than the Jimmy blower for the street, if you want to use a Roots-type supercharger, might be the B&M two-rotor miniblower. It fits under the hoods of many cars and

Pulling the air through the carbs causes its own problems. It would be better if the blower fed the carbs instead of the other way around.

A blown Bow Tie certainly wakes up this old Kaiser, but it's strictly a fair-weather show car.

A Whipple blower is a variation of a Roots type, except it compresses air before it reaches the intake manifold.

trucks, and it works fairly well carbureted while pumping up to 6–8 psi of boost. These are tough, dependable blowers but, as with any Roots-type blower, the vanes are machined to very tight tolerances, so good air filtration is a must.

My favorite Roots-type blower for the street is the Weiand Pro-Street 142 offered by Holley Weiand. They are small and fit nicely under most hoods. They also work well with Holley carbs or injection that is set up expressly for them. And Holley can help you custom-order your supercharger for your particular

application. These blowers are well made, durable, and produce awesome low-end torque as well as high-end horsepower.

SCREW-TYPE SUPERCHARGERS

Whipple offers some very nice screw-type blowers that are a variation on the Roots-type supercharger. They use two rotors that are like interlocking coarse-thread screws. The original design comes from Sweden, and the advantage of it is that the air is compressed before it enters the intake man-

This is what detonation looks like. Explosive shocks to pistons rapidly destroy them.

ifold, so there is less heat. Whipple superchargers have an excellent reputation.

TURBOCHARGERS

Turbochargers use the pressure of the escaping exhaust in an engine to spin a turbine that drives an impeller to force air into the intake manifold. Truly impressive horsepower gains can be obtained with turbochargers, but they also have a few drawbacks, including throttle lag. Anyone who has followed Indy car racing for a long time will remember when Kevin Cogan looped his car at the start of the race and took out Mario Andretti and A. J. Foyt in 1982. It was embarrassing for Cogan, but it was an easy mistake to make, as the throttle lag caused by the turbocharger made it difficult for Cogan to manage his car's power delivery.

Turbochargers don't provide boost at low rpms, and their bearings and turbines can suffer from the extreme heat generated by the exhaust system if not properly cooled. They also require more extensive plumbing than other types of superchargers. On the other hand, if used with an intercooler and with the oil in them properly cooled, they are incredible.

Late-model injected small-block engines have tremendous potential, thanks to precise fuel metering.

Garrett is my choice for turbochargers. They have been racing for years, particularly in Indy cars. They are also the turbo of choice in other venues where supercharging is allowed. Many major manufacturers have installed Garrett turbochargers on their offerings in the past 20 years and they have proven themselves very reliable. Around town in low rpm ranges, your car toddles along like any other car, but then when you put your foot in it out on the highway you get a real kick in the pants when the turbocharger spools up.

Turbos are really great for higher altitudes too. If you are building a street rod in the Colorado Rockies, you might as well consider adding one to your small block. Many diesel truck manufacturers run Garrett turbochargers and have found them reliable and indispensable in the mountains.

This radical small block will produce awesome power, but building such an engine is expensive, and requires very sophisticated tuning skills.

CENTRIFUGAL SUPERCHARGERS

These have been around for a long time (Graham used them in the 1930s), but they have become popular again with manufacturers such as Buick, Pontiac, and Ford. It is probably easiest to think of centrifugal superchargers as crankshaft-driven turbochargers. They give you boost at lower rpms and back off when you do, so there is no throttle lag. They are also easy to install, and they fit under the hoods of most vehicles.

Eaton makes bolt-on units for new cars and, when combined with modern fuel injection and ignition management systems, they are quite impressive. They are also quiet, reliable, and street legal in all 50 states. The only problem is that Eaton doesn't provide kits for the street rod builder, so a lot of fabrication would be required if you wanted to adapt one of their centrifugal superchargers to an older engine.

Powerdyne also sells centrifugal superchargers that are easily bolted on to newer (1993 and later) small-block engines, but they are not designed to fit older engines and no kits are available. Powerdyne superchargers are also too new at this writing for me to offer an evaluation. The other manufacturers mentioned have established good reputations over many years, but Powerdyne is the new kid on the block.

For most street uses, ample power can be generated from your Chevy small block without going to the expense of a supercharger. Many well-engineered aftermarket components are available for less money and they will really wake up your engine. Unless you have the time, expertise, and money, superchargers aren't worth the trouble. They are marvelous devices that provide awesome power, but if you don't know what you are doing, they can make awesome trouble for you as well.

BASIC ENGINE SPECIFICATIONS

Displacement/ Model Year	Bore	Stroke	Main Journal Diameter	Rod Journal Diameter	Main Bearings
262 1975–1976	3.671	3.10	2.45	2.1	Two Bolt
265 1955–1956	3.75	3.00	2.30	2.00	Two Bolt
267 1979–1981	3.50	3.48	2.45	2.10	Two Bolt
283 1957–1967	3.875	3.0	2.30	2.0	Two Bolt
302 1967	4.0	3.0	2.30	2.0	Two Bolt
302 1968–1969	4.0	3.0	2.45	2.1	Four Bolt
305 1976–1988	3.736	3.48	2.45	2.1	Two Bolt
307 1968–1973	3.875	3.25	2.45	2.1	Two Bolt
327 1962–1967	4.0	3.25	2.30	2.0	Two Bolt
327 1968–1969	4.0	3.25	2.45	2.1	Two Bolt
350 1967–1988	4.0	3.48	2.45	2.1	Two and Four Bolt
400 1970–1972	4.125	3.75	2.65	2.1	Four Bolt
400 1973–1980	4.125	3.75	2.65	2.1	Two Bolt

RECOMMENDED CLEARANCES

Piston to Bore:	.005"–0055" measured at centerline of wrist pin hole, perpendicular to pin.
Forged Pistons:	Finish bores with #500 grit stones or equivalent.
Piston Ring:	Minimum end clearance top- .022," second- .016," Oil- .016."
Wrist Pin:	.0004"–.0008" in piston; .0005"–.0007" in rod for floating pin.
Rod Bearing:	.002"–.0025"
Side Clearance:	.010"–.020."
Main Bearing:	.002"–.003," minimum preferred; .005"–.007" end play
Piston to Top of Block:	.015"–.020" average below deck. No part of piston except dome to be higher than deck of block.
Deck Height:	Deck height specified is for a .018" steel head gasket. If a thicker head gasket is used, piston-to-cylinder-head clearance of .035" should be considered minimum.
Valve Lash:	Follow camshaft manufacturer's recommendations.
Valve to Piston	.020" exhaust and intake at 0 valve lash. Note: These are to be considered minimum clearances
Clearance:	for an engine that runs below 8,000 rpm. If you intend to run higher than that, more clearance should be allowed.

RECOMMENDED BOLT TORQUE AND LUBRICANT SPECIFICATIONS FOR CAST-IRON SMALL-BLOCK V-8 ENGINES

	Torque	Lubricant
Main Bearing	Inner 70-ft-lb	Molykote
	Outer 65	Molykote
Con. Rod Bolt 3/8"	45–50 ft-lb (.006" stretch preferred)	Oil
Con. Rod Bolt 7/16"	60–65 ft-lb	Oil
Cylinder Head Bolt	65 ft-lb	Sealant
Rocker Arm Stud (Late HP Head)	50 ft-lb	Sealant
Camshaft Sprocket	20 ft-lb	Oil
Intake Manifold	30 ft-lb	Oil
Flywheel	60 ft-lb	Oil
Spark Plugs (Conventional Gasket)	25 ft-lb	Dry
Spark Plugs (Tapered Seat)	15 ft-lb	Dry
Exhaust Manifold	25 ft-lb	Anti-seize
Oil Pan Bolt	165 in-lb	Oil
Front Cover Bolt	75 in-lb	Oil
Rocker Cover	25 in-lb	Oil

RECOMMENDED BOLT TORQUE AND LUBRICANT FOR ALUMINUM SMALL-BLOCK V-8 ENGINES

Torque		Lubricant
Main Bearing Studs	70 ft-lb	Oil
Main Bearing Bolts	70 ft-lb	Molykote
Con. Rod Bolt 7/16"	67–73 ft-lb (.009" stretch)	Oil
Cylinder Head Bolt with Hardened Washer		
Long	65 ft-lb	Sealant
Short	60 ft-lb	Sealant
Head Studs 7/16"		
Long	65 ft-lb	Oil
Short	60 ft-lb	Oil
Rocker Arm Stud	50 ft-lb	Oil
Camshaft Sprocket	20 ft-lb	Oil
Intake Manifold	25 ft-lb	Anti-seize
Flywheel	60 ft-lb	Oil
Bellhousing	25 ft-lb	Anti-seize
Spark Plugs	25 ft-lb	Anti-seize
Exhaust Manifold	20 ft-lb	Anti-seize
Oil Pan Bolt	165 in-lb	Anti-seize
Front Cover Bolt	75 in-lb	Anti-seize
Rocker Cover	25 in-lb	Anti-seize

BLOCK CASTING IDENTIFICATION

CASTING NO.	CID	YEARS USED	USED IN
360851	262	1974–1976	Monza
*3703524	265	1955	Passenger cars
3720991	265	1956–1957	Truck & passenger cars
14010280			Passenger cars
14016376	267	1979–1982	
471511			
3731548	283	1957	
3556519			Trucks &
3737739	283	1958–1961	passenger cars
3849852			
3789935			Trucks &
3849852	283	1962–1964	passenger cars
3864812			
3849852			Trucks &
3849935	283	1965–1967	passenger cars
3896944			
393288			
See Note 1	302	1967	302 Camaro
See Note 2	302	1968–1969	302 Camaro
389257			
14010201			

CASTING NO.	CID	YEARS USED	USED IN
14016381	305	1980–1984	Passenger cars & light trucks
14010202			"
14010203			"
460776			Passenger cars
460777	305	1978–1979	& light trucks
460778			
361979			
3914653			Trucks &
3914636	307	1968–1973	passenger
3932373			cars
3970020			
3959512	327	1962–1963	
3782870			Trucks
3789817	327	1962–1964	&
3794460			passenger
3852174			cars
3858180			
3892657			Trucks
3782870	327	1964–1967	&
3903352			passenger
3789817			cars
3858174			
3892657			
3791362	327	1965–1967	Chevy II
3970041			Corvette
3814660			Camaro and other
3970010	327	1968–1969	high-performance
3914678			applications
3932386			
3955618			
3855961			Passenger
3932388			cars
3958618	350	1968–1976	(2-bolt mains)
3970014			
6259425			
3955618			Truck and high-
+3970010	350	1968–1979	performance applications
3932386			(4-bolt mains)
14016379	350	1978–1979	Passenger cars
366245	350	1978–1979	& light trucks (dip stick in pan)
140029	350	1980–1984	Passenger cars
14010207	350		
3951511	400	1970–1973	Heavy-duty trucks & passenger cars (4-bolt mains)
3951509	400	1974–1976	(2-bolt mains)
3030817			

*First six-month's production used mechanical cams, not hydraulic.

+Sometimes machined for 2-bolt mains.

Note 1: Small-journal 302-CID engine uses 327 block.

Note 2: Large-journal 302-CID engine uses 350 block.

CRANKSHAFTS

Year	Stroke (in.)	Construction and materials	Casting or forging number
1968–1969	3.000	Forged steel	1178–3279
	3.250	Forged steel	1130–4672
1968–1973	3.250	Cast nodular iron	3911001 or 3941174
1968–1975	3.480	Forged steel	2690
1968–1985	3.480	Cast nodular iron	3932442
		Forged steel 1182	3941182 or
1970–1980	3.750	Cast nodular iron	3951529*
1975–1976	3.100	Cast nodular iron	354431
1986–1988	3.480	Cast nodular iron	14088526
		Forged steel	14088552

*Needs main bearing journal modification before interchange is possible. (Works only in a 1986 or later block.)

RESOURCES

L&R Automotive Supply Company
13731 Bora Drive
Santa Fe Springs, CA 90670
(562) 802-0443
FAX (562) 802-8684

Ed Iskenderian Racing Cams
16020 S. Broadway, Box 30
Gardena, CA 90247-9990
(323) 770-0930
FAX (310) 515-5730
www.iskycams.com

California Discount Warehouse, Inc
2320 E. Artesia Blvd.
Long Beach, CA 90805
(562) 423-4346
FAX (562) 428-2060

T. D. Performance Products
16410 Manning Way
Cerritos, CA 90703
(562) 921-0404
www.TDperformance.com

Holley Performance Products, Inc.
1801 Russellville Rd., P.O. Box 10360
Bowling Green, KY 42102-7360
(800) HOLLEY-1
www.holley.com

MSD Ignition/Autotronic Controls Corporation
1490 Henry Brennan Drive
El Paso, TX 79936
(915) 857-5200
FAX (915) 857-3344
www.msdignition.com

K&N Filters
P.O. Box 1329
Riverside, CA 92502
(800) 700-0256
wwwknfilters.com

World Products
35330 Stanley
Sterling Heights, MI 48312
(810) 939-9628
FAX (810) 939-8153
www.gr8ride.com

Doug's Headers
2349 W. La Palma Ave, Suite 101
Anaheim, CA 92841
(714) 502-0286
FAX (714) 502-0287
www.dougsheaders.com

Carb Shop
1461 E. Philadelphia St.
Ontario, CA 91761
(909) 947-3575
www.customcarbs.com

Vrbancic Bros. Racing
1463 E. Philadelphia St.
Ontario, CA 91761
(909) 930-9980
FAX (909) 923-3950

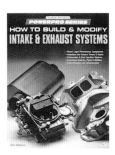

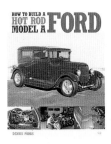
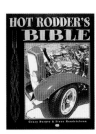
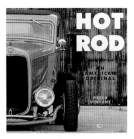
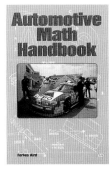

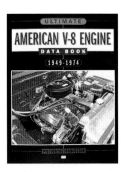